QUINCREDIBLE

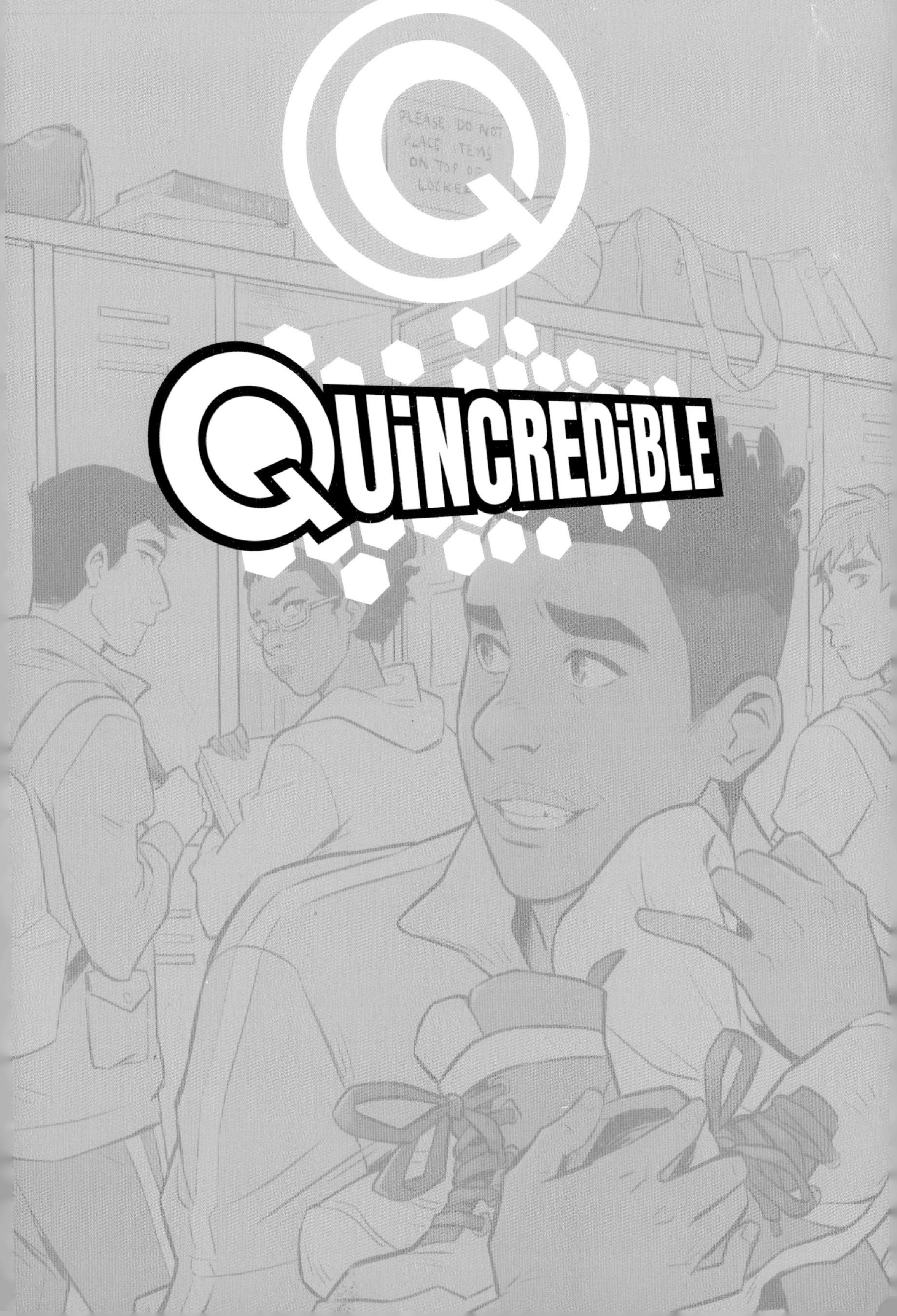
PLEASE DO NOT PLACE ITEMS ON TOP OF LOCKER

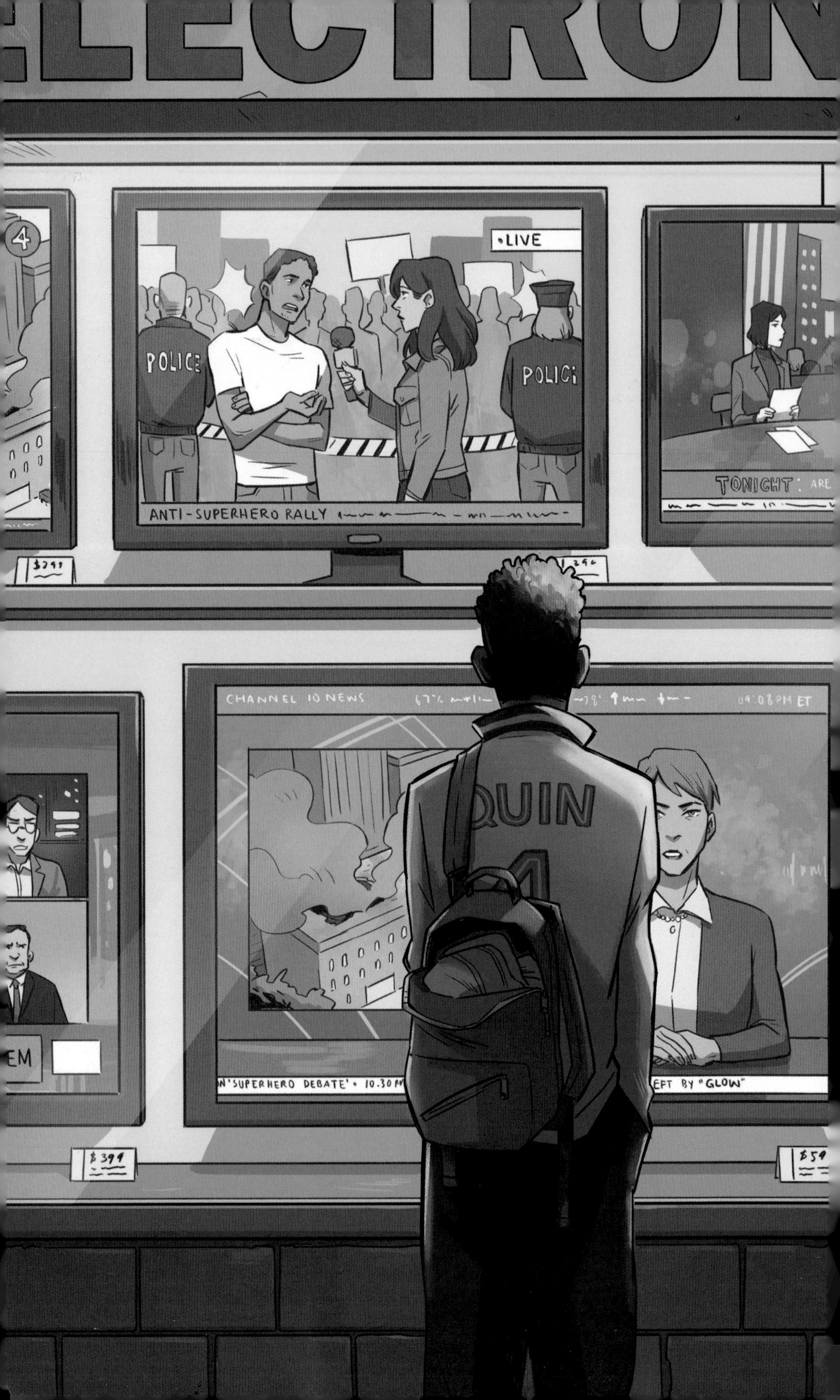

ELECTRON
LIVE
POLICE
POLICE
ANTI-SUPERHERO RALLY
TONIGHT: ARE
CHANNEL 10 NEWS
09:08PM ET
QUIN
'SUPERHERO DEBATE' • 10.30
EFT BY "GLOW"
EM
$399

THE RIGHT SOLUTION?
DOZENS DISPLACED IN

CATALYST PRIME

QUINCREDIBLE

QUEST TO BE THE BEST!

written by **RODNEY BARNES**
illustrated by **SELINA ESPIRITU**
colored by **KELLY FITZPATRICK**
lettered by **AW'S TOM NAPOLITANO**
cover by **SELINA ESPIRITU**

JASMINE AMIRI AND STEENZ • editors
ZOE MAFFITT AND KAT VENDETTI • assistant editors

LION FORGE

ISBN 978-1-5493-0282-4

Librayr of Congress Control Number: 2018962461

Quincredible Vol. 1, published 2019 by The Lion Forge, LLC.

CHAPTER ONE

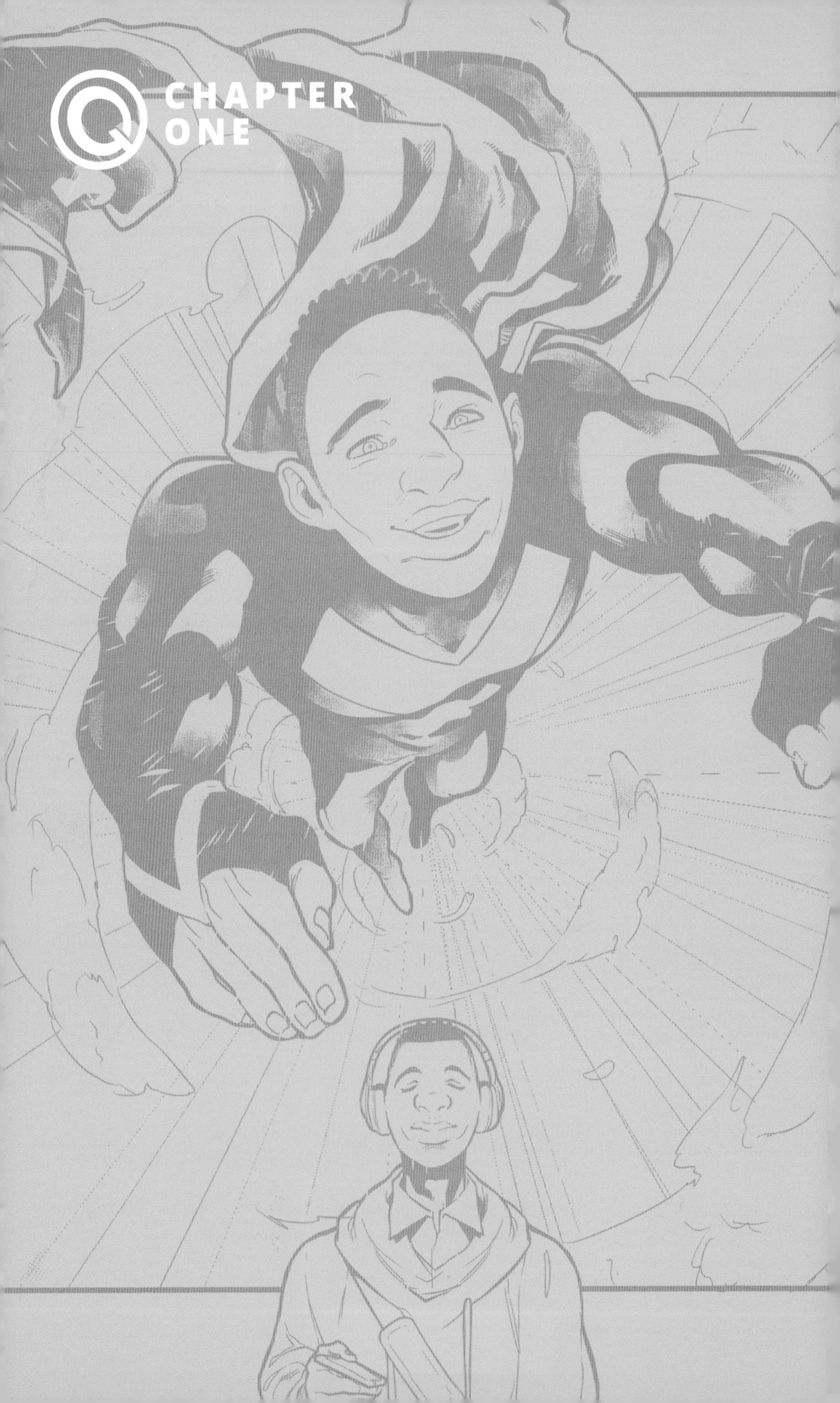

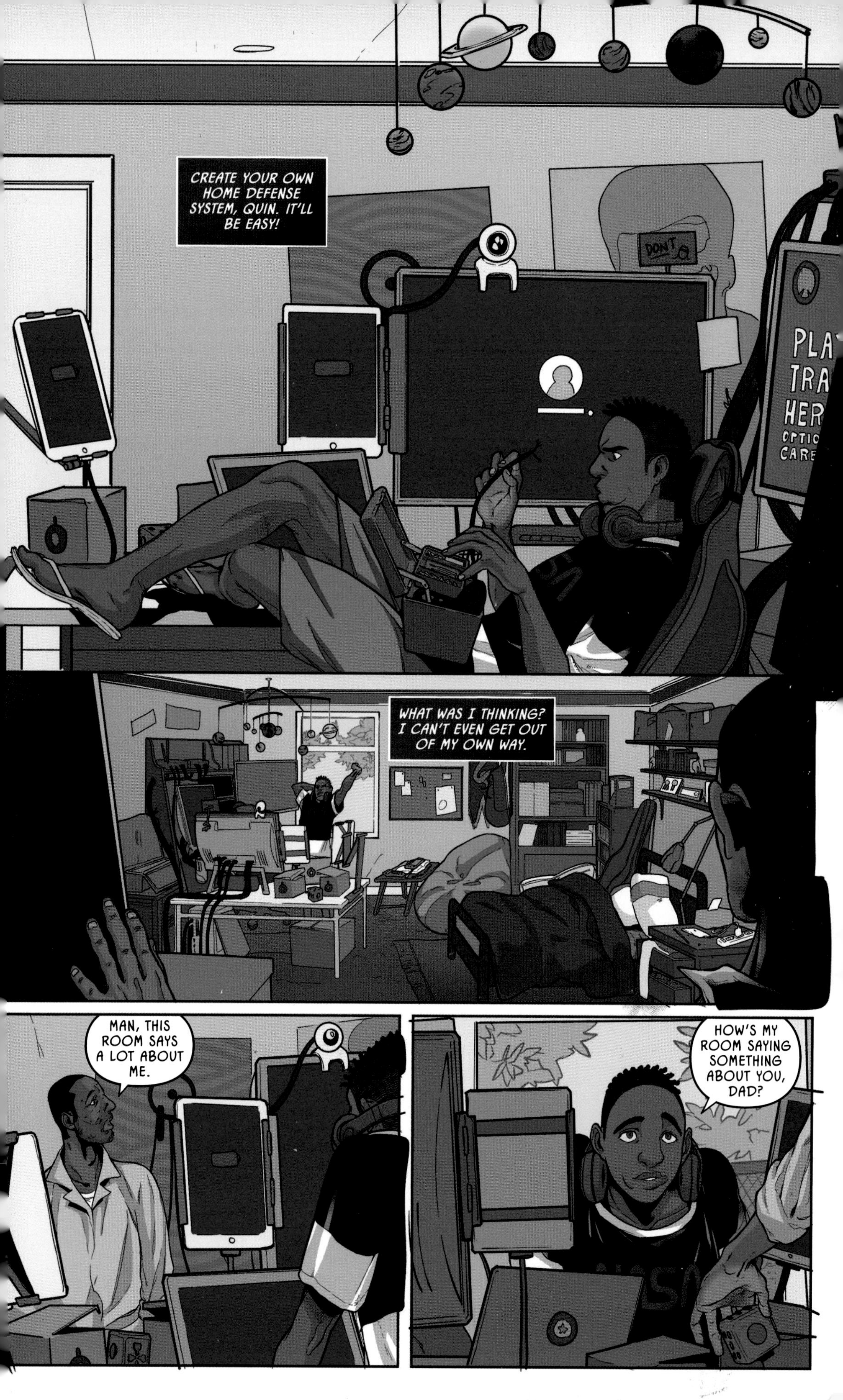
CREATE YOUR OWN HOME DEFENSE SYSTEM, QUIN. IT'LL BE EASY!
WHAT WAS I THINKING? I CAN'T EVEN GET OUT OF MY OWN WAY.
MAN, THIS ROOM SAYS A LOT ABOUT ME.
HOW'S MY ROOM SAYING SOMETHING ABOUT YOU, DAD?

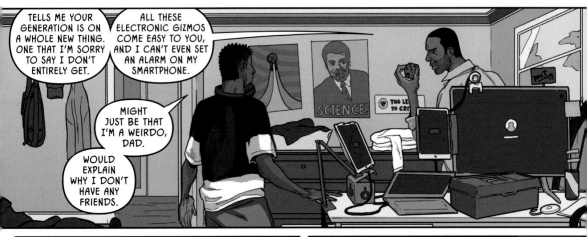

TELLS ME YOUR GENERATION IS ON A WHOLE NEW THING. ONE THAT I'M SORRY TO SAY I DON'T ENTIRELY GET.

ALL THESE ELECTRONIC GIZMOS COME EASY TO YOU, AND I CAN'T EVEN SET AN ALARM ON MY SMARTPHONE.

MIGHT JUST BE THAT I'M A WEIRDO, DAD.

WOULD EXPLAIN WHY I DON'T HAVE ANY FRIENDS.

QUIN. YOU'VE GOT PLENTY OF FRIENDS.

WHO?

AND DON'T SAY UNCLE TIM, 'CAUSE THAT'S FAMILY.

GIVE IT TIME. YOU'LL FIND YOUR TRIBE, QUIN.

UNTIL I DO, IS IT OKAY IF I'M MY OWN TRIBE?

IT'S MORE THAN OKAY, SON.

WHY DON'T YOU GO HAVE SOME WEEKEND FUN? I'M SURE WE CAN GO WITHOUT TOP-NOTCH SECURITY FOR A FEW HOURS.

MOM WILL WANT ME TO DO SOME CHORES, STUDY... SOMETHING OTHER THAN FUN.

I'LL DEAL WITH YOUR MOM.

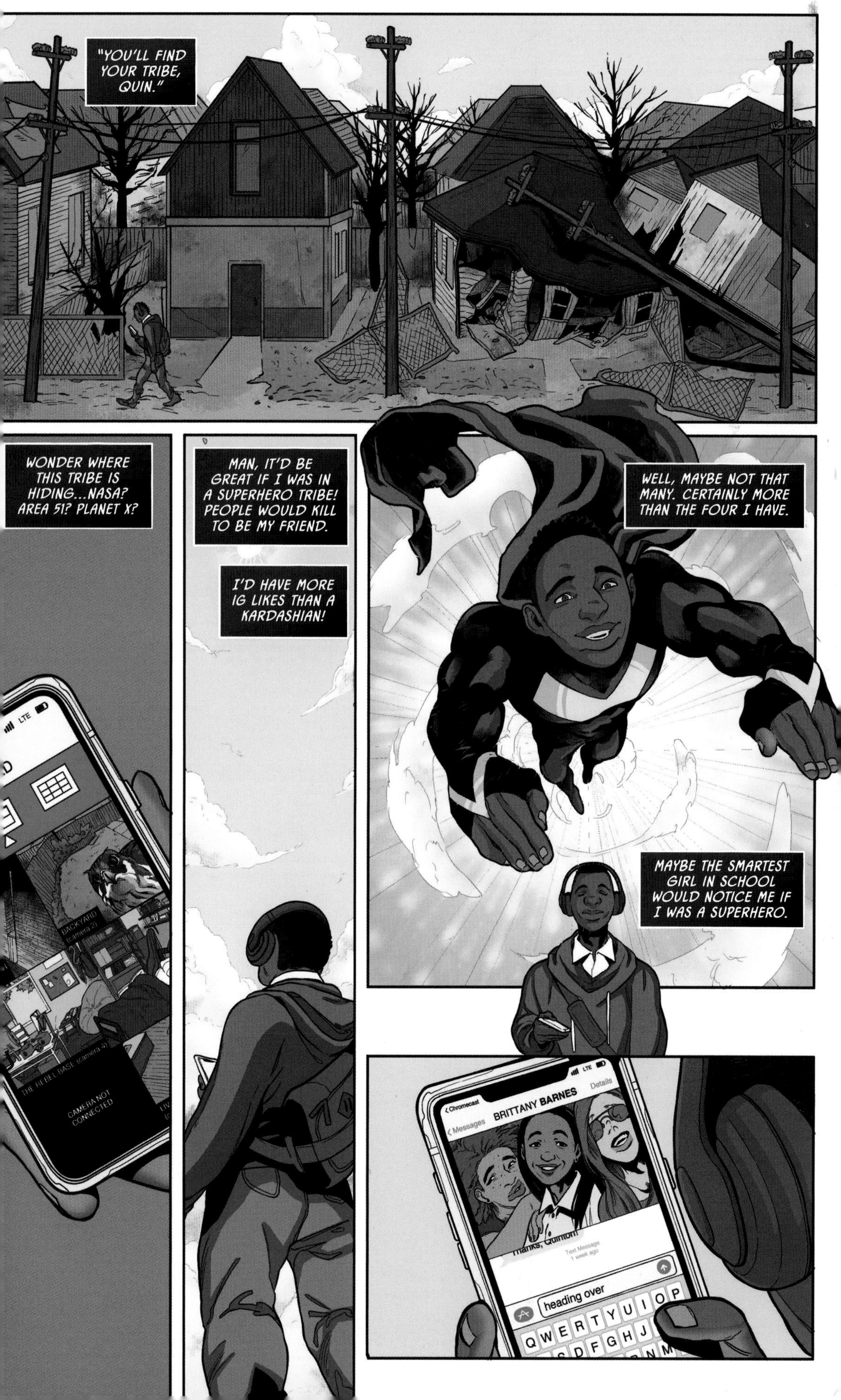
"YOU'LL FIND YOUR TRIBE, QUIN."
WONDER WHERE THIS TRIBE IS HIDING...NASA? AREA 51? PLANET X?
BACKYARD (camera 2)
THE REBEL BASE (camera 4)
CAMERA NOT CONNECTED
MAN, IT'D BE GREAT IF I WAS IN A SUPERHERO TRIBE! PEOPLE WOULD KILL TO BE MY FRIEND.
I'D HAVE MORE IG LIKES THAN A KARDASHIAN!
WELL, MAYBE NOT THAT MANY. CERTAINLY MORE THAN THE FOUR I HAVE.
MAYBE THE SMARTEST GIRL IN SCHOOL WOULD NOTICE ME IF I WAS A SUPERHERO.
Chromecast
Messages
BRITTANY BARNES
Details
Thanks, Quinton!
Text Message
1 week ago
heading over

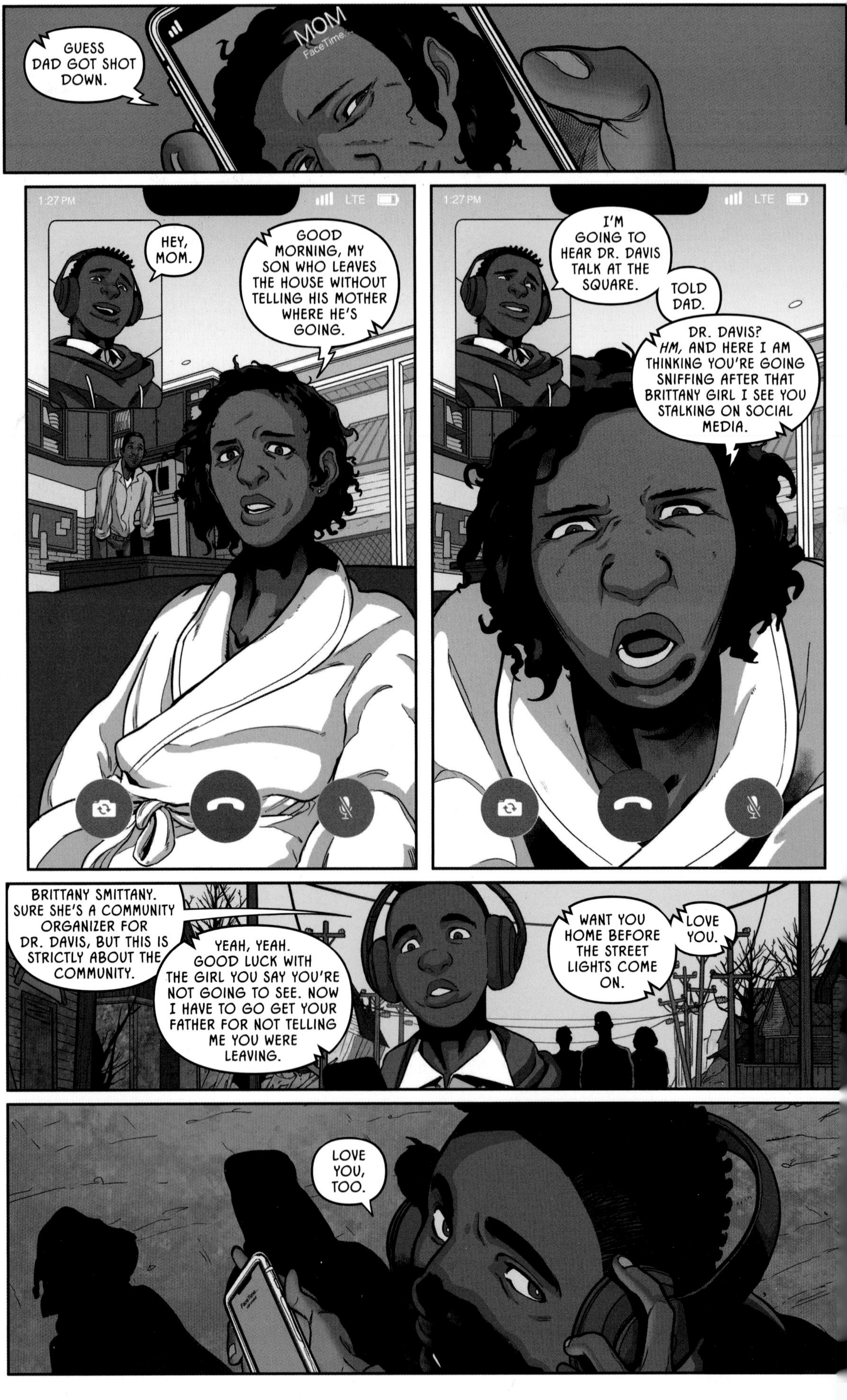

MOM
FaceTime...
GUESS DAD GOT SHOT DOWN.
1:27 PM
LTE
HEY, MOM.
GOOD MORNING, MY SON WHO LEAVES THE HOUSE WITHOUT TELLING HIS MOTHER WHERE HE'S GOING.
1:27 PM
LTE
I'M GOING TO HEAR DR. DAVIS TALK AT THE SQUARE.
TOLD DAD.
DR. DAVIS? *HM,* AND HERE I AM THINKING YOU'RE GOING SNIFFING AFTER THAT BRITTANY GIRL I SEE YOU STALKING ON SOCIAL MEDIA.
BRITTANY SMITTANY. SURE SHE'S A COMMUNITY ORGANIZER FOR DR. DAVIS, BUT THIS IS STRICTLY ABOUT THE COMMUNITY.
YEAH, YEAH. GOOD LUCK WITH THE GIRL YOU SAY YOU'RE NOT GOING TO SEE. NOW I HAVE TO GO GET YOUR FATHER FOR NOT TELLING ME YOU WERE LEAVING.
WANT YOU HOME BEFORE THE STREET LIGHTS COME ON.
LOVE YOU.
LOVE YOU, TOO.

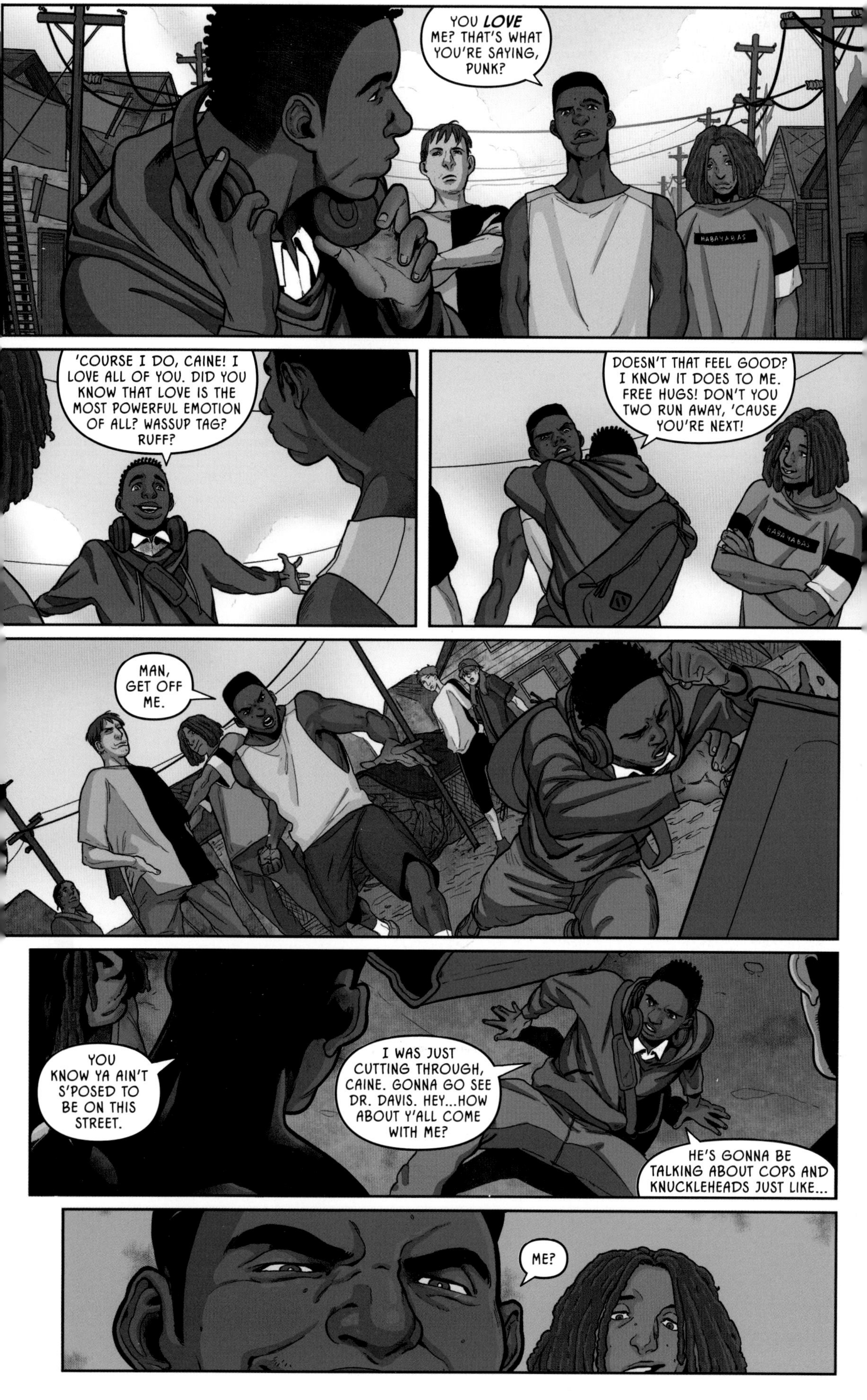

YOU *LOVE* ME? THAT'S WHAT YOU'RE SAYING, PUNK?
HABAYABAS
'COURSE I DO, CAINE! I LOVE ALL OF YOU. DID YOU KNOW THAT LOVE IS THE MOST POWERFUL EMOTION OF ALL? WASSUP TAG? RUFF?
DOESN'T THAT FEEL GOOD? I KNOW IT DOES TO ME. FREE HUGS! DON'T YOU TWO RUN AWAY, 'CAUSE YOU'RE NEXT!
HABAYABAS
MAN, GET OFF ME.
YOU KNOW YA AIN'T S'POSED TO BE ON THIS STREET.
I WAS JUST CUTTING THROUGH, CAINE. GONNA GO SEE DR. DAVIS. HEY...HOW ABOUT Y'ALL COME WITH ME?
HE'S GONNA BE TALKING ABOUT COPS AND KNUCKLEHEADS JUST LIKE...
ME?

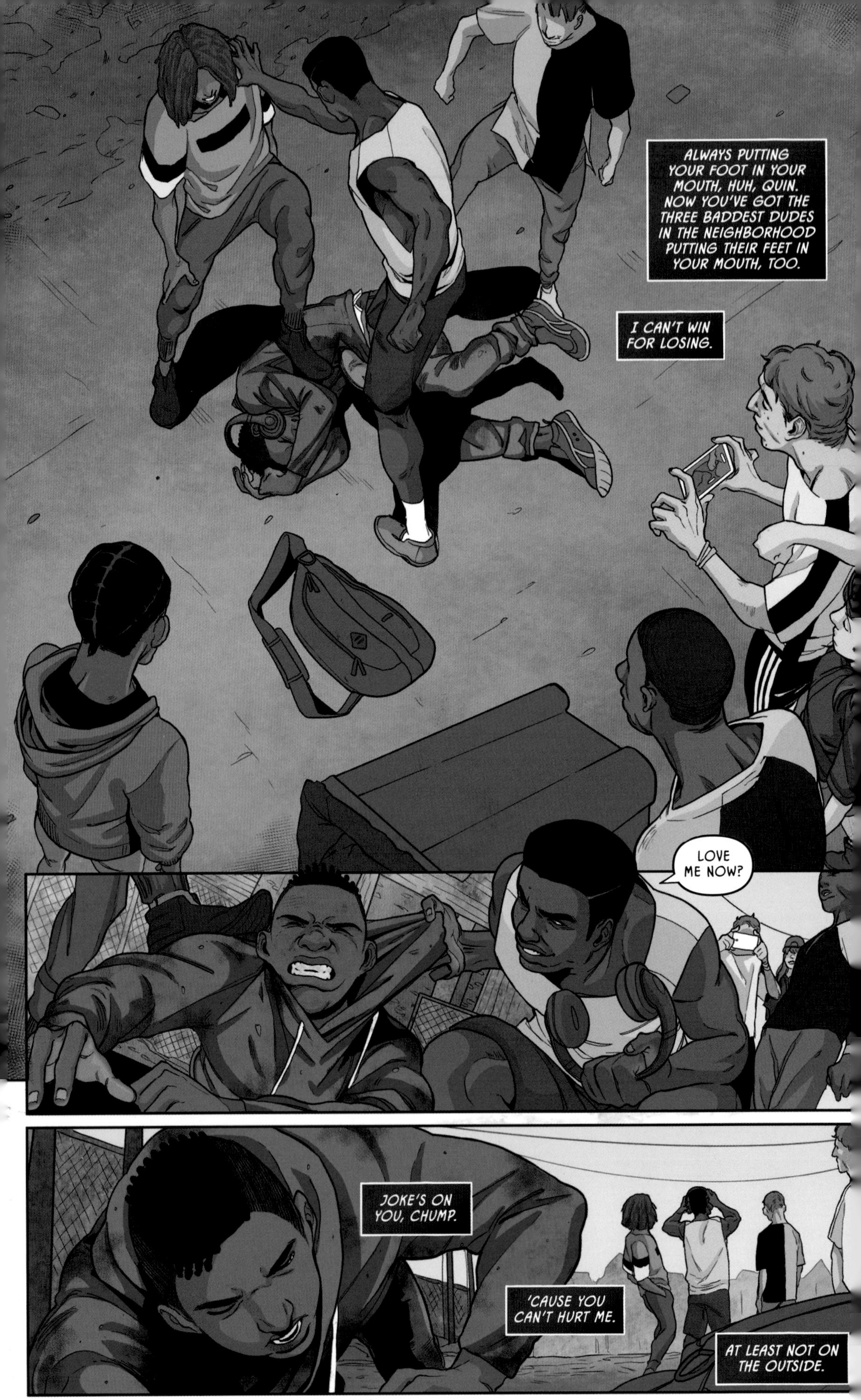
ALWAYS PUTTING YOUR FOOT IN YOUR MOUTH, HUH, QUIN. NOW YOU'VE GOT THE THREE BADDEST DUDES IN THE NEIGHBORHOOD PUTTING THEIR FEET IN YOUR MOUTH, TOO.
I CAN'T WIN FOR LOSING.
LOVE ME NOW?
JOKE'S ON YOU, CHUMP.
'CAUSE YOU CAN'T HURT ME.
AT LEAST NOT ON THE OUTSIDE.

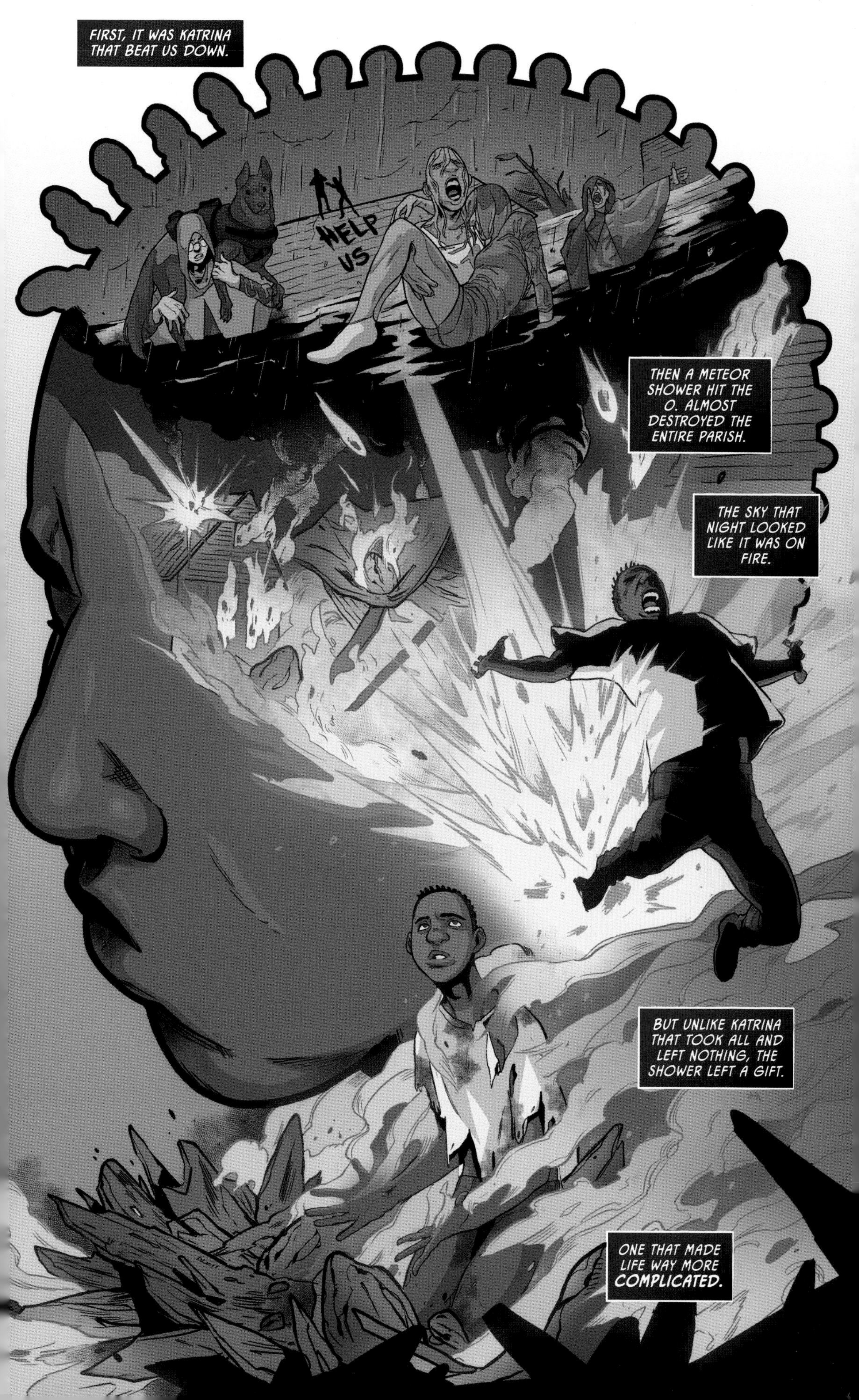
FIRST, IT WAS KATRINA THAT BEAT US DOWN.
HELP US
THEN A METEOR SHOWER HIT THE O. ALMOST DESTROYED THE ENTIRE PARISH.
THE SKY THAT NIGHT LOOKED LIKE IT WAS ON FIRE.
BUT UNLIKE KATRINA THAT TOOK ALL AND LEFT NOTHING, THE SHOWER LEFT A GIFT.
ONE THAT MADE LIFE WAY MORE COMPLICATED.

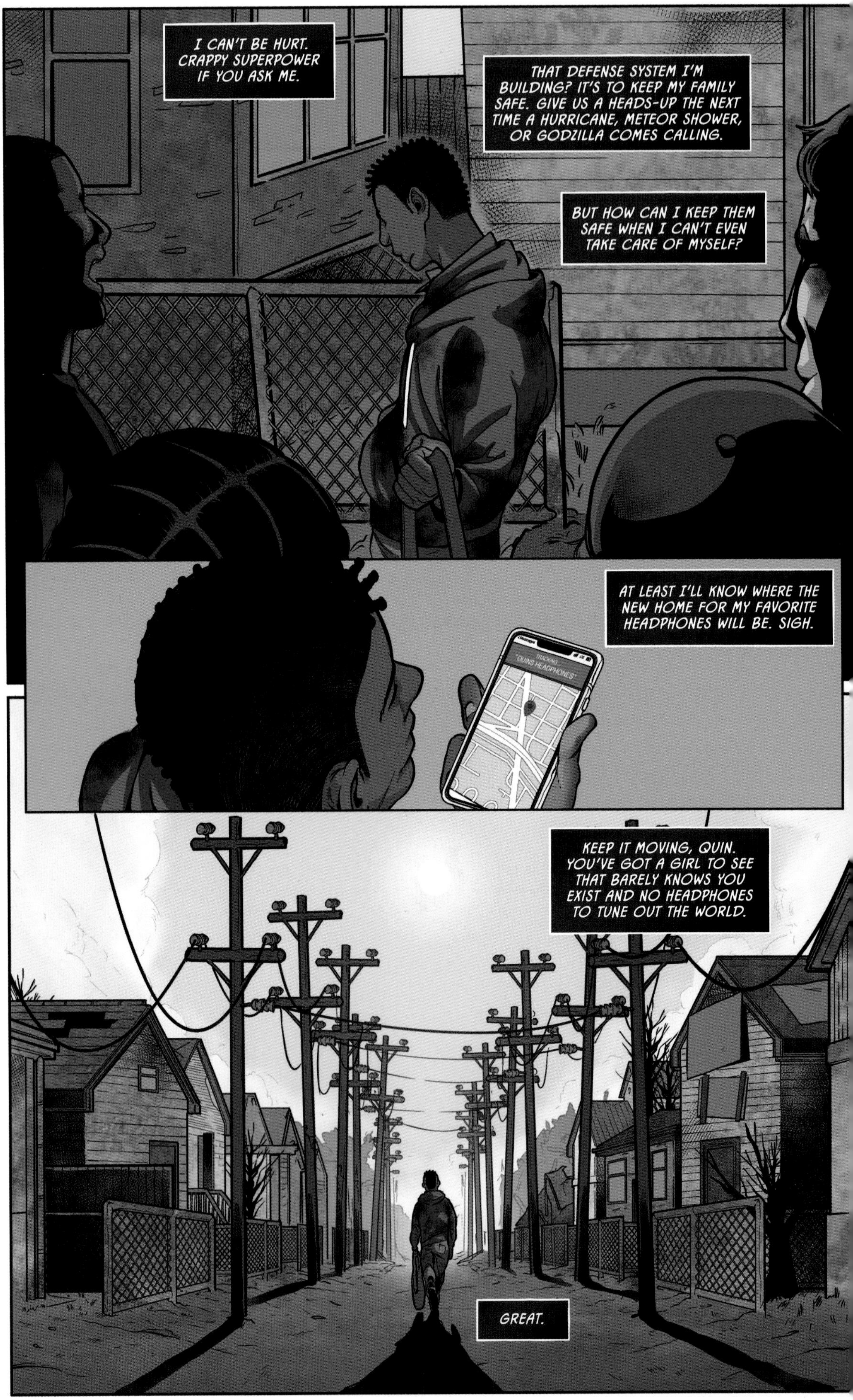
I CAN'T BE HURT. CRAPPY SUPERPOWER IF YOU ASK ME.
THAT DEFENSE SYSTEM I'M BUILDING? IT'S TO KEEP MY FAMILY SAFE. GIVE US A HEADS-UP THE NEXT TIME A HURRICANE, METEOR SHOWER, OR GODZILLA COMES CALLING.
BUT HOW CAN I KEEP THEM SAFE WHEN I CAN'T EVEN TAKE CARE OF MYSELF?
AT LEAST I'LL KNOW WHERE THE NEW HOME FOR MY FAVORITE HEADPHONES WILL BE. SIGH.
TRACKING...
"QUIN'S HEADPHONES"
KEEP IT MOVING, QUIN. YOU'VE GOT A GIRL TO SEE THAT BARELY KNOWS YOU EXIST AND NO HEADPHONES TO TUNE OUT THE WORLD.
GREAT.

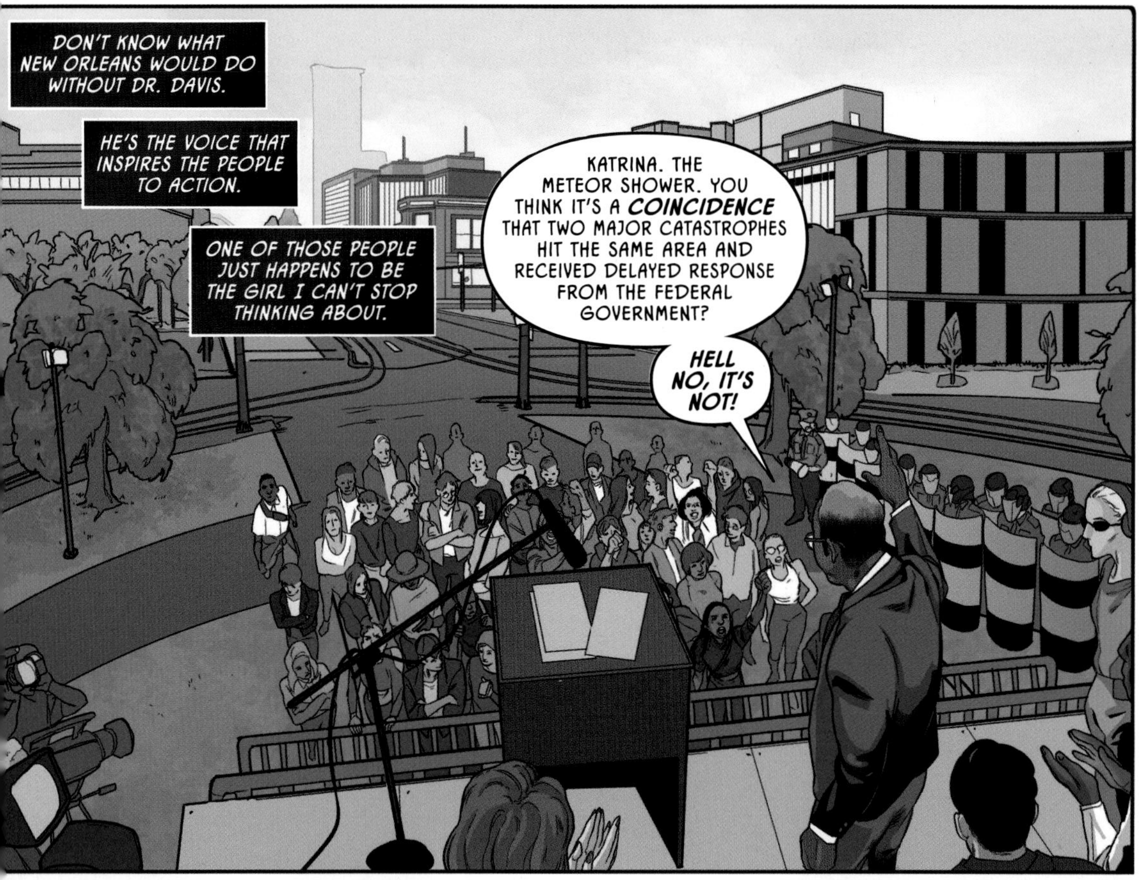
DON'T KNOW WHAT NEW ORLEANS WOULD DO WITHOUT DR. DAVIS.
HE'S THE VOICE THAT INSPIRES THE PEOPLE TO ACTION.
ONE OF THOSE PEOPLE JUST HAPPENS TO BE THE GIRL I CAN'T STOP THINKING ABOUT.
KATRINA. THE METEOR SHOWER. YOU THINK IT'S A COINCIDENCE THAT TWO MAJOR CATASTROPHES HIT THE SAME AREA AND RECEIVED DELAYED RESPONSE FROM THE FEDERAL GOVERNMENT?
HELL NO, IT'S NOT!

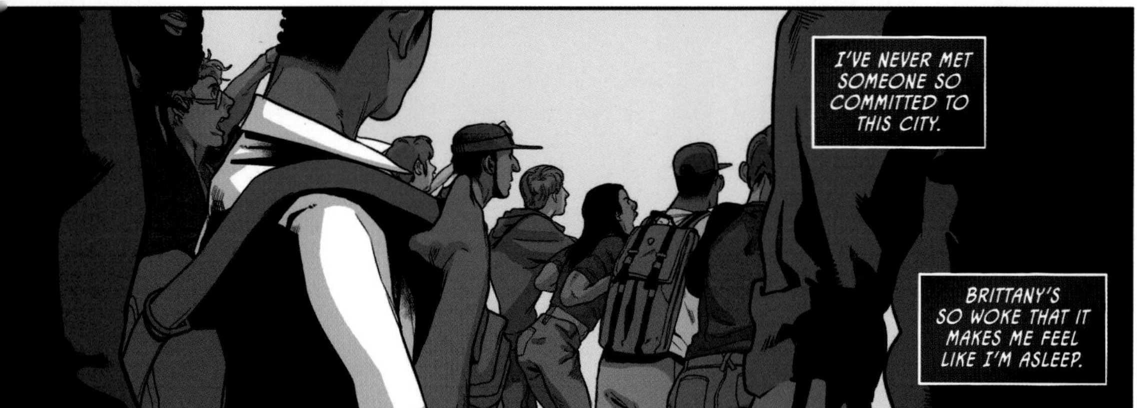
I'VE NEVER MET SOMEONE SO COMMITTED TO THIS CITY.
BRITTANY'S SO WOKE THAT IT MAKES ME FEEL LIKE I'M ASLEEP.

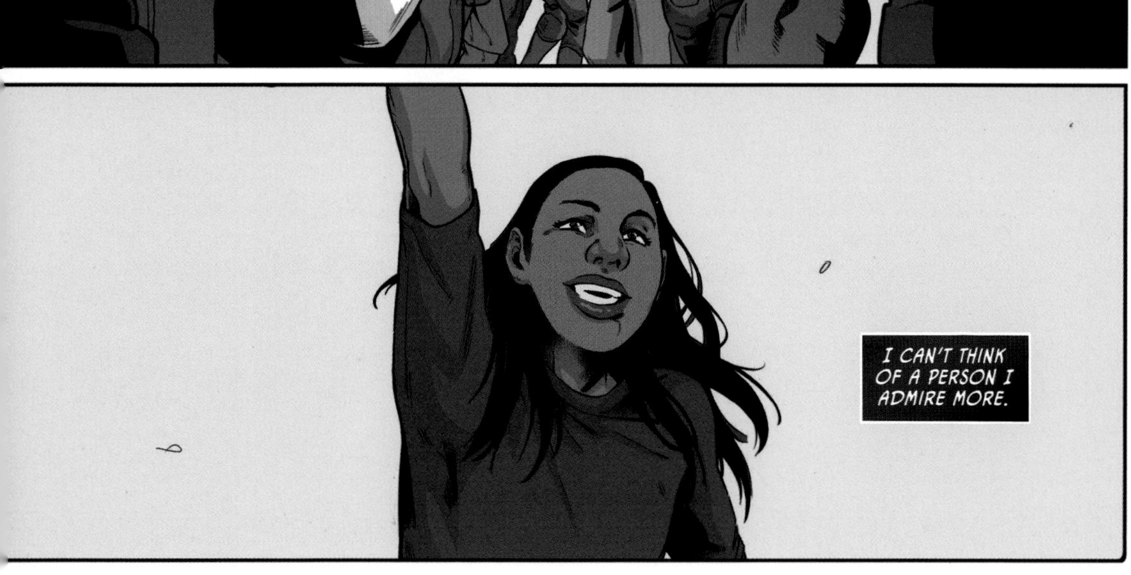
I CAN'T THINK OF A PERSON I ADMIRE MORE.

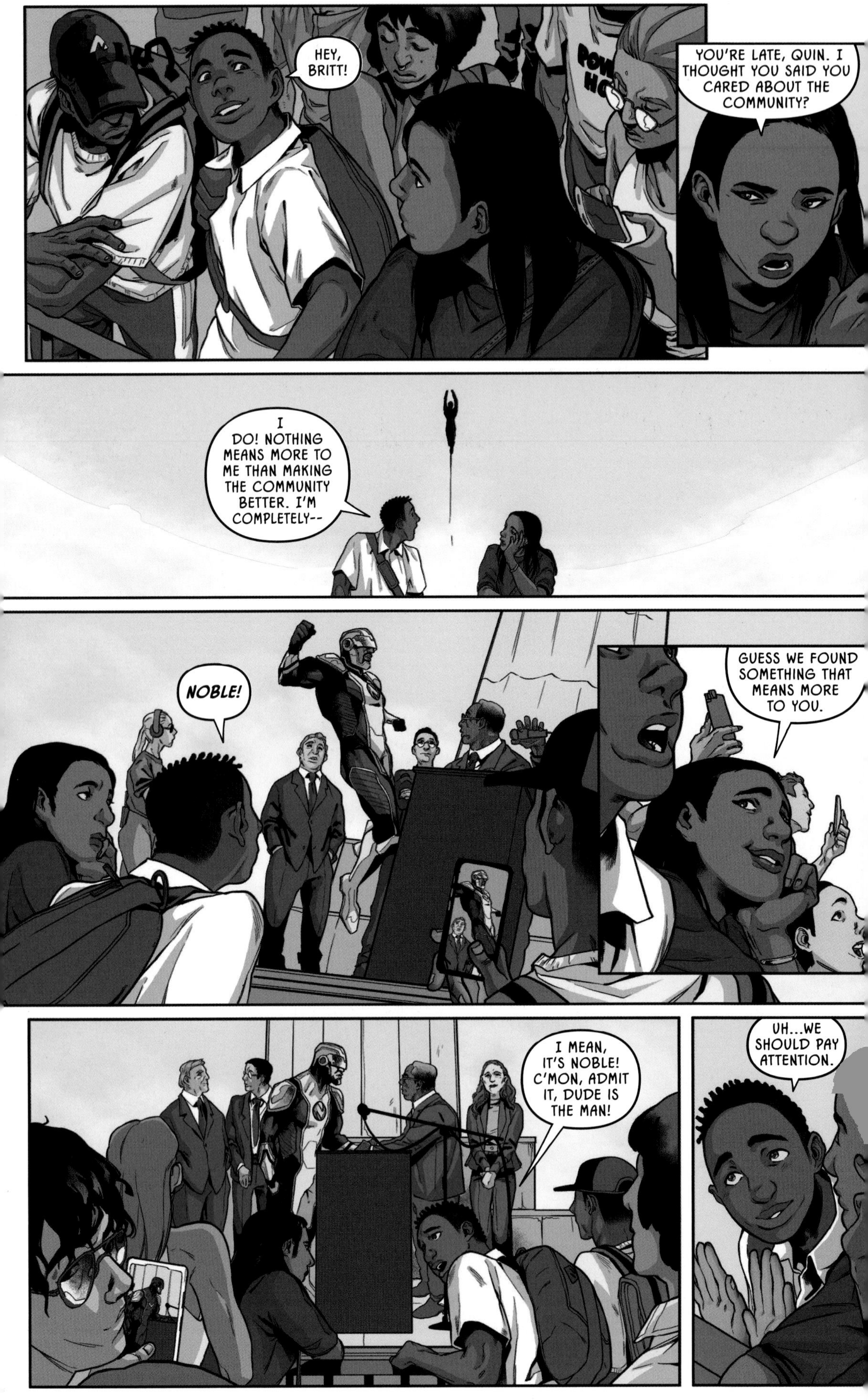
HEY, BRITT!
YOU'RE LATE, QUIN. I THOUGHT YOU SAID YOU CARED ABOUT THE COMMUNITY?
I DO! NOTHING MEANS MORE TO ME THAN MAKING THE COMMUNITY BETTER. I'M COMPLETELY--
NOBLE!
GUESS WE FOUND SOMETHING THAT MEANS MORE TO YOU.
I MEAN, IT'S NOBLE! C'MON, ADMIT IT, DUDE IS THE MAN!
UH...WE SHOULD PAY ATTENTION.

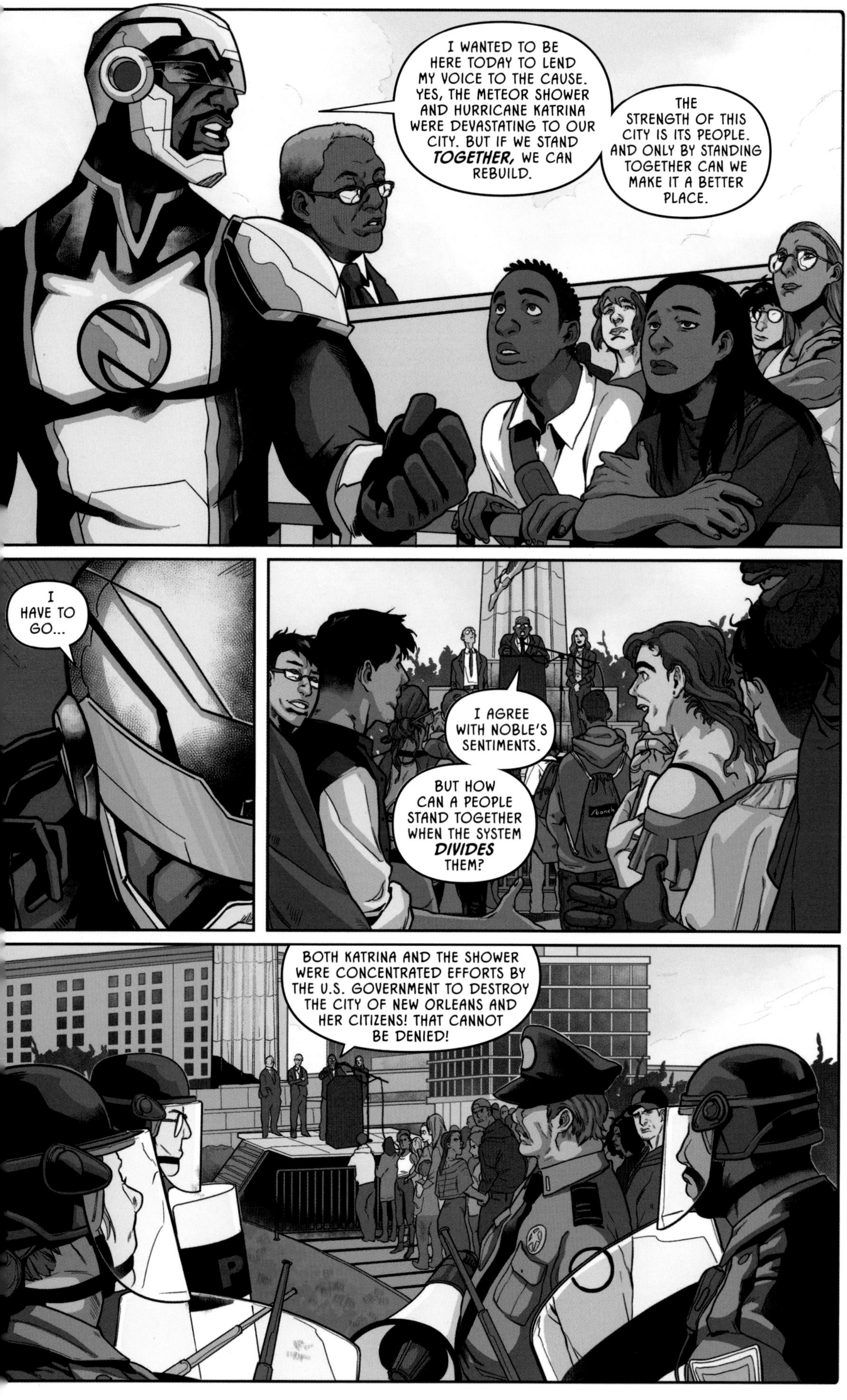
I WANTED TO BE HERE TODAY TO LEND MY VOICE TO THE CAUSE. YES, THE METEOR SHOWER AND HURRICANE KATRINA WERE DEVASTATING TO OUR CITY. BUT IF WE STAND *TOGETHER,* WE CAN REBUILD.
THE STRENGTH OF THIS CITY IS ITS PEOPLE. AND ONLY BY STANDING TOGETHER CAN WE MAKE IT A BETTER PLACE.
I HAVE TO GO...
I AGREE WITH NOBLE'S SENTIMENTS.
BUT HOW CAN A PEOPLE STAND TOGETHER WHEN THE SYSTEM *DIVIDES* THEM?
BOTH KATRINA AND THE SHOWER WERE CONCENTRATED EFFORTS BY THE U.S. GOVERNMENT TO DESTROY THE CITY OF NEW ORLEANS AND HER CITIZENS! THAT CANNOT BE DENIED!

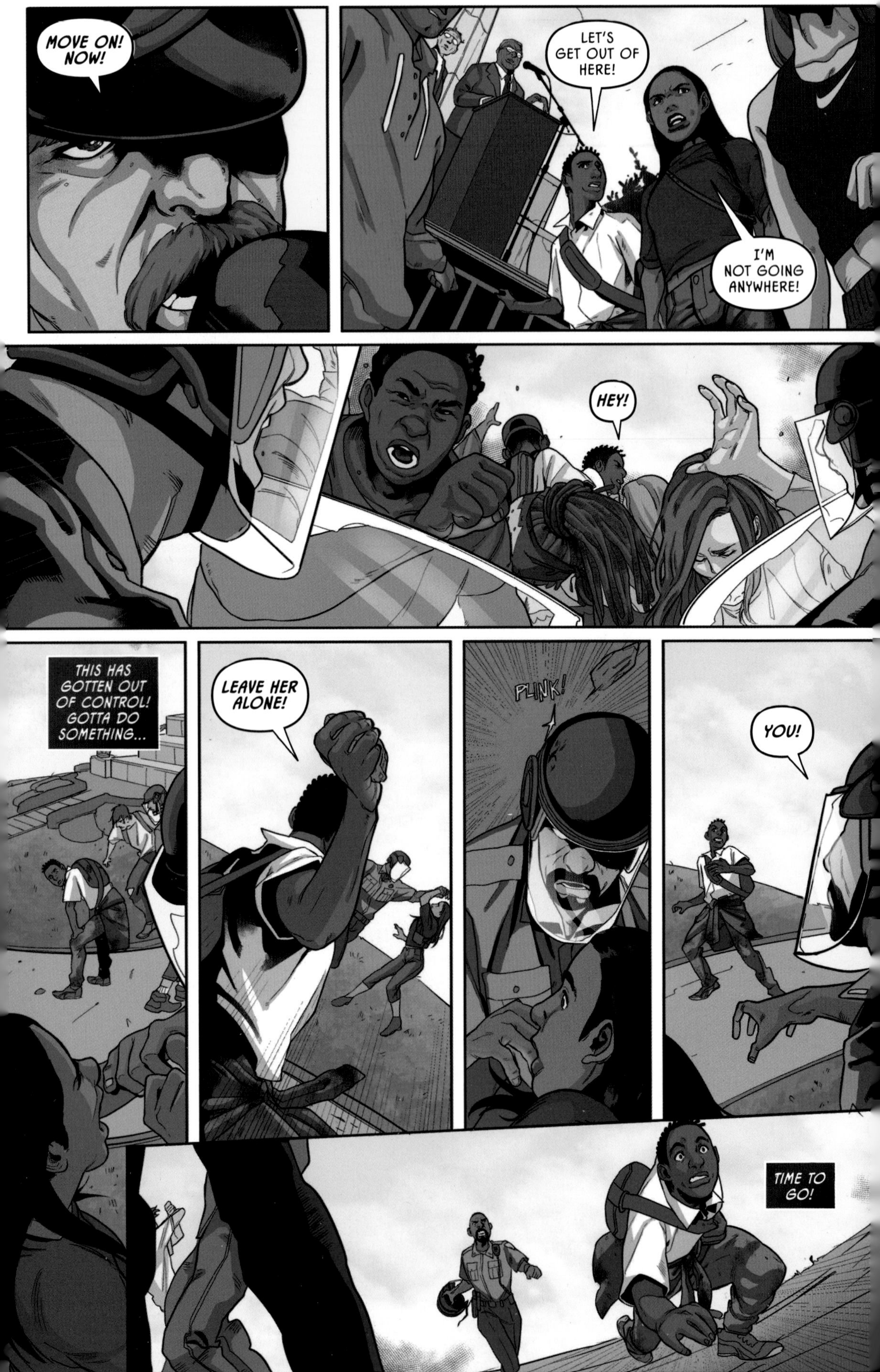
MOVE ON! NOW!
LET'S GET OUT OF HERE!
I'M NOT GOING ANYWHERE!
HEY!
THIS HAS GOTTEN OUT OF CONTROL! GOTTA DO SOMETHING...
LEAVE HER ALONE!
PLINK!
YOU!
TIME TO GO!

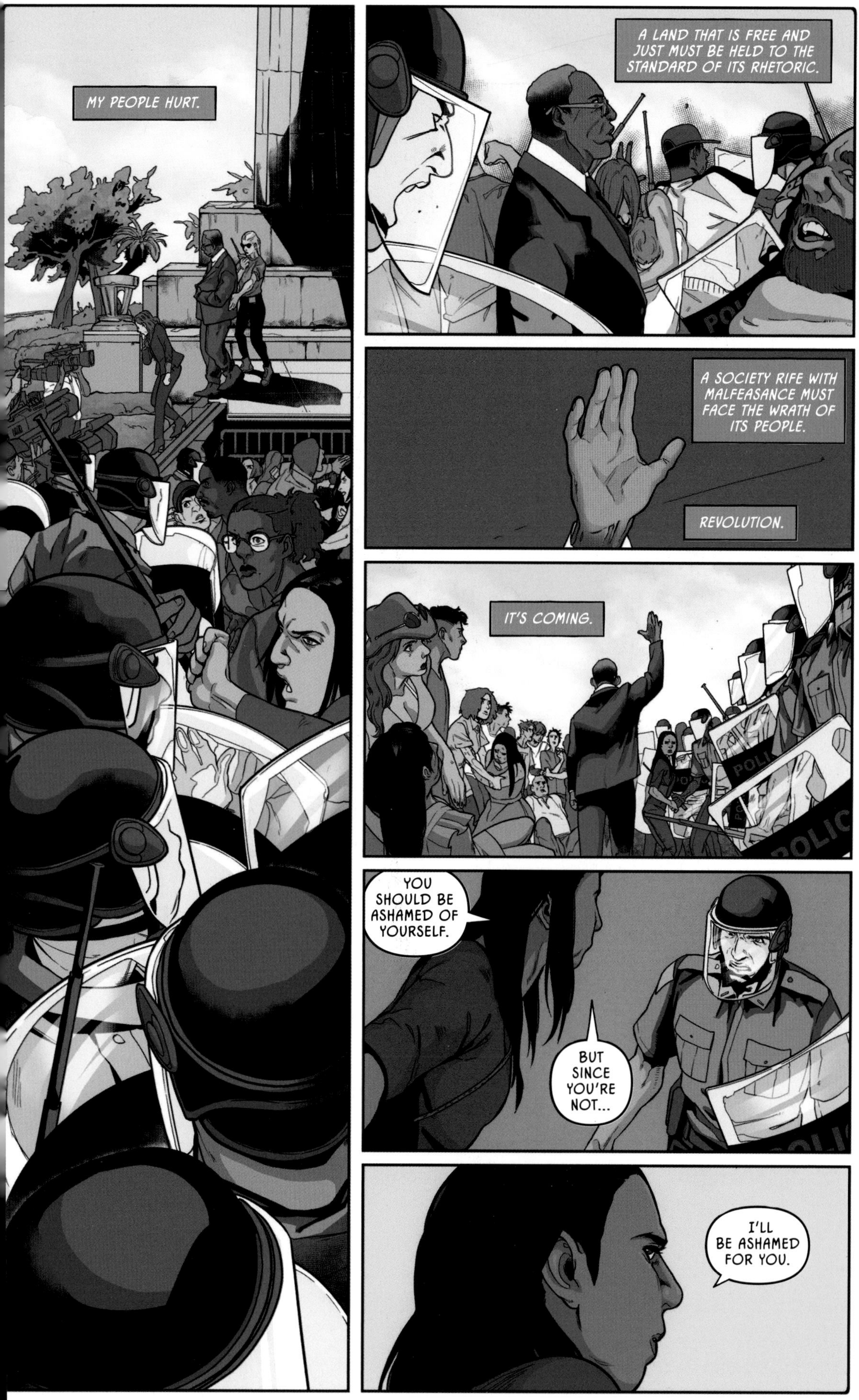
MY PEOPLE HURT.
A LAND THAT IS FREE AND JUST MUST BE HELD TO THE STANDARD OF ITS RHETORIC.
A SOCIETY RIFE WITH MALFEASANCE MUST FACE THE WRATH OF ITS PEOPLE.
REVOLUTION.
IT'S COMING.
YOU SHOULD BE ASHAMED OF YOURSELF.
BUT SINCE YOU'RE NOT...
I'LL BE ASHAMED FOR YOU.

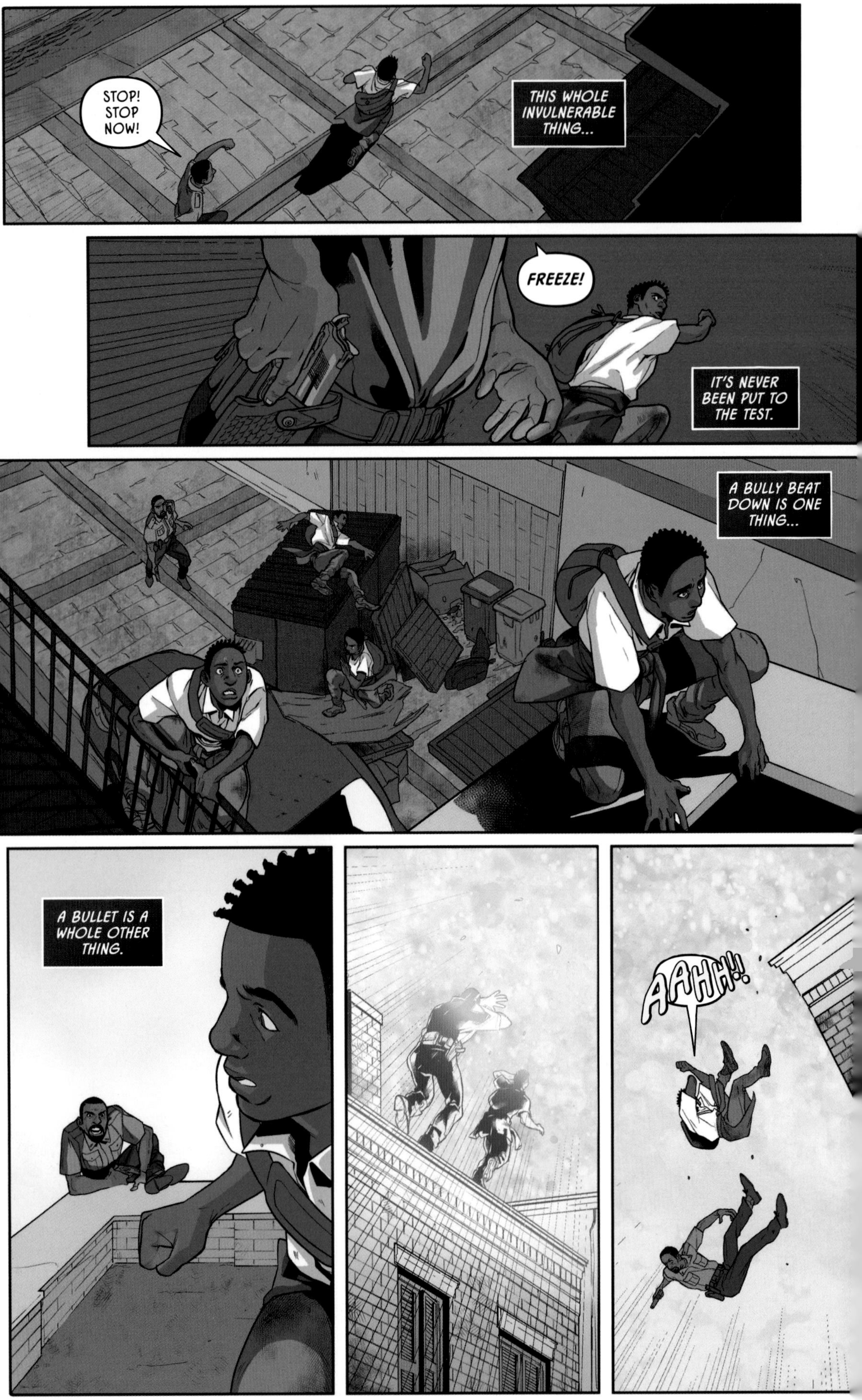
STOP! STOP NOW!
THIS WHOLE INVULNERABLE THING...
FREEZE!
IT'S NEVER BEEN PUT TO THE TEST.
A BULLY BEAT DOWN IS ONE THING...
A BULLET IS A WHOLE OTHER THING.
AAHH!!

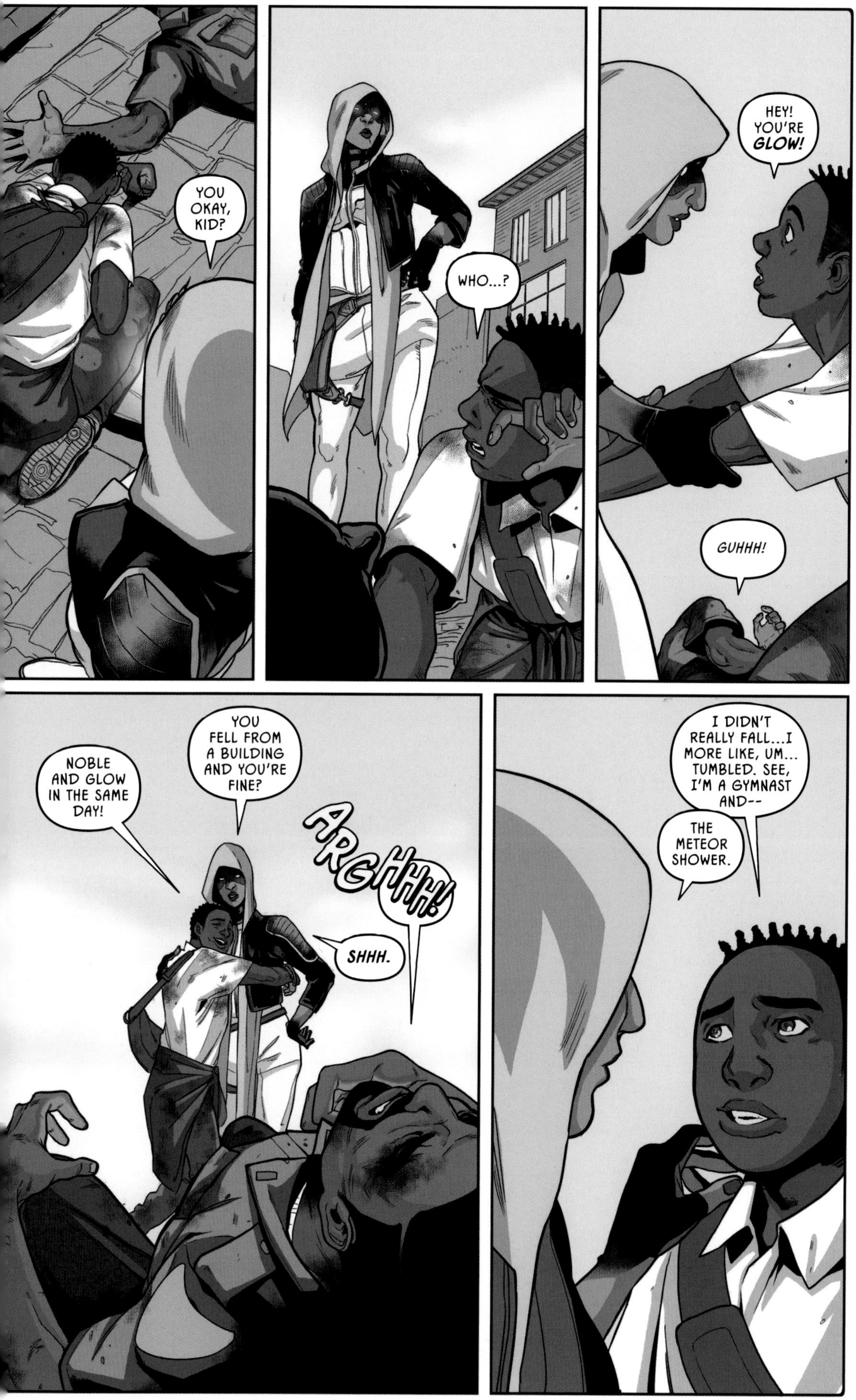
YOU OKAY, KID?
WHO...?
HEY! YOU'RE GLOW!
GUHHH!
NOBLE AND GLOW IN THE SAME DAY!
YOU FELL FROM A BUILDING AND YOU'RE FINE?
ARGHHH!
SHHH.
I DIDN'T REALLY FALL...I MORE LIKE, UM... TUMBLED. SEE, I'M A GYMNAST AND--
THE METEOR SHOWER.

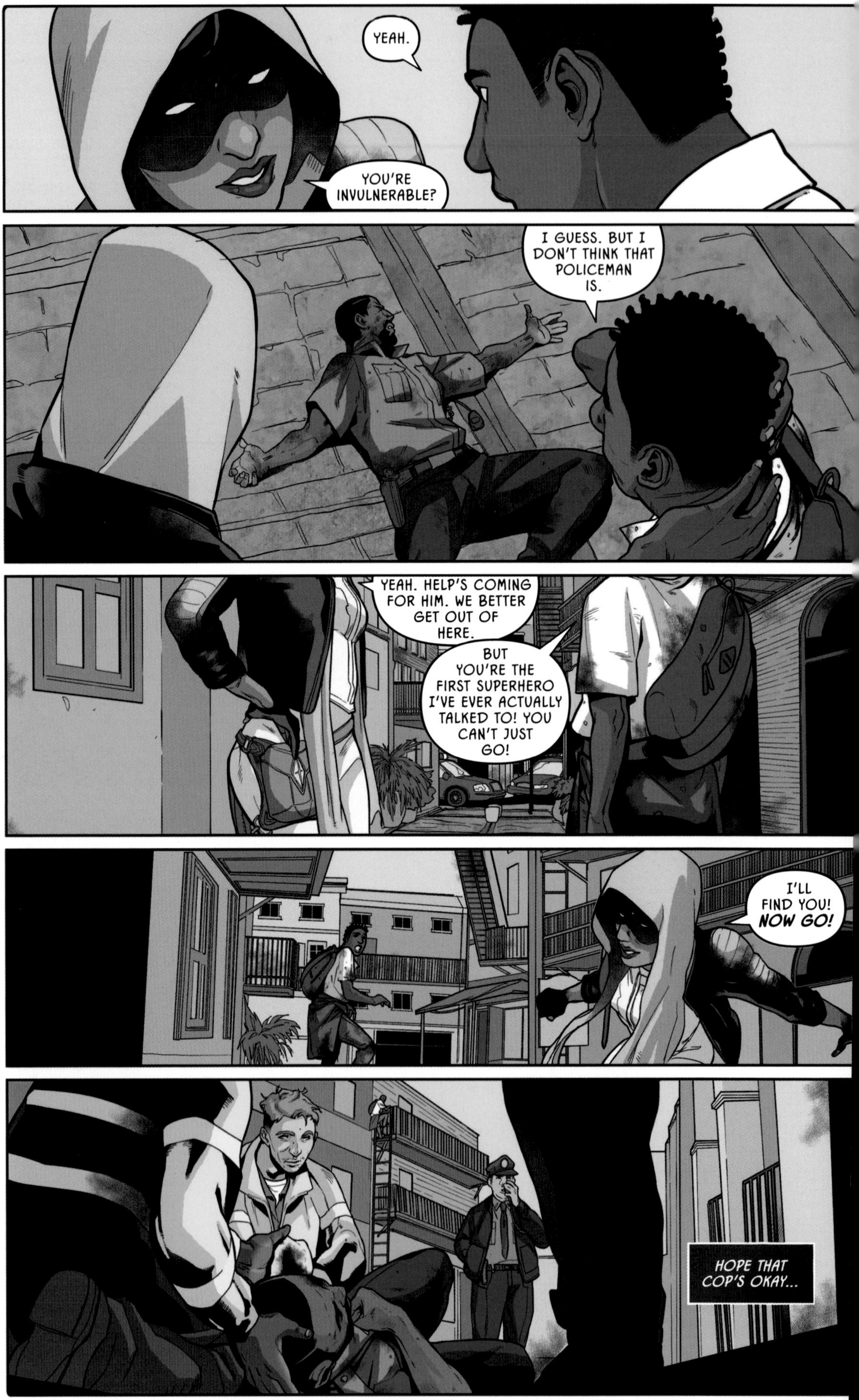
YEAH.
YOU'RE INVULNERABLE?
I GUESS. BUT I DON'T THINK THAT POLICEMAN IS.
YEAH. HELP'S COMING FOR HIM. WE BETTER GET OUT OF HERE.
BUT YOU'RE THE FIRST SUPERHERO I'VE EVER ACTUALLY TALKED TO! YOU CAN'T JUST GO!
I'LL FIND YOU! **NOW GO!**
HOPE THAT COP'S OKAY...

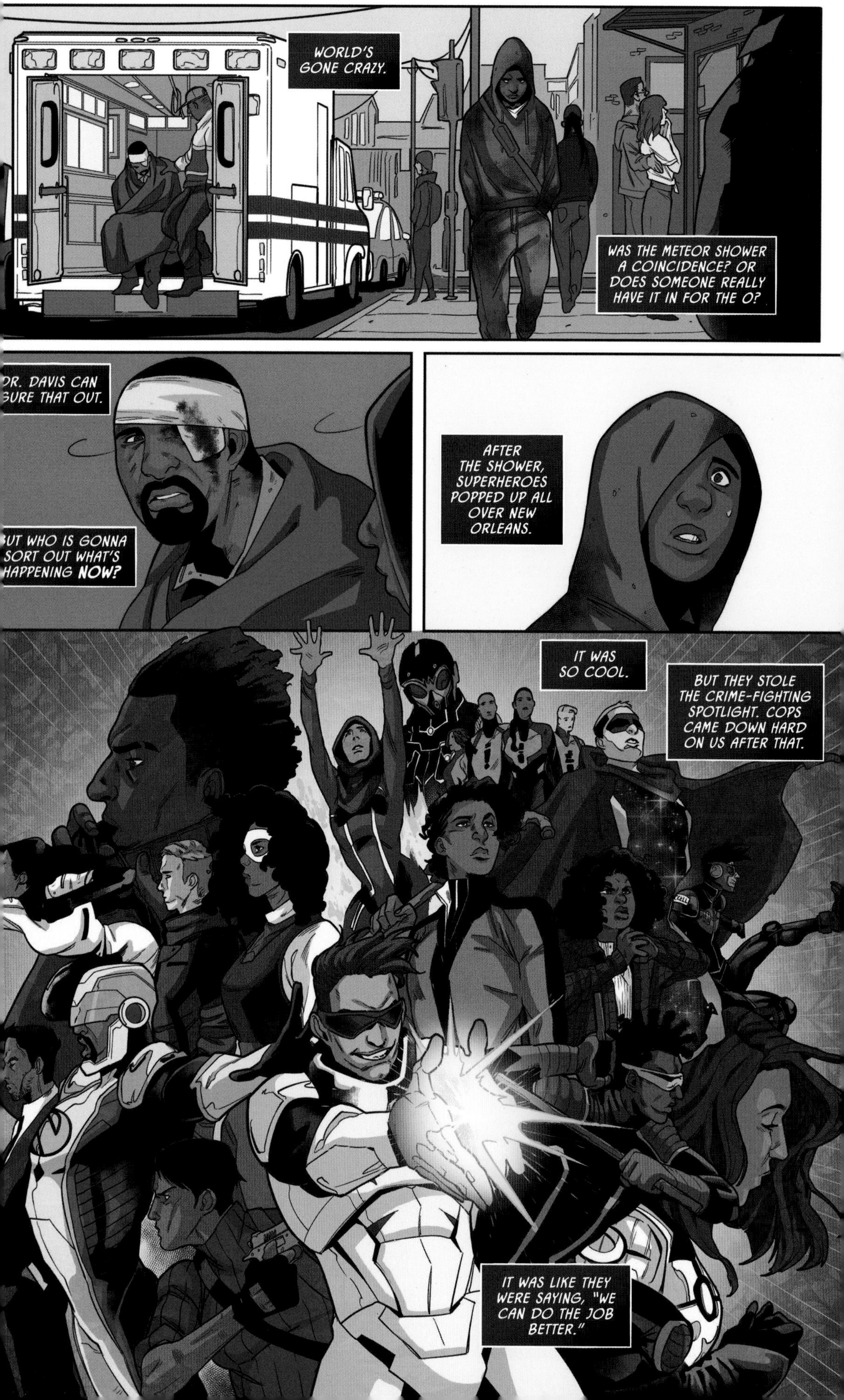

WORLD'S GONE CRAZY.
WAS THE METEOR SHOWER A COINCIDENCE? OR DOES SOMEONE REALLY HAVE IT IN FOR THE O?
R. DAVIS CAN GURE THAT OUT.
UT WHO IS GONNA SORT OUT WHAT'S HAPPENING **NOW?**
AFTER THE SHOWER, SUPERHEROES POPPED UP ALL OVER NEW ORLEANS.
IT WAS SO COOL.
BUT THEY STOLE THE CRIME-FIGHTING SPOTLIGHT. COPS CAME DOWN HARD ON US AFTER THAT.
IT WAS LIKE THEY WERE SAYING, "WE CAN DO THE JOB BETTER."

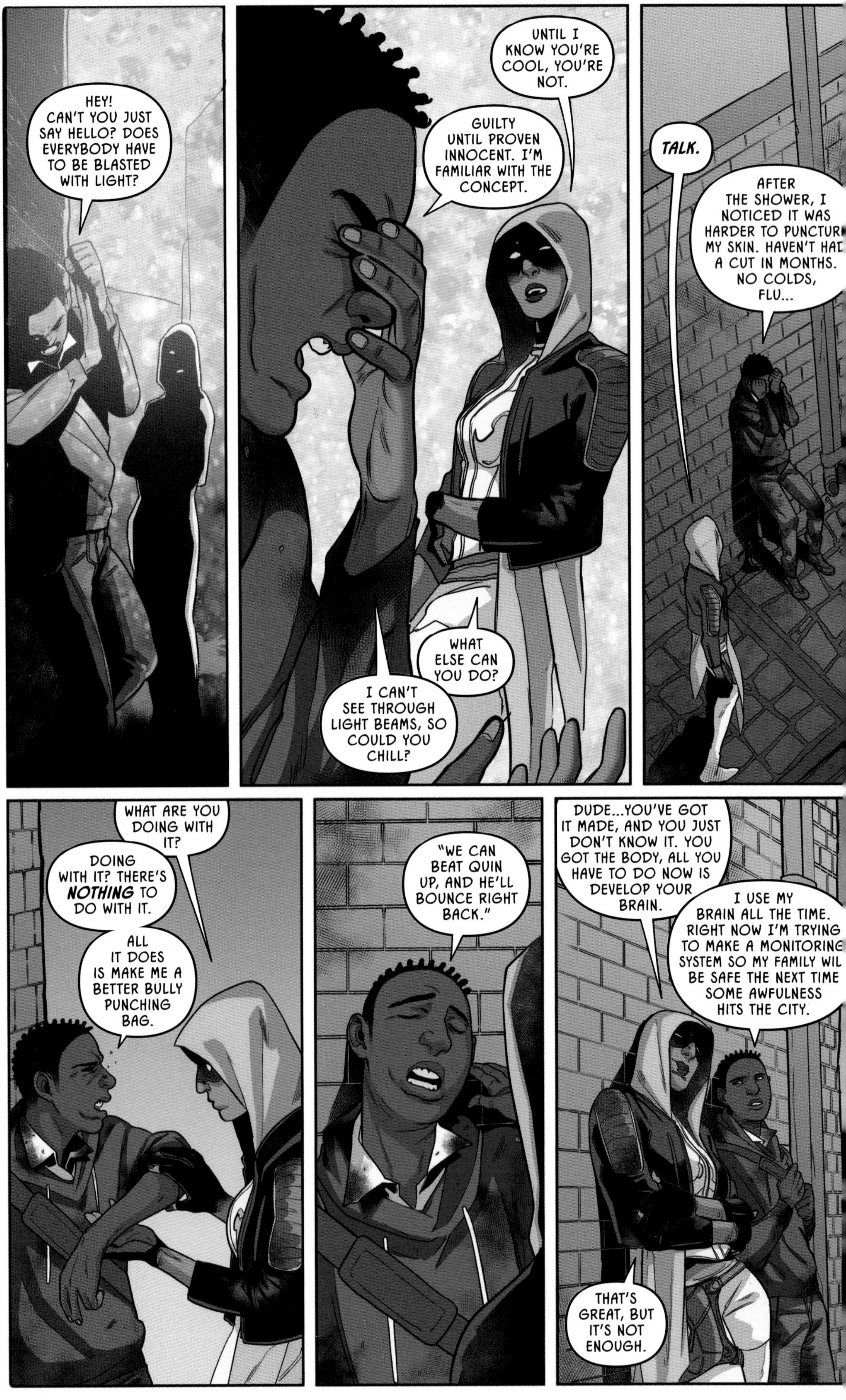
HEY! CAN'T YOU JUST SAY HELLO? DOES EVERYBODY HAVE TO BE BLASTED WITH LIGHT?
UNTIL I KNOW YOU'RE COOL, YOU'RE NOT.
GUILTY UNTIL PROVEN INNOCENT. I'M FAMILIAR WITH THE CONCEPT.
WHAT ELSE CAN YOU DO?
I CAN'T SEE THROUGH LIGHT BEAMS, SO COULD YOU CHILL?
TALK.
AFTER THE SHOWER, I NOTICED IT WAS HARDER TO PUNCTUR MY SKIN. HAVEN'T HAD A CUT IN MONTHS. NO COLDS, FLU...
WHAT ARE YOU DOING WITH IT?
DOING WITH IT? THERE'S NOTHING TO DO WITH IT.
ALL IT DOES IS MAKE ME A BETTER BULLY PUNCHING BAG.
"WE CAN BEAT QUIN UP, AND HE'LL BOUNCE RIGHT BACK."
DUDE...YOU'VE GOT IT MADE, AND YOU JUST DON'T KNOW IT. YOU GOT THE BODY, ALL YOU HAVE TO DO NOW IS DEVELOP YOUR BRAIN.
I USE MY BRAIN ALL THE TIME. RIGHT NOW I'M TRYING TO MAKE A MONITORING SYSTEM SO MY FAMILY WIL BE SAFE THE NEXT TIME SOME AWFULNESS HITS THE CITY.
THAT'S GREAT, BUT IT'S NOT ENOUGH.

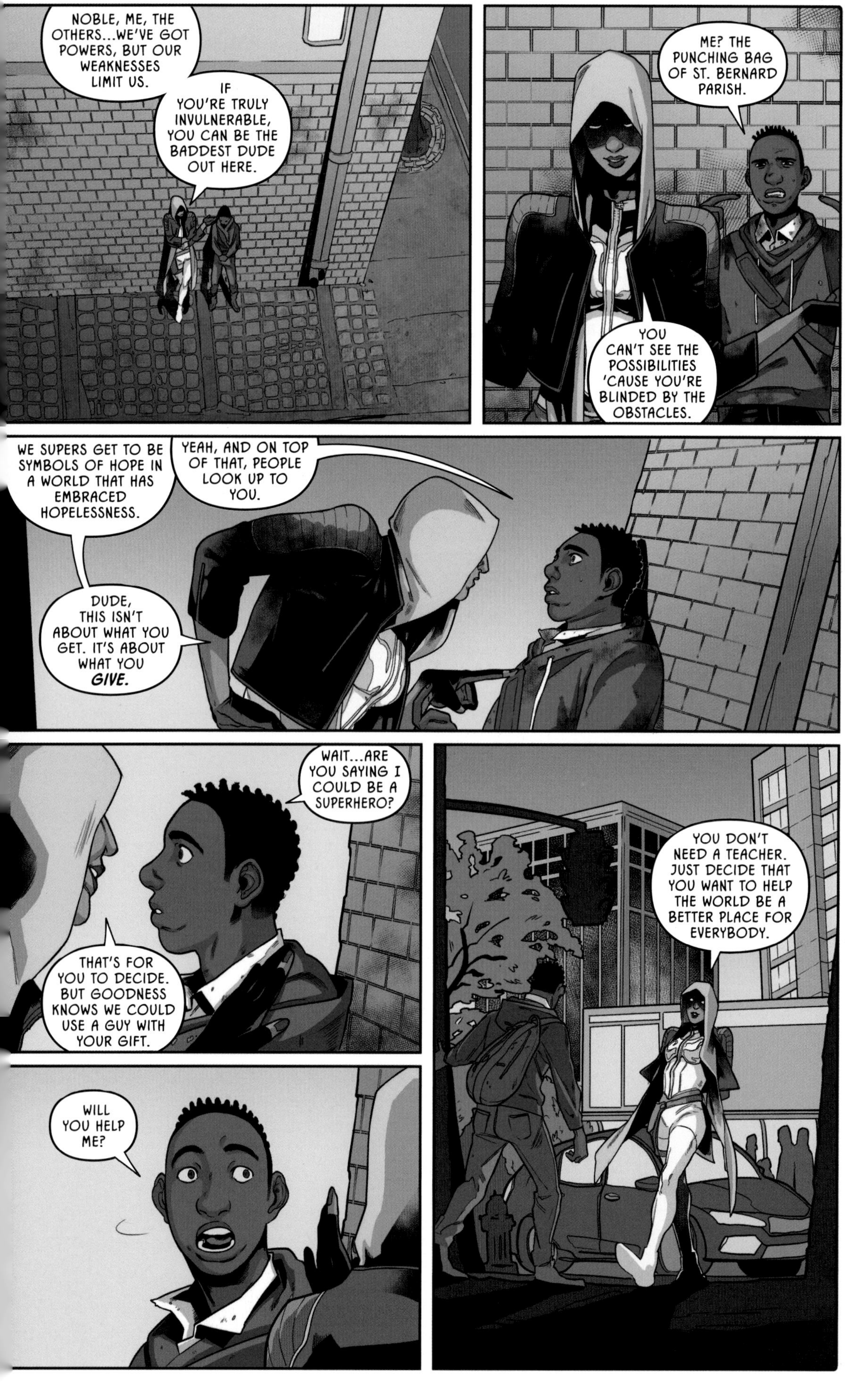

NOBLE, ME, THE OTHERS...WE'VE GOT POWERS, BUT OUR WEAKNESSES LIMIT US.
IF YOU'RE TRULY INVULNERABLE, YOU CAN BE THE BADDEST DUDE OUT HERE.
ME? THE PUNCHING BAG OF ST. BERNARD PARISH.
YOU CAN'T SEE THE POSSIBILITIES 'CAUSE YOU'RE BLINDED BY THE OBSTACLES.
WE SUPERS GET TO BE SYMBOLS OF HOPE IN A WORLD THAT HAS EMBRACED HOPELESSNESS.
YEAH, AND ON TOP OF THAT, PEOPLE LOOK UP TO YOU.
DUDE, THIS ISN'T ABOUT WHAT YOU GET. IT'S ABOUT WHAT YOU ***GIVE.***
WAIT...ARE YOU SAYING I COULD BE A SUPERHERO?
THAT'S FOR YOU TO DECIDE. BUT GOODNESS KNOWS WE COULD USE A GUY WITH YOUR GIFT.
WILL YOU HELP ME?
YOU DON'T NEED A TEACHER. JUST DECIDE THAT YOU WANT TO HELP THE WORLD BE A BETTER PLACE FOR EVERYBODY.

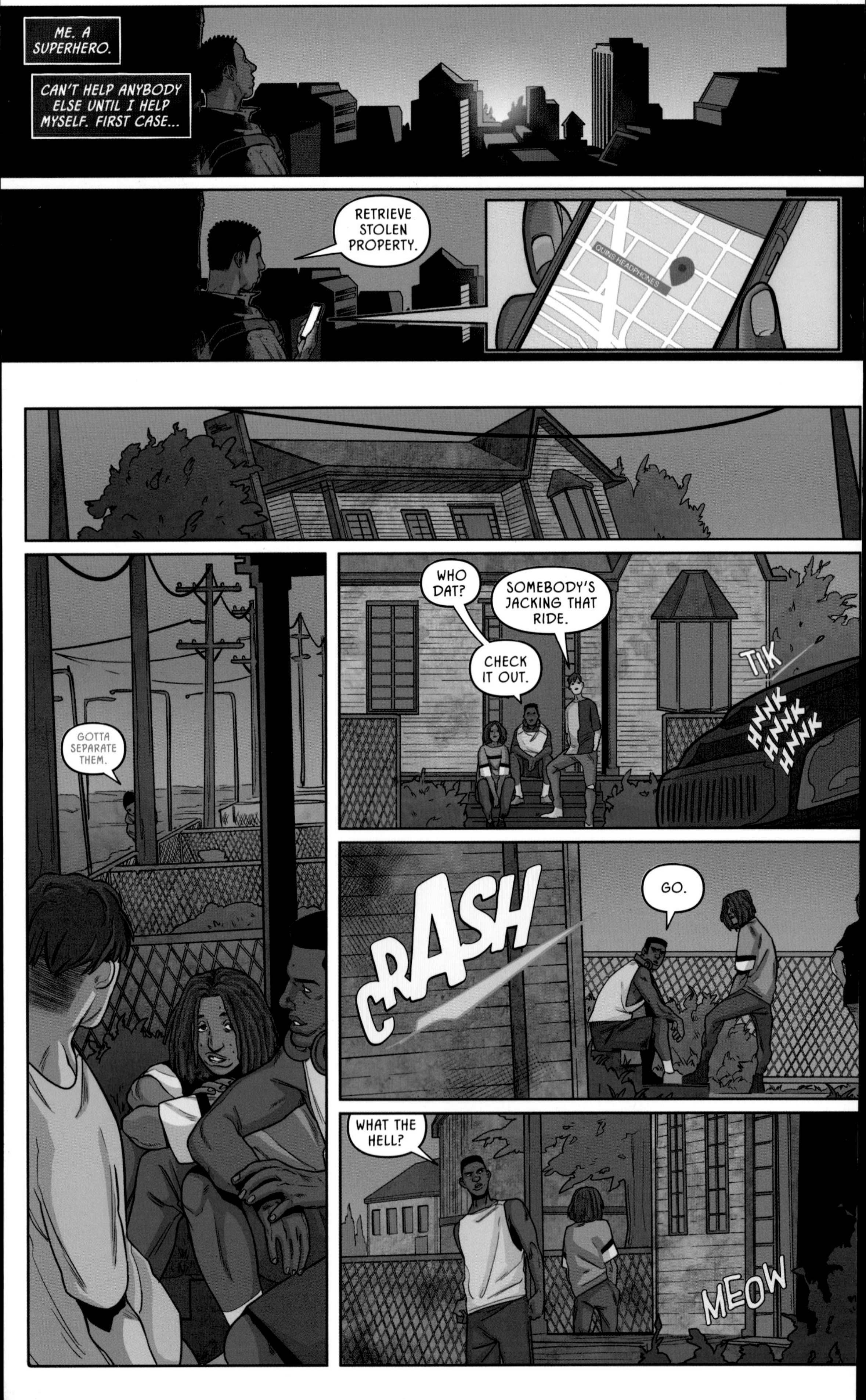
ME. A SUPERHERO.
CAN'T HELP ANYBODY ELSE UNTIL I HELP MYSELF. FIRST CASE...
RETRIEVE STOLEN PROPERTY.
QUINS HEADPHONES
GOTTA SEPARATE THEM.
WHO DAT?
SOMEBODY'S JACKING THAT RIDE.
CHECK IT OUT.
TIK
HNNK HNNK HNNK
CRASH
GO.
WHAT THE HELL?
MEOW

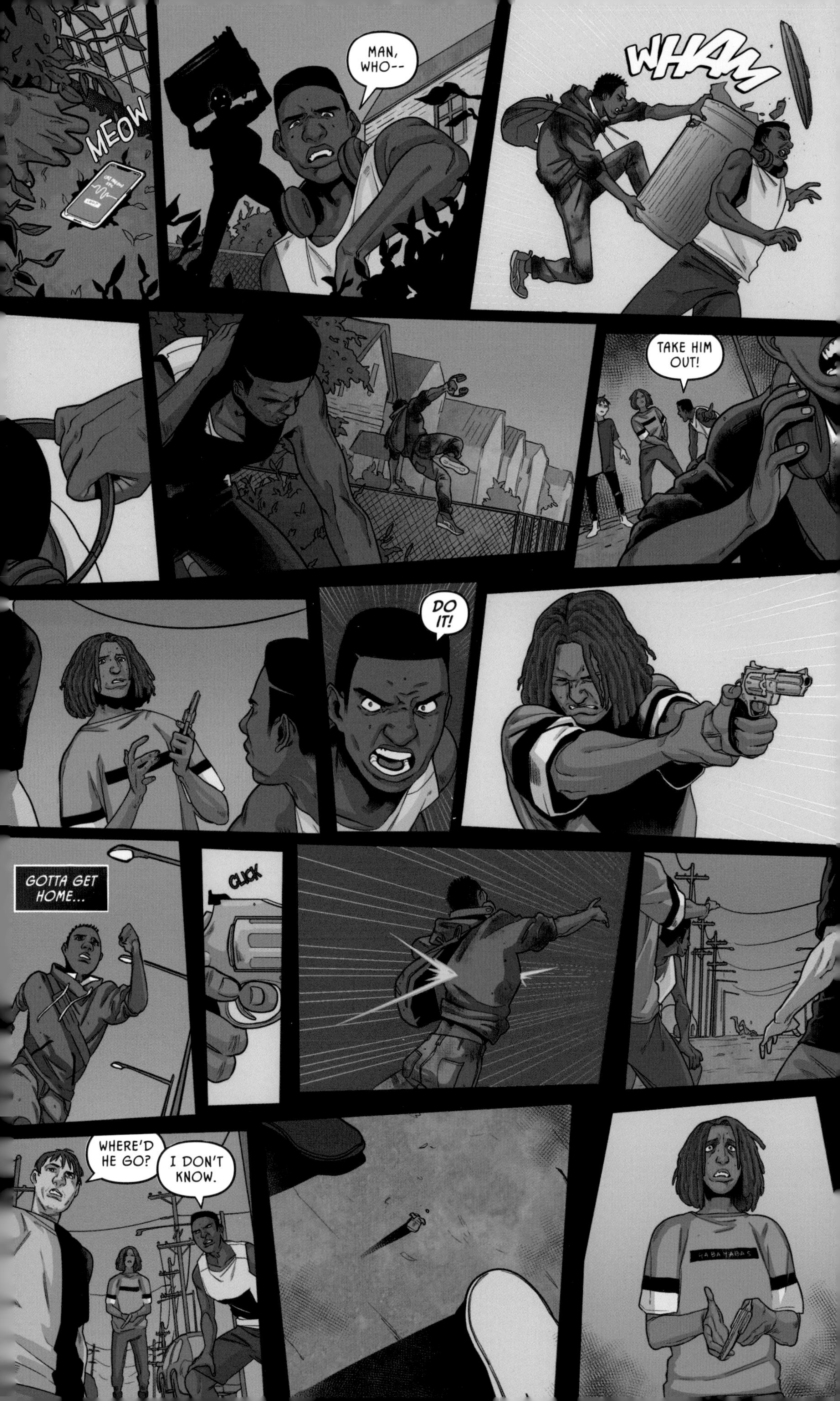
MEOW
MAN, WHO--
WHAM
TAKE HIM OUT!
DO IT!
GOTTA GET HOME...
CLICK
WHERE'D HE GO?
I DON'T KNOW.

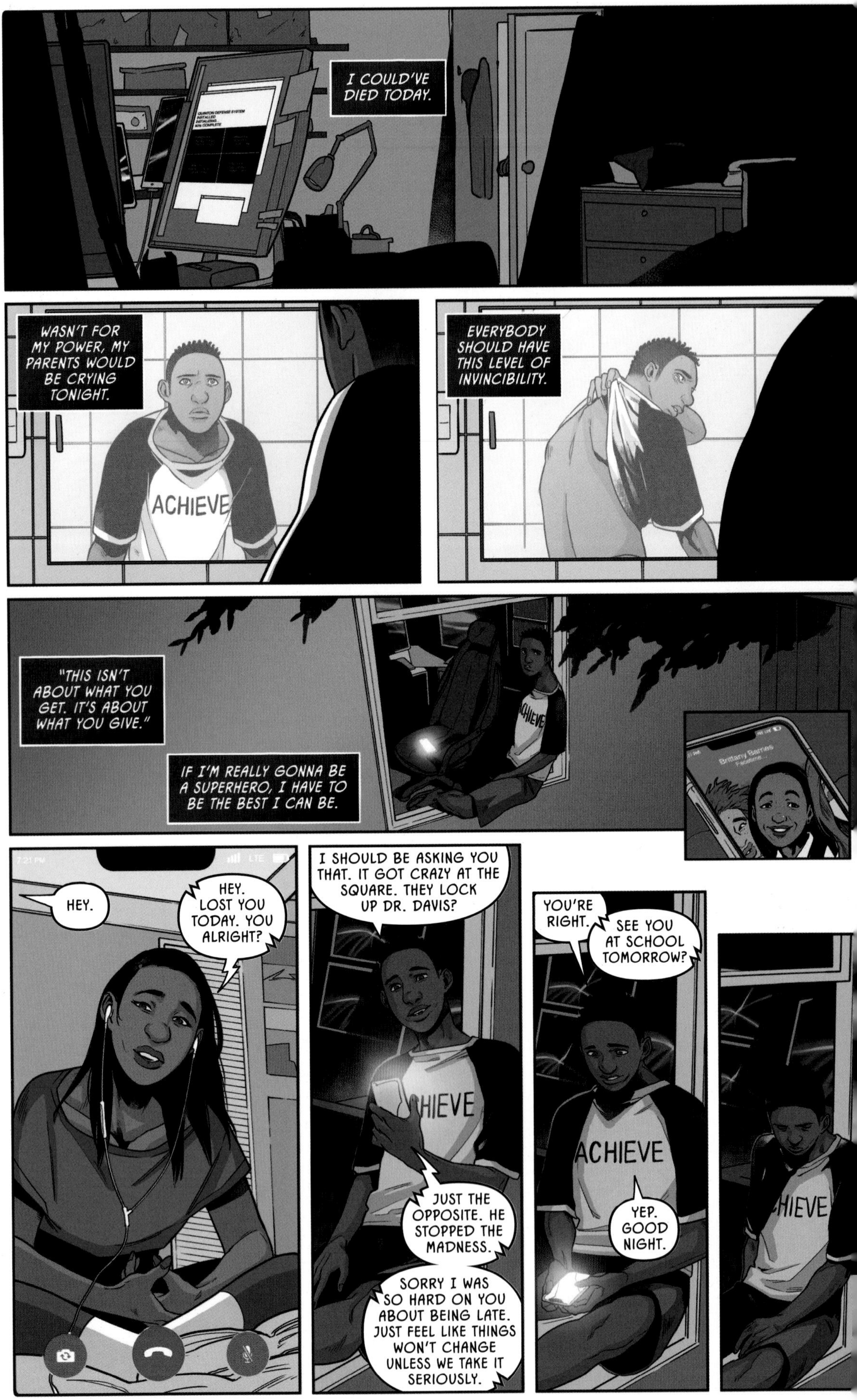
I COULD'VE DIED TODAY.
QUINTON DEFENSE SYSTEM INSTALLED INITIALIZING 80% COMPLETE
WASN'T FOR MY POWER, MY PARENTS WOULD BE CRYING TONIGHT.
ACHIEVE
EVERYBODY SHOULD HAVE THIS LEVEL OF INVINCIBILITY.
"THIS ISN'T ABOUT WHAT YOU GET. IT'S ABOUT WHAT YOU GIVE."
IF I'M REALLY GONNA BE A SUPERHERO, I HAVE TO BE THE BEST I CAN BE.
ACHIEVE
Brittany Barnes
HEY.
HEY. LOST YOU TODAY. YOU ALRIGHT?
I SHOULD BE ASKING YOU THAT. IT GOT CRAZY AT THE SQUARE. THEY LOCK UP DR. DAVIS?
JUST THE OPPOSITE. HE STOPPED THE MADNESS.
SORRY I WAS SO HARD ON YOU ABOUT BEING LATE. JUST FEEL LIKE THINGS WON'T CHANGE UNLESS WE TAKE IT SERIOUSLY.
YOU'RE RIGHT.
SEE YOU AT SCHOOL TOMORROW?
ACHIEVE
YEP. GOOD NIGHT.

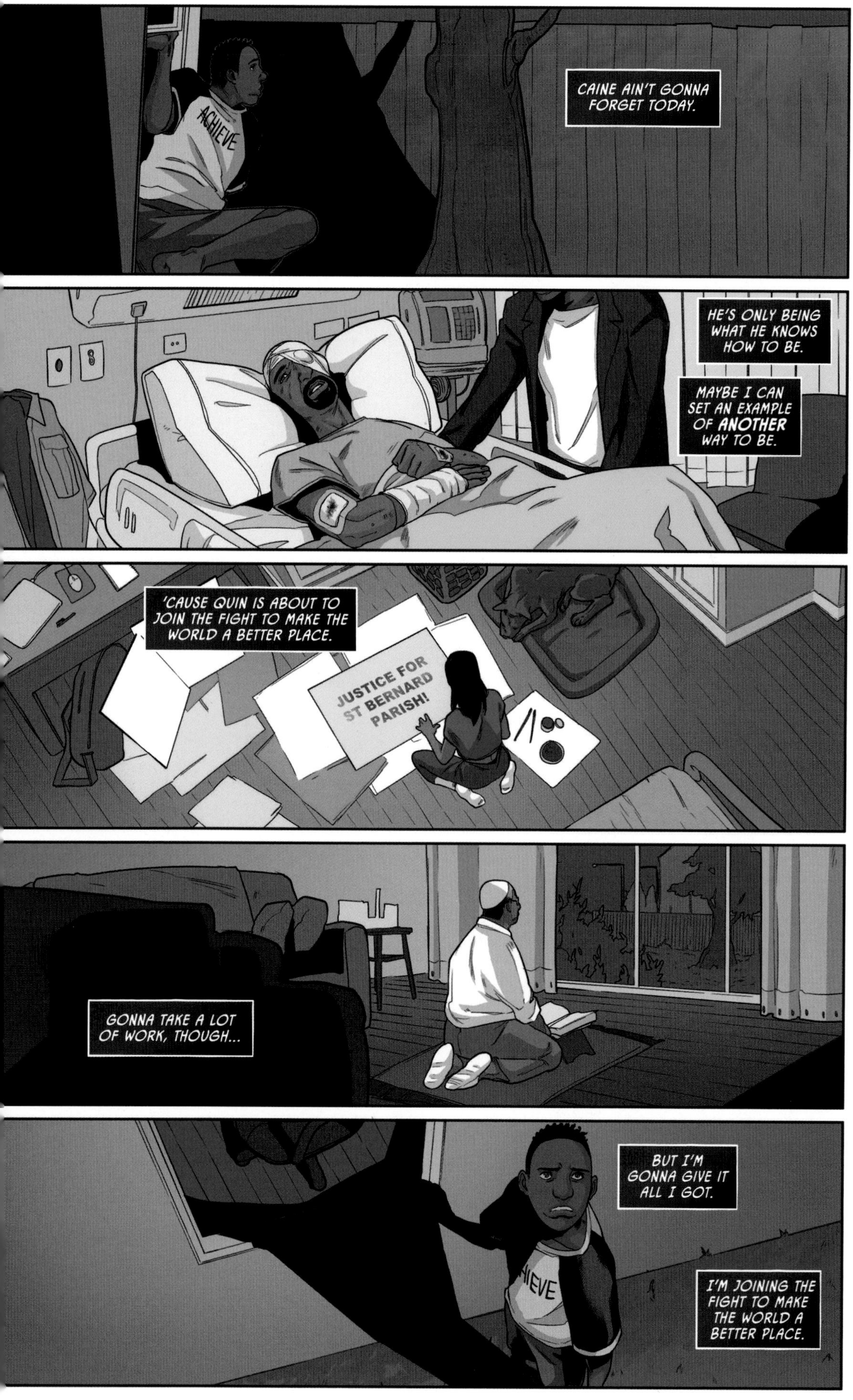
ACHIEVE
CAINE AIN'T GONNA FORGET TODAY.
HE'S ONLY BEING WHAT HE KNOWS HOW TO BE.
MAYBE I CAN SET AN EXAMPLE OF **ANOTHER** WAY TO BE.
'CAUSE QUIN IS ABOUT TO JOIN THE FIGHT TO MAKE THE WORLD A BETTER PLACE.
JUSTICE FOR ST BERNARD PARISH!
GONNA TAKE A LOT OF WORK, THOUGH...
BUT I'M GONNA GIVE IT ALL I GOT.
HIEVE
I'M JOINING THE FIGHT TO MAKE THE WORLD A BETTER PLACE.

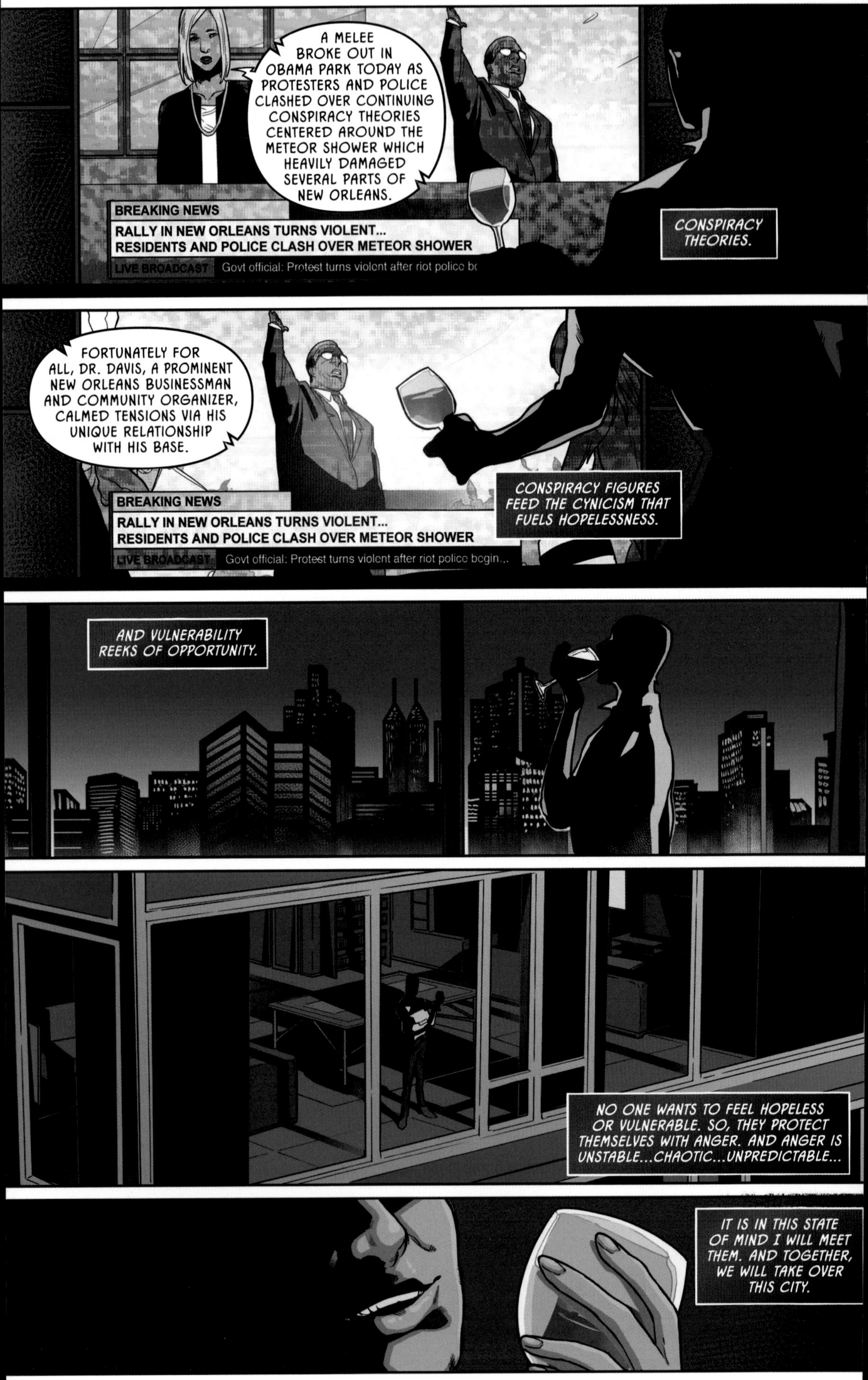
A MELEE BROKE OUT IN OBAMA PARK TODAY AS PROTESTERS AND POLICE CLASHED OVER CONTINUING CONSPIRACY THEORIES CENTERED AROUND THE METEOR SHOWER WHICH HEAVILY DAMAGED SEVERAL PARTS OF NEW ORLEANS.
BREAKING NEWS
RALLY IN NEW ORLEANS TURNS VIOLENT...
RESIDENTS AND POLICE CLASH OVER METEOR SHOWER
LIVE BROADCAST
Govt official: Protest turns violent after riot police bc
CONSPIRACY THEORIES.
FORTUNATELY FOR ALL, DR. DAVIS, A PROMINENT NEW ORLEANS BUSINESSMAN AND COMMUNITY ORGANIZER, CALMED TENSIONS VIA HIS UNIQUE RELATIONSHIP WITH HIS BASE.
BREAKING NEWS
RALLY IN NEW ORLEANS TURNS VIOLENT...
RESIDENTS AND POLICE CLASH OVER METEOR SHOWER
LIVE BROADCAST
Govt official: Protest turns violent after riot police begin...
CONSPIRACY FIGURES FEED THE CYNICISM THAT FUELS HOPELESSNESS.
AND VULNERABILITY REEKS OF OPPORTUNITY.
NO ONE WANTS TO FEEL HOPELESS OR VULNERABLE. SO, THEY PROTECT THEMSELVES WITH ANGER. AND ANGER IS UNSTABLE...CHAOTIC...UNPREDICTABLE...
IT IS IN THIS STATE OF MIND I WILL MEET THEM. AND TOGETHER, WE WILL TAKE OVER THIS CITY.

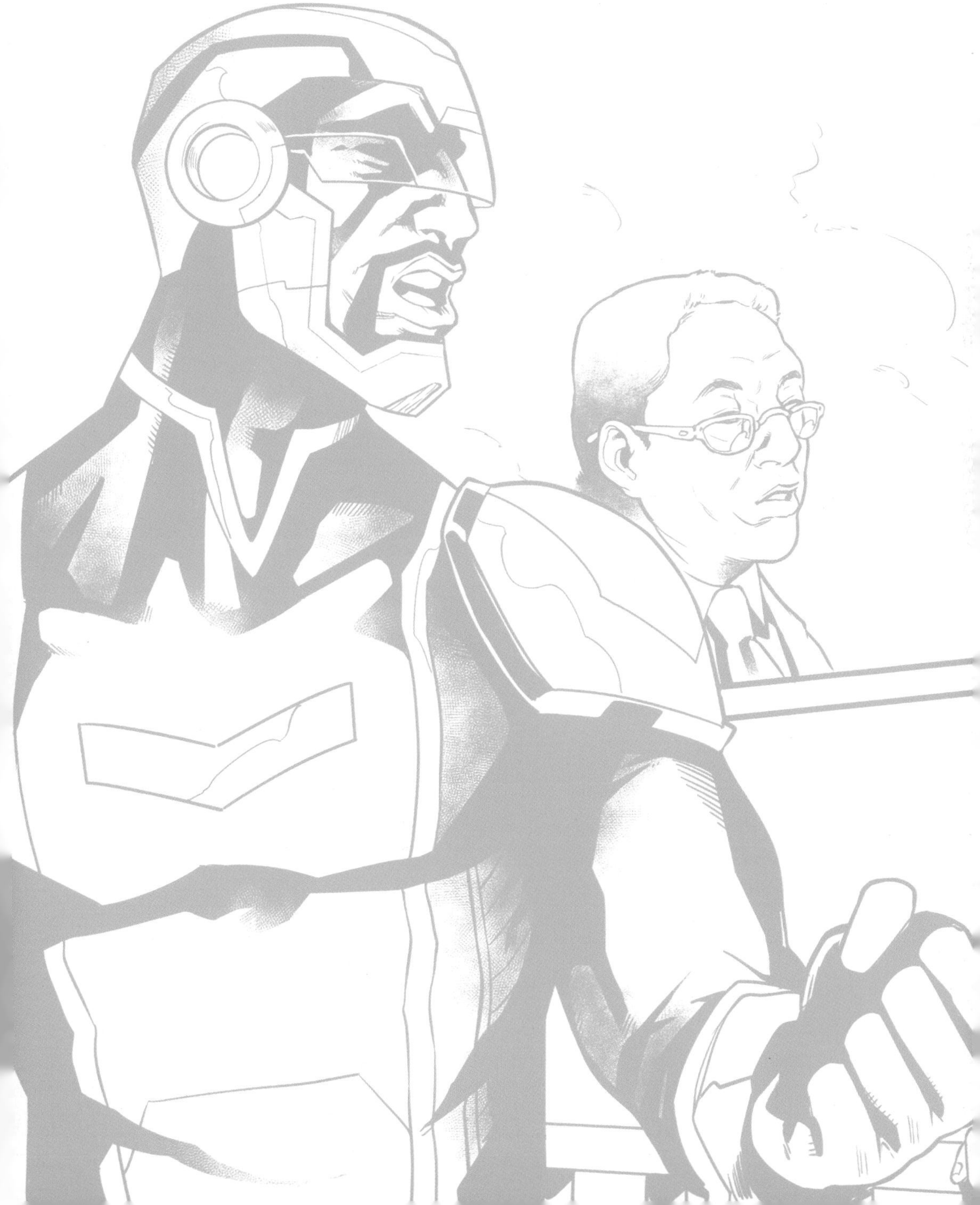

CHAPTER TWO

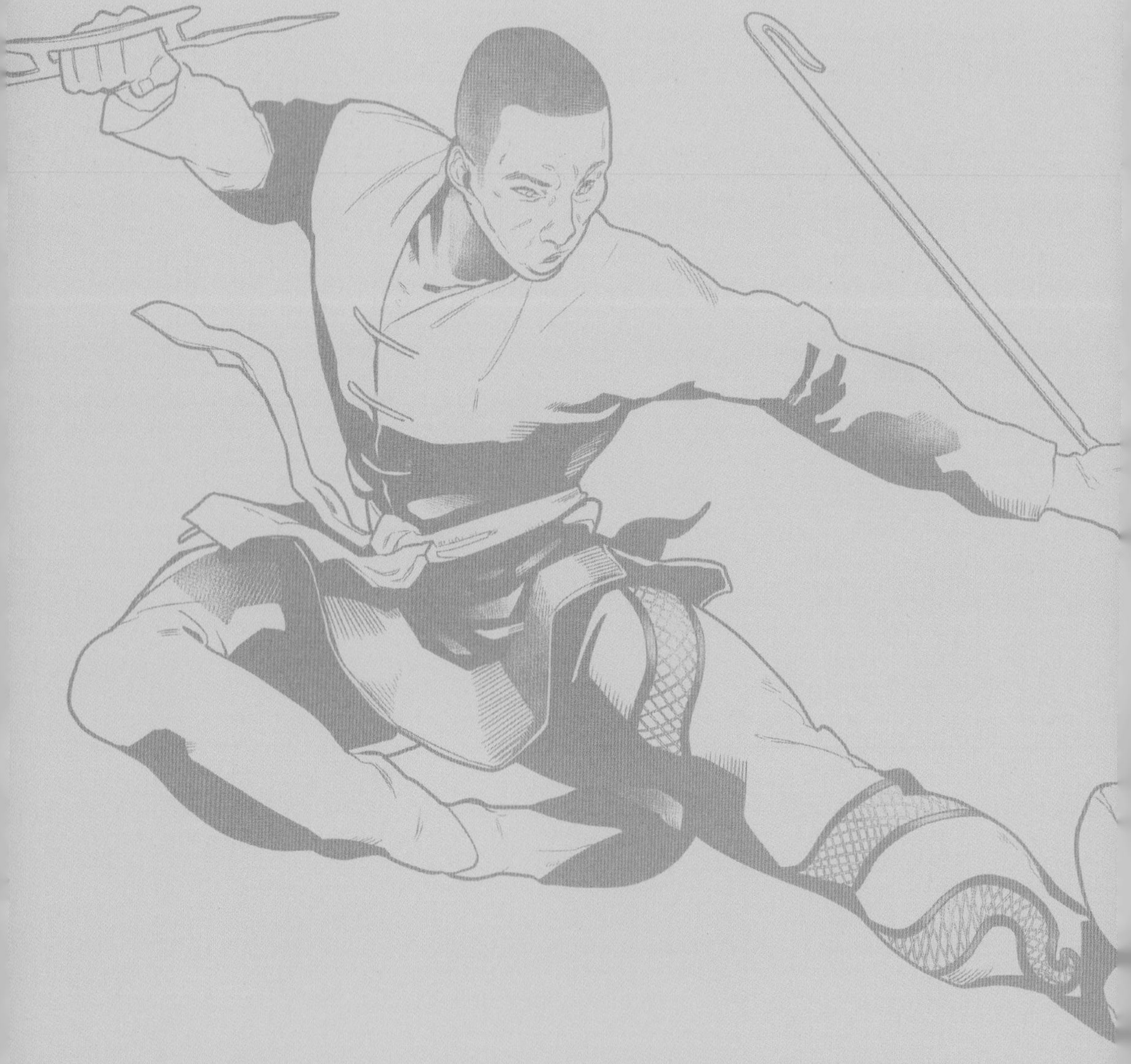

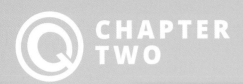

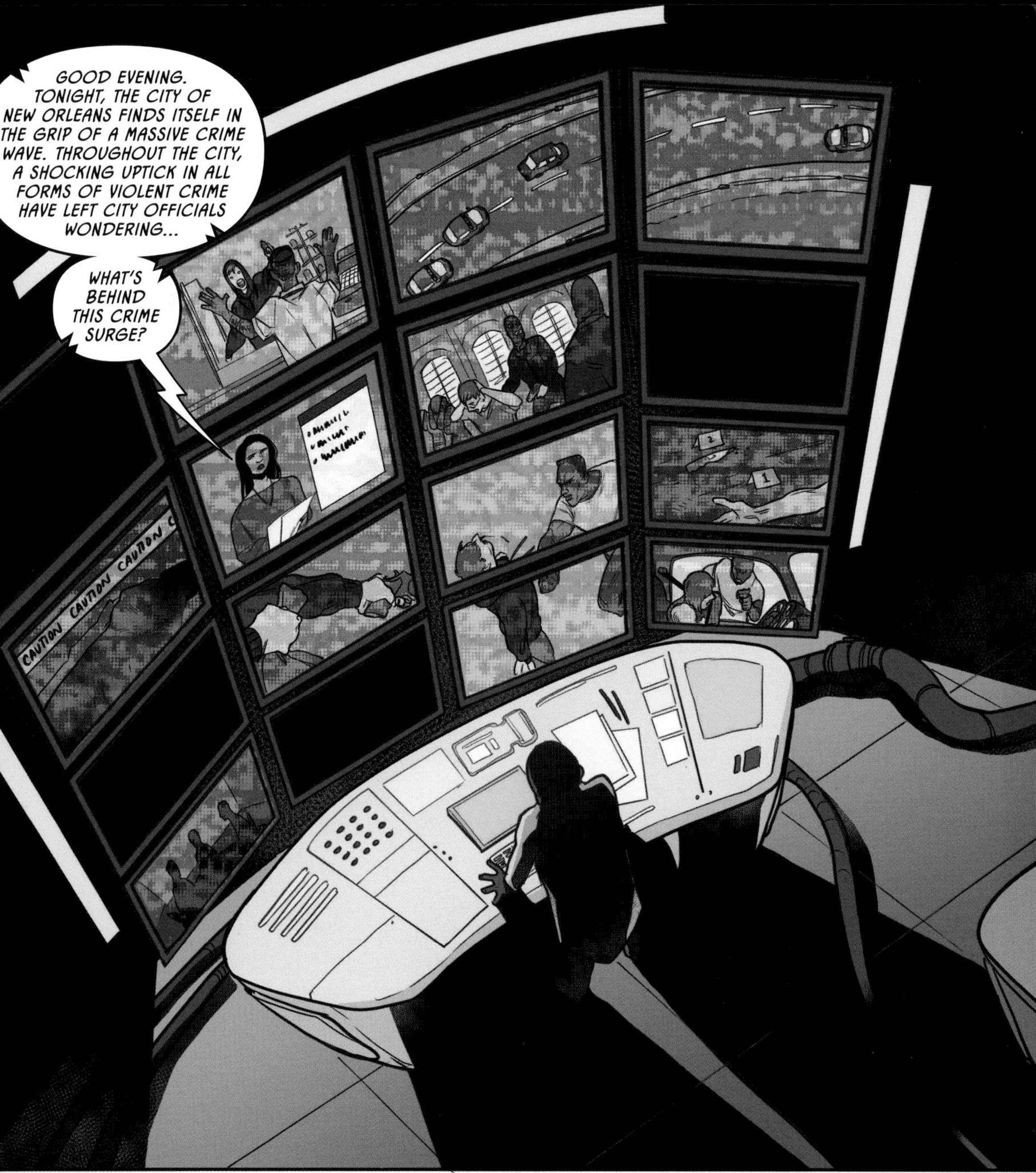
GOOD EVENING. TONIGHT, THE CITY OF NEW ORLEANS FINDS ITSELF IN THE GRIP OF A MASSIVE CRIME WAVE. THROUGHOUT THE CITY, A SHOCKING UPTICK IN ALL FORMS OF VIOLENT CRIME HAVE LEFT CITY OFFICIALS WONDERING...
WHAT'S BEHIND THIS CRIME SURGE?
CAUTION CAUTION CAUTION

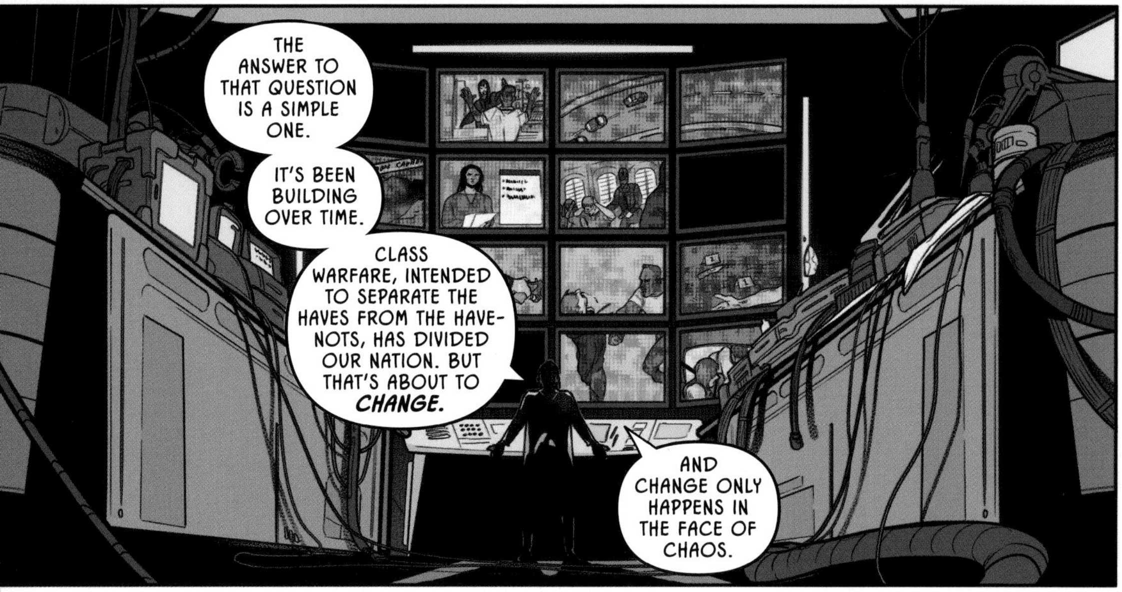
THE ANSWER TO THAT QUESTION IS A SIMPLE ONE.
IT'S BEEN BUILDING OVER TIME.
CLASS WARFARE, INTENDED TO SEPARATE THE HAVES FROM THE HAVE-NOTS, HAS DIVIDED OUR NATION. BUT THAT'S ABOUT TO **CHANGE.**
AND CHANGE ONLY HAPPENS IN THE FACE OF CHAOS.

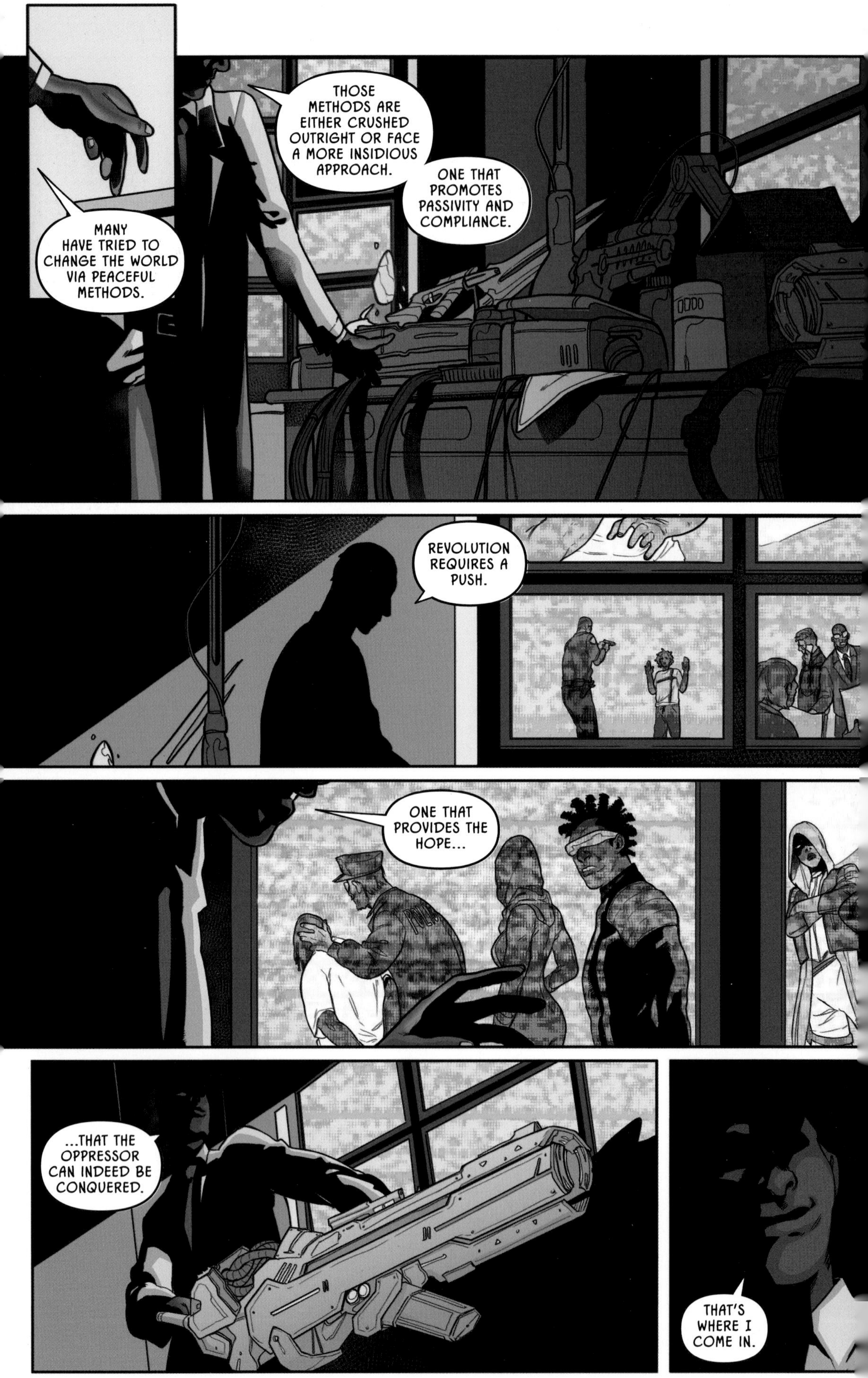
MANY HAVE TRIED TO CHANGE THE WORLD VIA PEACEFUL METHODS.
THOSE METHODS ARE EITHER CRUSHED OUTRIGHT OR FACE A MORE INSIDIOUS APPROACH.
ONE THAT PROMOTES PASSIVITY AND COMPLIANCE.
REVOLUTION REQUIRES A PUSH.
ONE THAT PROVIDES THE HOPE...
...THAT THE OPPRESSOR CAN INDEED BE CONQUERED.
THAT'S WHERE I COME IN.

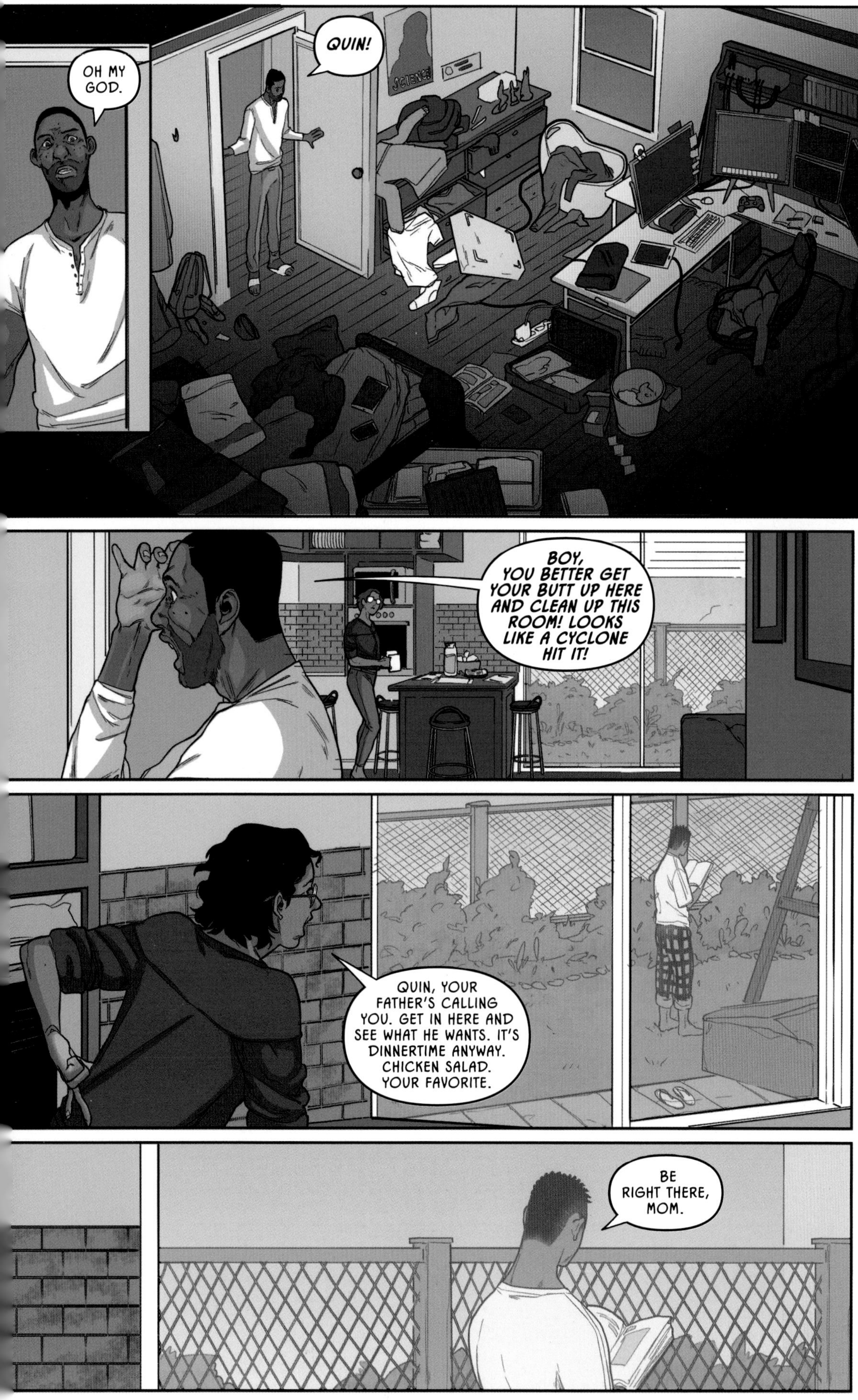
OH MY GOD.
QUIN!
JCIENCE!
BOY, YOU BETTER GET YOUR BUTT UP HERE AND CLEAN UP THIS ROOM! LOOKS LIKE A CYCLONE HIT IT!
QUIN, YOUR FATHER'S CALLING YOU. GET IN HERE AND SEE WHAT HE WANTS. IT'S DINNERTIME ANYWAY. CHICKEN SALAD. YOUR FAVORITE.
BE RIGHT THERE, MOM.

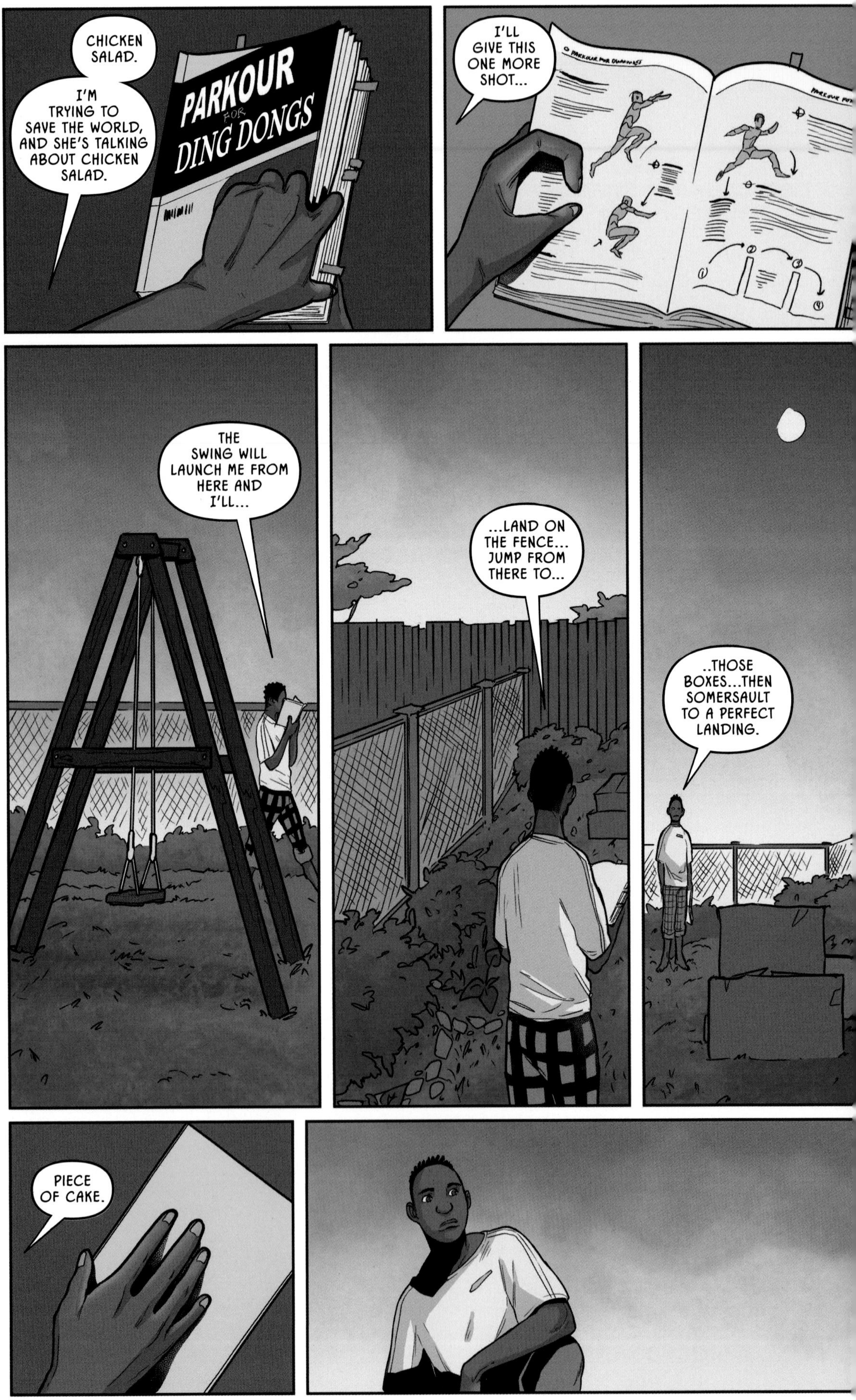
CHICKEN SALAD.
I'M TRYING TO SAVE THE WORLD, AND SHE'S TALKING ABOUT CHICKEN SALAD.
PARKOUR FOR DING DONGS
I'LL GIVE THIS ONE MORE SHOT...
THE SWING WILL LAUNCH ME FROM HERE AND I'LL...
...LAND ON THE FENCE... JUMP FROM THERE TO...
..THOSE BOXES...THEN SOMERSAULT TO A PERFECT LANDING.
PIECE OF CAKE.

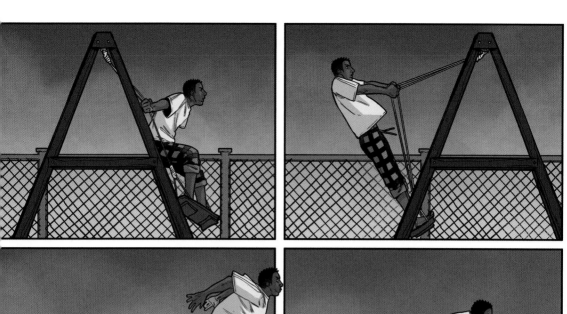

OWFF!

DING DONGS

CHICKEN SALAD DOESN'T SOUND TOO BAD RIGHT ABOUT NOW.

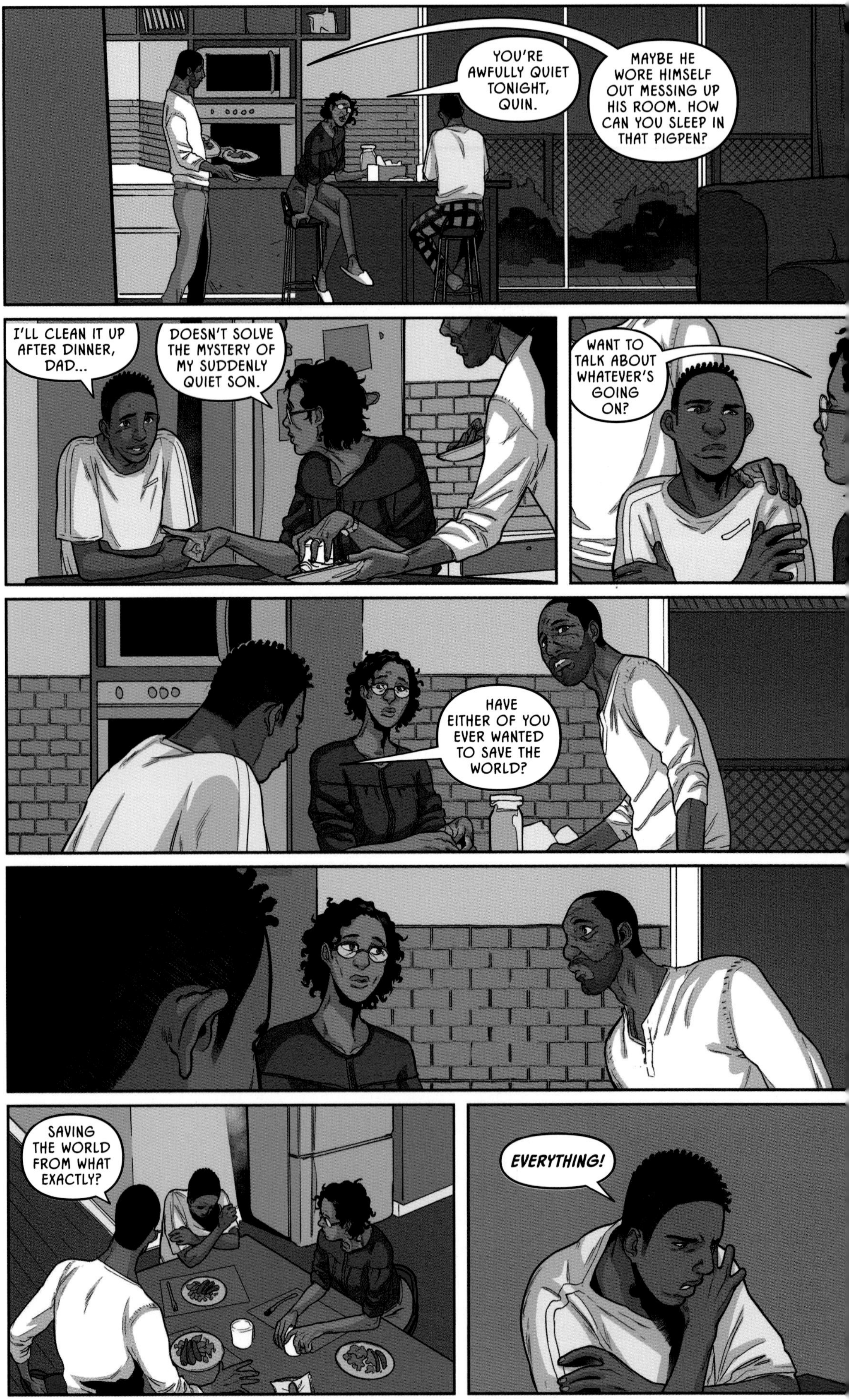
YOU'RE AWFULLY QUIET TONIGHT, QUIN.
MAYBE HE WORE HIMSELF OUT MESSING UP HIS ROOM. HOW CAN YOU SLEEP IN THAT PIGPEN?
I'LL CLEAN IT UP AFTER DINNER, DAD...
DOESN'T SOLVE THE MYSTERY OF MY SUDDENLY QUIET SON.
WANT TO TALK ABOUT WHATEVER'S GOING ON?
HAVE EITHER OF YOU EVER WANTED TO SAVE THE WORLD?
SAVING THE WORLD FROM WHAT EXACTLY?
EVERYTHING!

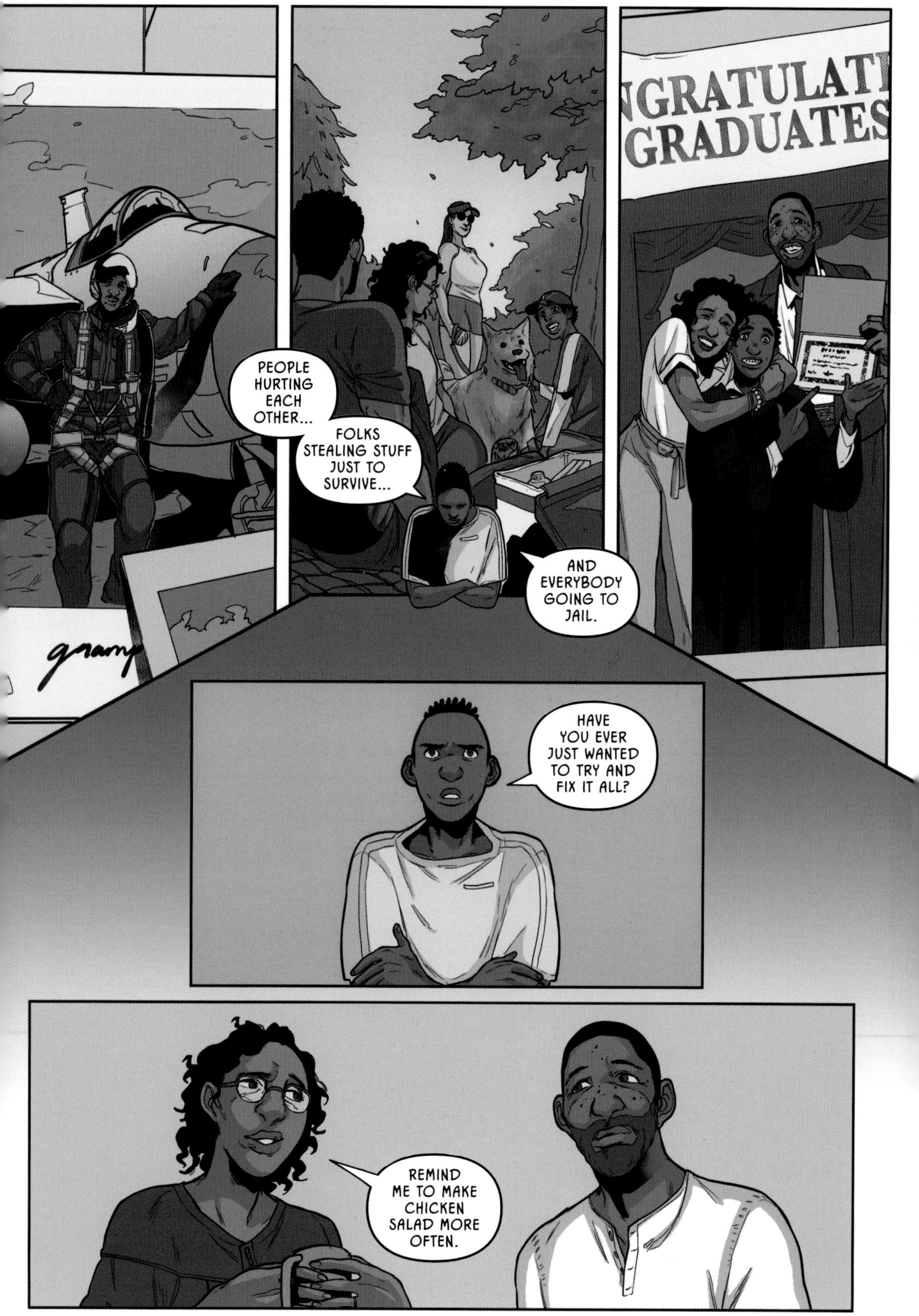
NGRATULATI
GRADUATES
gramp
PEOPLE HURTING EACH OTHER...
FOLKS STEALING STUFF JUST TO SURVIVE...
AND EVERYBODY GOING TO JAIL.
HAVE YOU EVER JUST WANTED TO TRY AND FIX IT ALL?
REMIND ME TO MAKE CHICKEN SALAD MORE OFTEN.

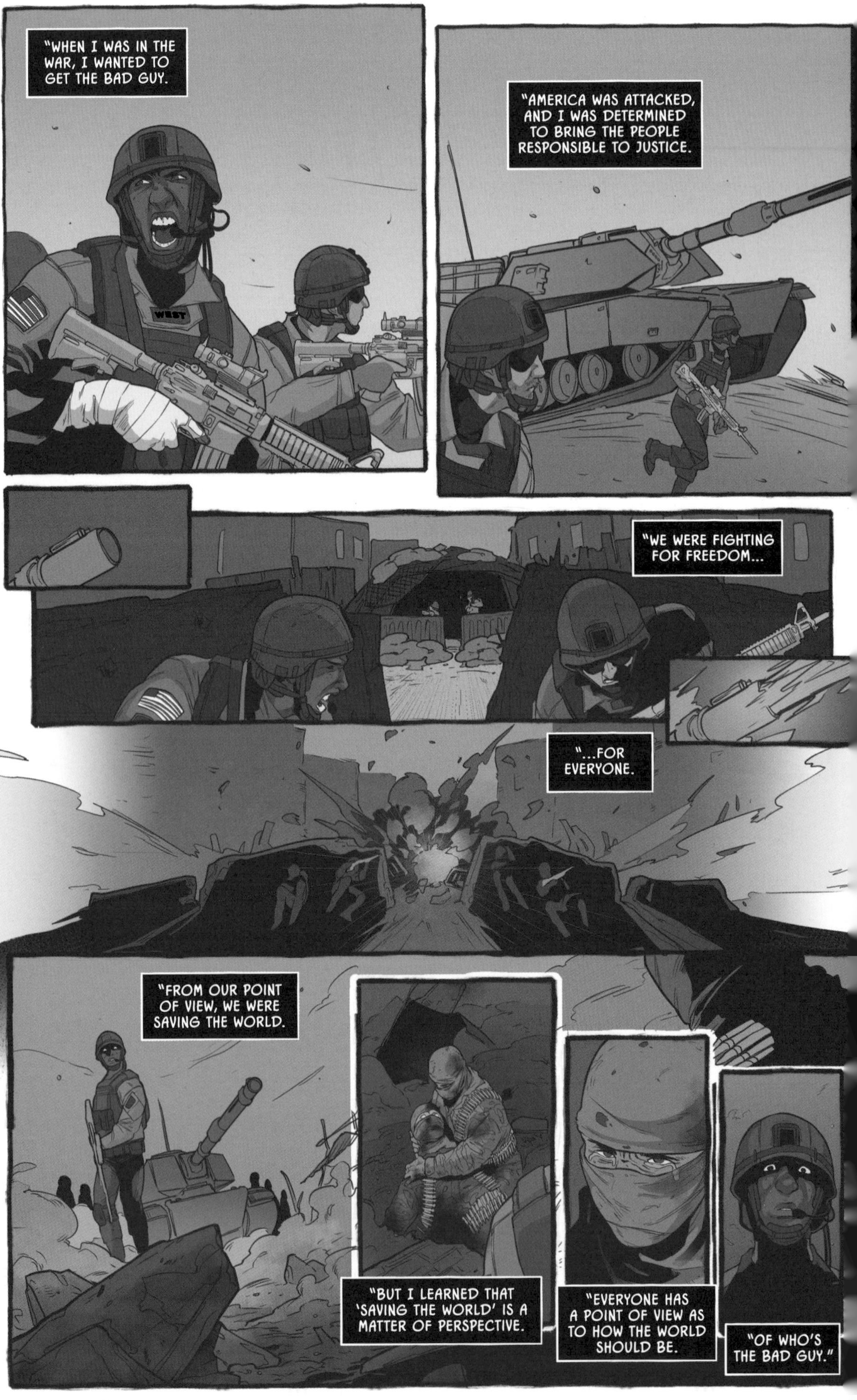
"WHEN I WAS IN THE WAR, I WANTED TO GET THE BAD GUY.
WEST
"AMERICA WAS ATTACKED, AND I WAS DETERMINED TO BRING THE PEOPLE RESPONSIBLE TO JUSTICE.
"WE WERE FIGHTING FOR FREEDOM...
"...FOR EVERYONE.
"FROM OUR POINT OF VIEW, WE WERE SAVING THE WORLD.
"BUT I LEARNED THAT 'SAVING THE WORLD' IS A MATTER OF PERSPECTIVE.
"EVERYONE HAS A POINT OF VIEW AS TO HOW THE WORLD SHOULD BE.
"OF WHO'S THE BAD GUY."

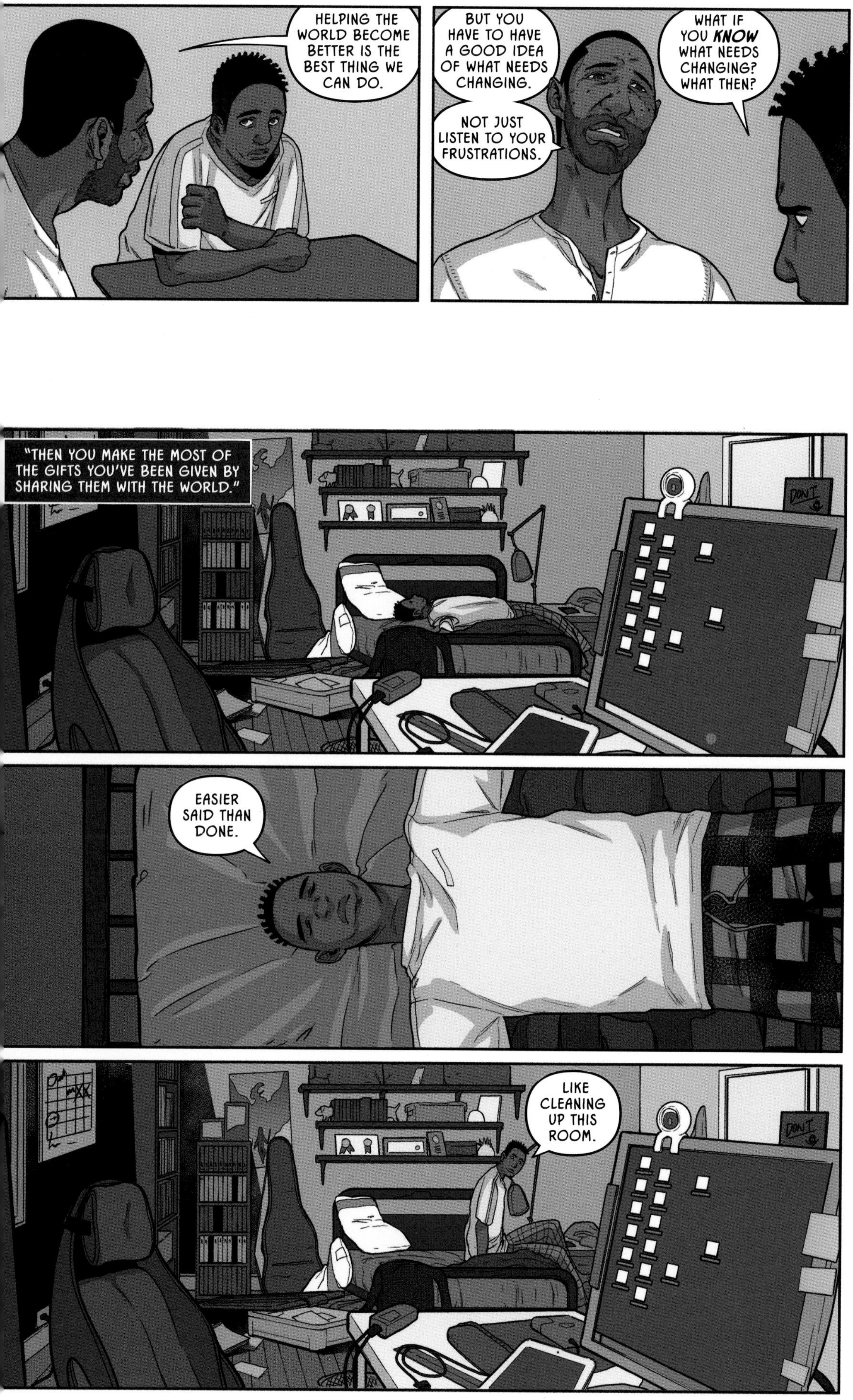
HELPING THE WORLD BECOME BETTER IS THE BEST THING WE CAN DO.
BUT YOU HAVE TO HAVE A GOOD IDEA OF WHAT NEEDS CHANGING.
NOT JUST LISTEN TO YOUR FRUSTRATIONS.
WHAT IF YOU ***KNOW*** WHAT NEEDS CHANGING? WHAT THEN?
"THEN YOU MAKE THE MOST OF THE GIFTS YOU'VE BEEN GIVEN BY SHARING THEM WITH THE WORLD."
EASIER SAID THAN DONE.
LIKE CLEANING UP THIS ROOM.

I'M NOT GOING TO BEAT UP ANYONE ANYTIME SOON.

SO I'VE GOT TO FIGURE OUT HOW TO GET THEM WITHOUT THEM KNOWING THEY'RE GETTING GOT.

HEY...

WHAT IF I CAN STAY THREE STEPS AHEAD OF THE BAD GUYS? MIGHT HAVE TO GET IN THE LINE OF FIRE, BUT IT'S NOT LIKE THEY CAN HURT ME. LET'S GET SOME INFO, AS DAD WOULD SAY...

CRIME STATS FOR THE PARISH...WHO'S BEEN GETTING HIT THE HARDEST?

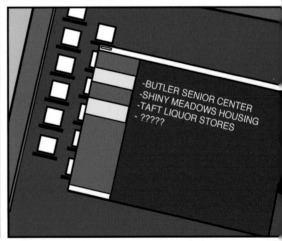

-BUTLER SENIOR CENTER
-SHINY MEADOWS HOUSING
-TAFT LIQUOR STORES
- ?????

WELL, FOLKS, GET READY FOR A SIGNIFICANT DROP IN CRIME.

HOPEFULLY.

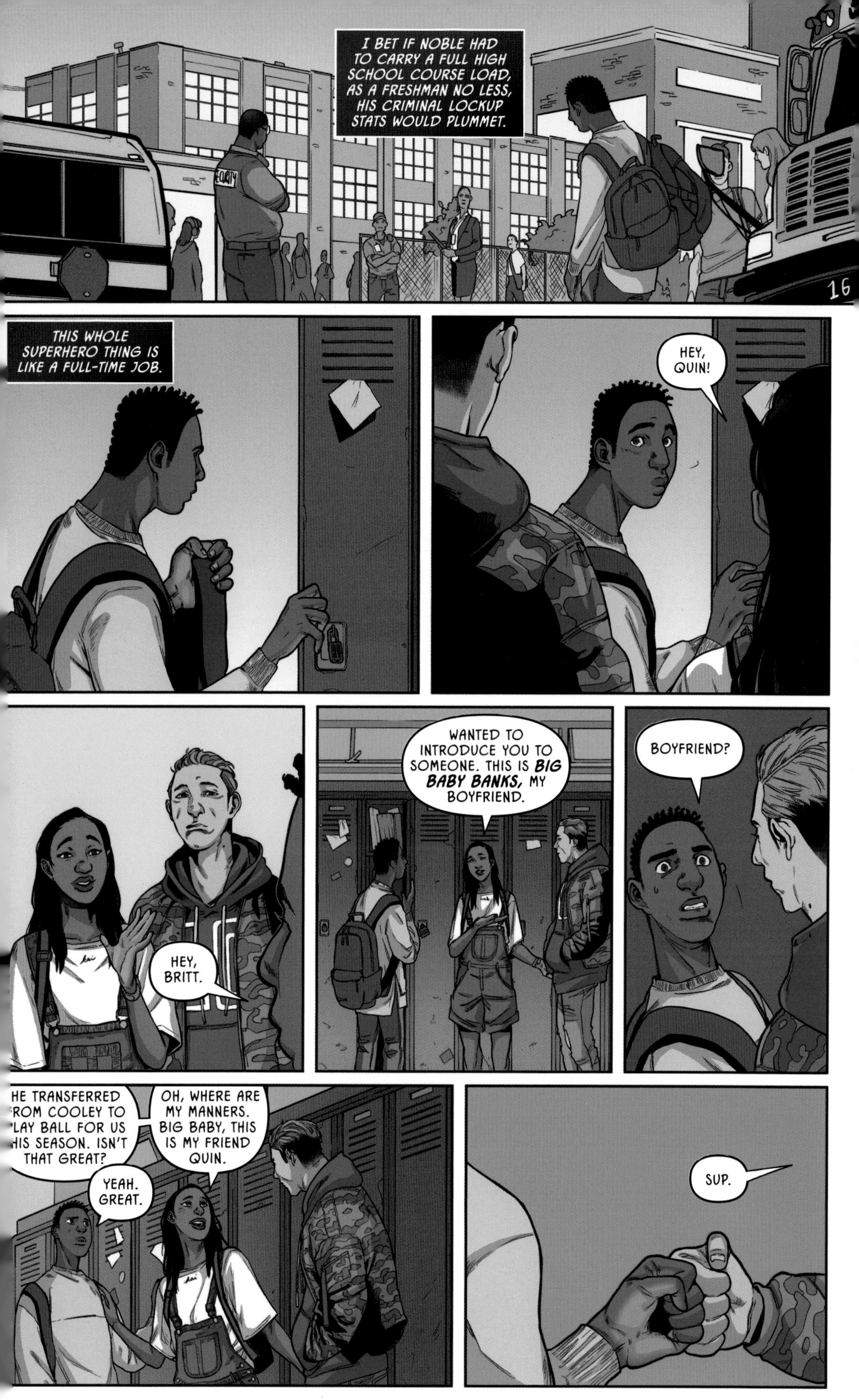
I BET IF NOBLE HAD TO CARRY A FULL HIGH SCHOOL COURSE LOAD, AS A FRESHMAN NO LESS, HIS CRIMINAL LOCKUP STATS WOULD PLUMMET.
SECURITY
16
THIS WHOLE SUPERHERO THING IS LIKE A FULL-TIME JOB.
HEY, QUIN!
HEY, BRITT.
WANTED TO INTRODUCE YOU TO SOMEONE. THIS IS BIG BABY BANKS, MY BOYFRIEND.
BOYFRIEND?
HE TRANSFERRED FROM COOLEY TO PLAY BALL FOR US THIS SEASON. ISN'T THAT GREAT?
OH, WHERE ARE MY MANNERS. BIG BABY, THIS IS MY FRIEND QUIN.
YEAH. GREAT.
SUP.

SUP, MAN. SO, YOU'RE A BALL PLAYER?

VARSITY. 22 POINTS A GAME. SECOND BEST PPG IN THE CITY.

DOPE. ME? 3.7 GPA. 14TH IN MY CLASS.

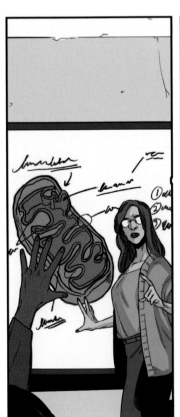

IF SHE KNEW I WAS HELPING THE CITY, WOULD IT MAKE A DIFFERENCE?

WOULD I STILL BE JUST A "FRIEND?"

OR IS 22 POINTS A GAME ALL THAT MATTERS?

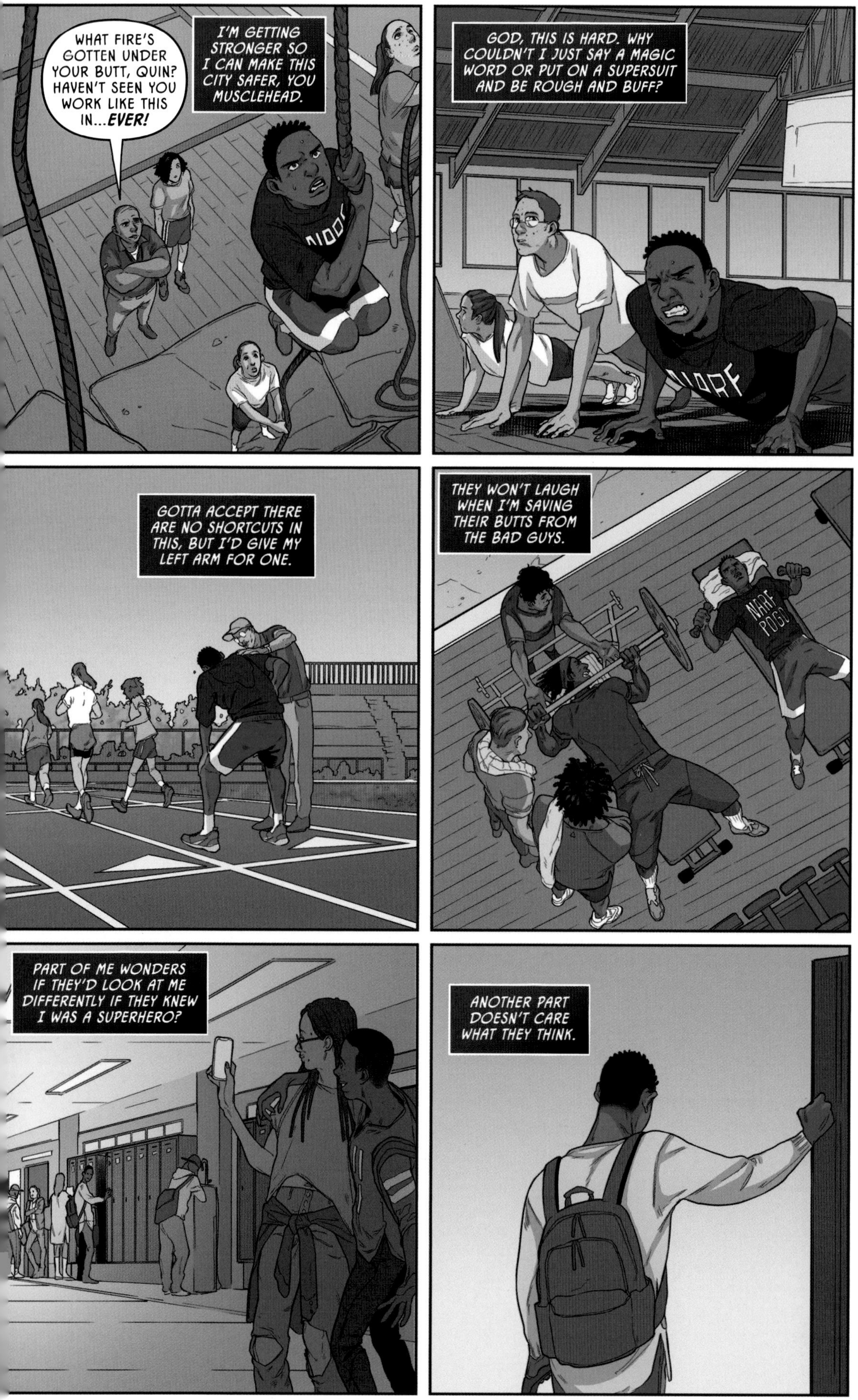

WHAT FIRE'S GOTTEN UNDER YOUR BUTT, QUIN? HAVEN'T SEEN YOU WORK LIKE THIS IN...EVER!
I'M GETTING STRONGER SO I CAN MAKE THIS CITY SAFER, YOU MUSCLEHEAD.
GOD, THIS IS HARD. WHY COULDN'T I JUST SAY A MAGIC WORD OR PUT ON A SUPERSUIT AND BE ROUGH AND BUFF?
GOTTA ACCEPT THERE ARE NO SHORTCUTS IN THIS, BUT I'D GIVE MY LEFT ARM FOR ONE.
THEY WON'T LAUGH WHEN I'M SAVING THEIR BUTTS FROM THE BAD GUYS.
NARF POGO
PART OF ME WONDERS IF THEY'D LOOK AT ME DIFFERENTLY IF THEY KNEW I WAS A SUPERHERO?
ANOTHER PART DOESN'T CARE WHAT THEY THINK.

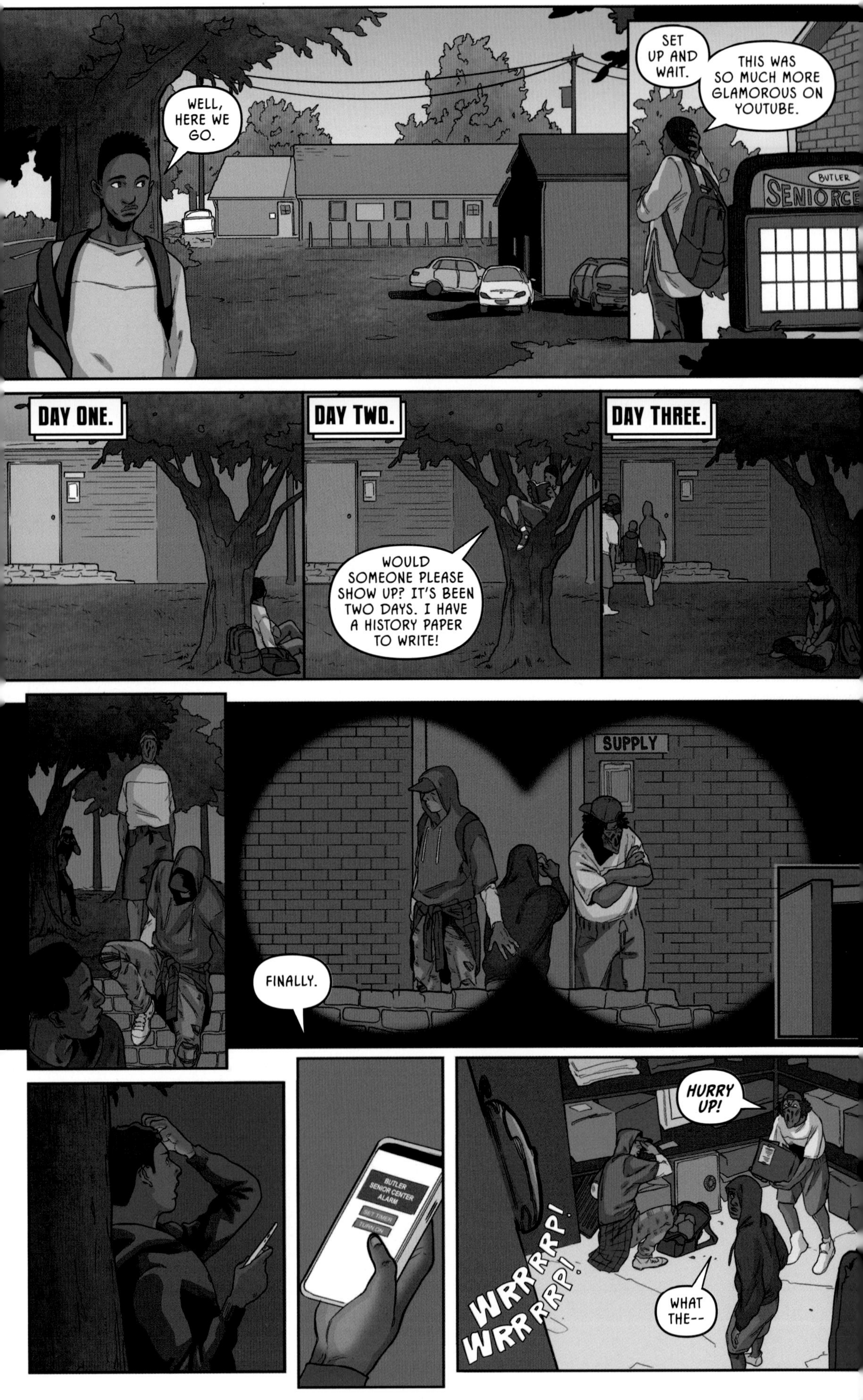
WELL, HERE WE GO.
SET UP AND WAIT.
THIS WAS SO MUCH MORE GLAMOROUS ON YOUTUBE.
BUTLER
SENIOR CE
DAY ONE.
DAY TWO.
WOULD SOMEONE PLEASE SHOW UP? IT'S BEEN TWO DAYS. I HAVE A HISTORY PAPER TO WRITE!
DAY THREE.
SUPPLY
FINALLY.
BUTLER SENIOR CENTER ALARM
SET TIMER
TURN ON
HURRY UP!
WRRRRRP! WRRRRRP!
WHAT THE--

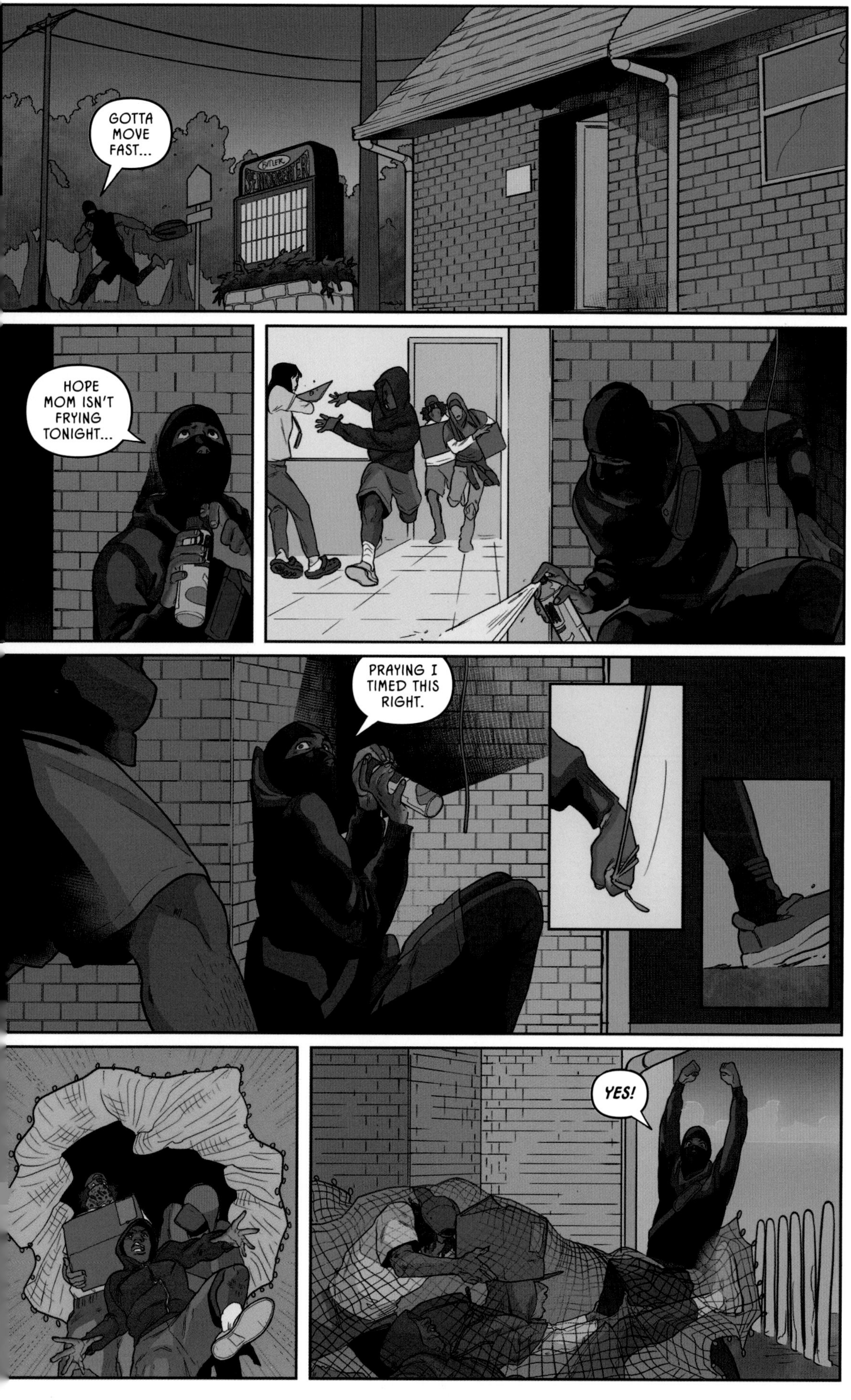
GOTTA MOVE FAST...
HOPE MOM ISN'T FRYING TONIGHT...
PRAYING I TIMED THIS RIGHT.
YES!

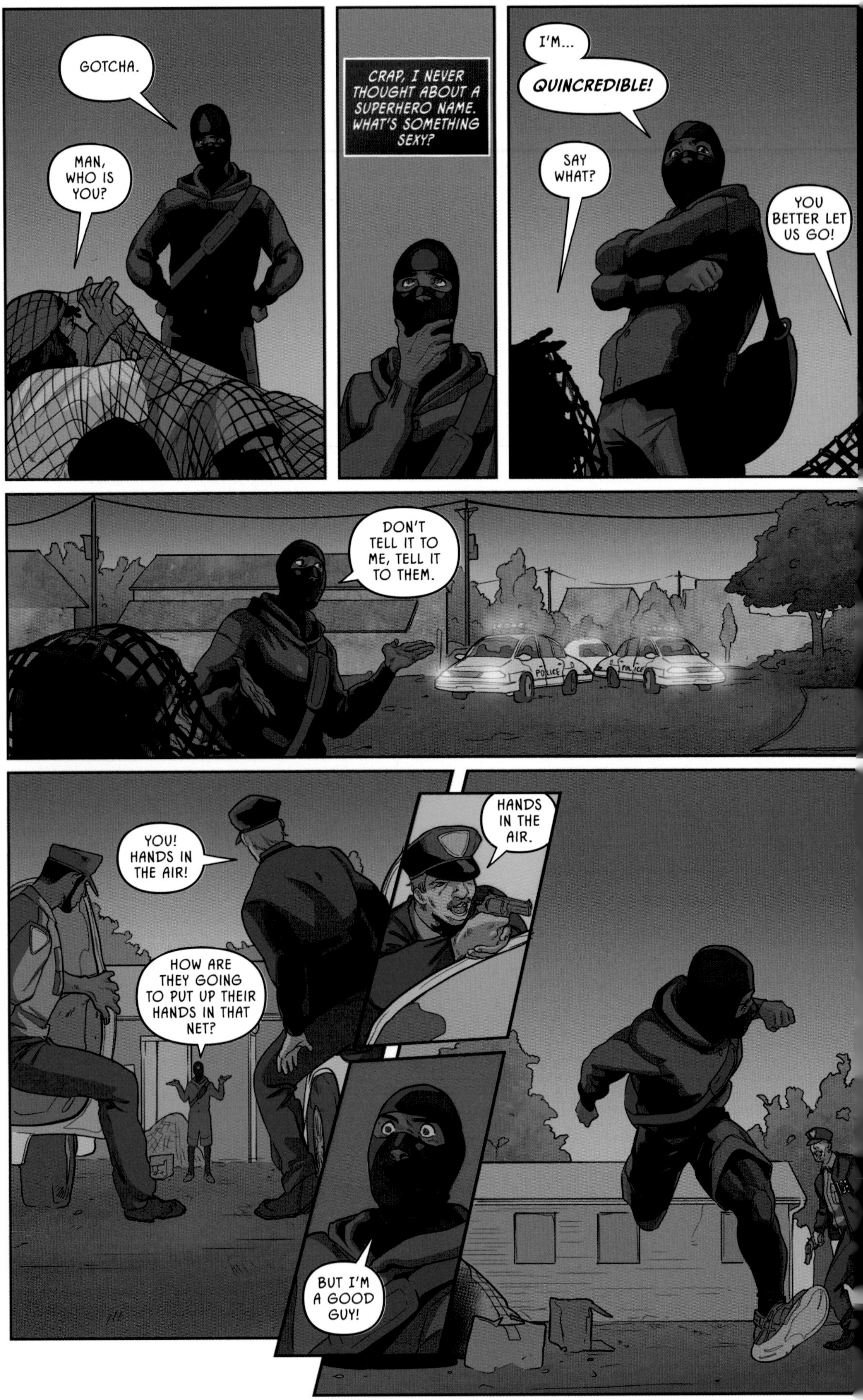
GOTCHA.
MAN, WHO IS YOU?
CRAP, I NEVER THOUGHT ABOUT A SUPERHERO NAME. WHAT'S SOMETHING SEXY?
I'M...
QUINCREDIBLE!
SAY WHAT?
YOU BETTER LET US GO!
DON'T TELL IT TO ME, TELL IT TO THEM.
POLICE
YOU! HANDS IN THE AIR!
HANDS IN THE AIR.
HOW ARE THEY GOING TO PUT UP THEIR HANDS IN THAT NET?
BUT I'M A GOOD GUY!

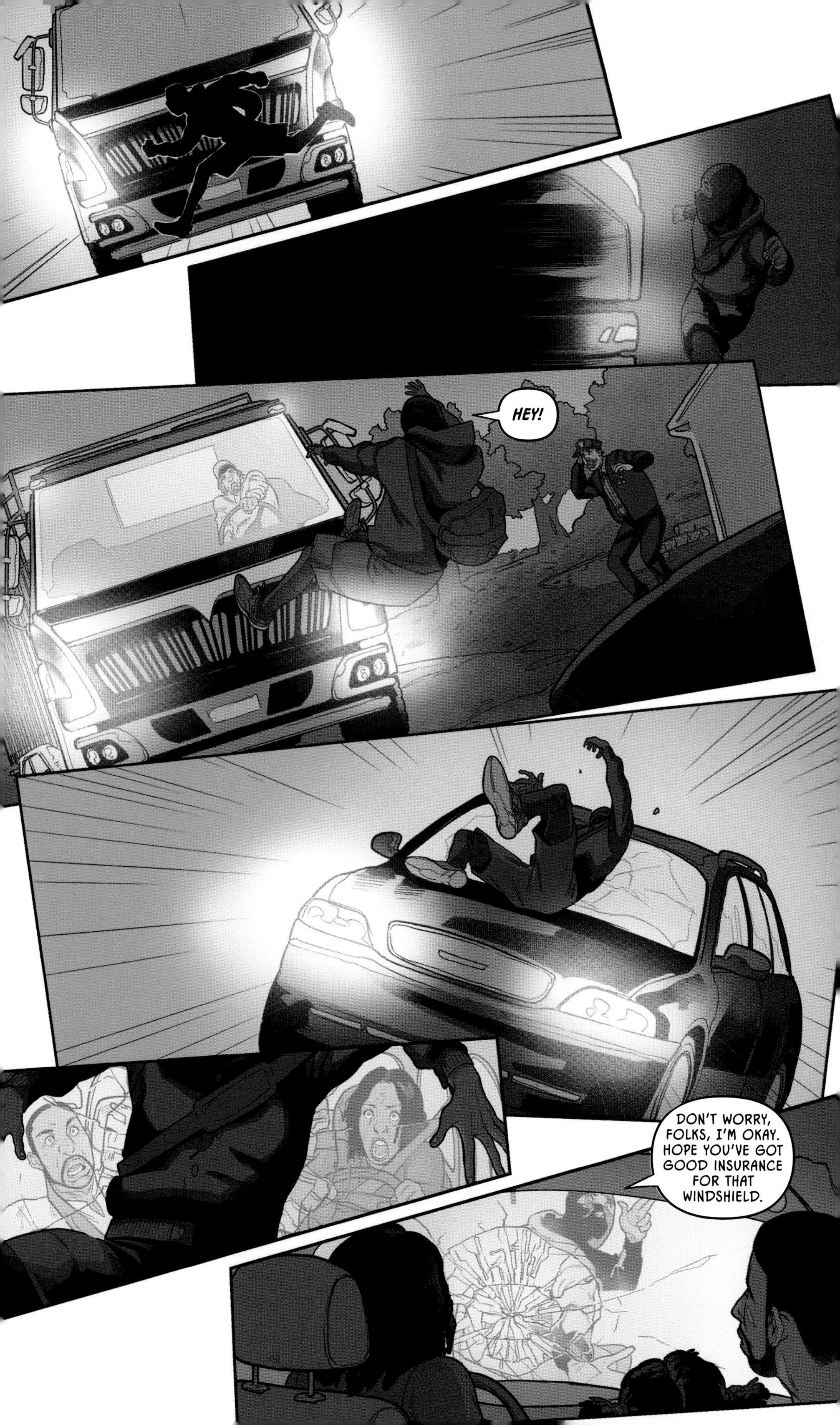
HEY!
DON'T WORRY, FOLKS, I'M OKAY. HOPE YOU'VE GOT GOOD INSURANCE FOR THAT WINDSHIELD.

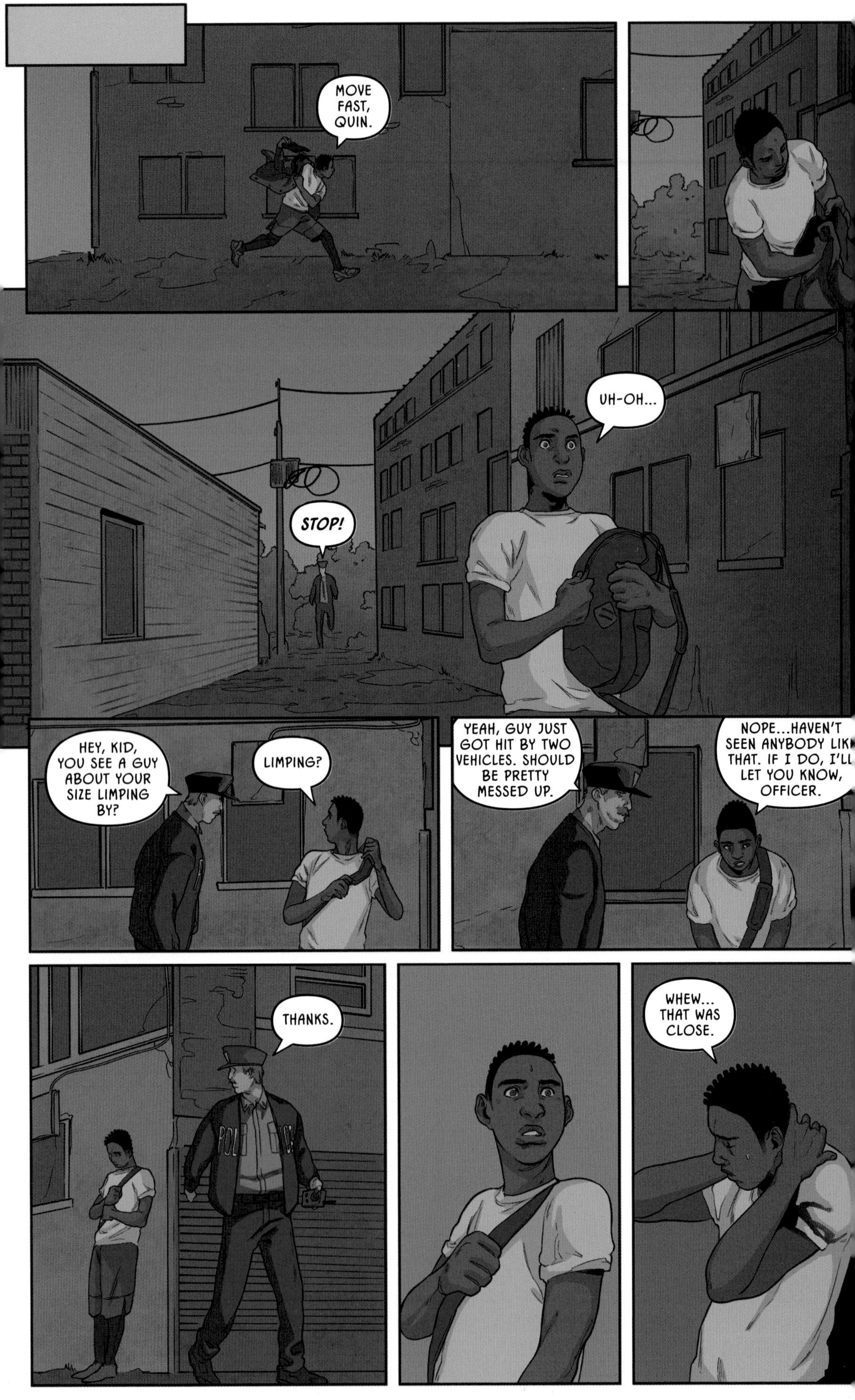
MOVE FAST, QUIN.
UH-OH...
STOP!
HEY, KID, YOU SEE A GUY ABOUT YOUR SIZE LIMPING BY?
LIMPING?
YEAH, GUY JUST GOT HIT BY TWO VEHICLES. SHOULD BE PRETTY MESSED UP.
NOPE...HAVEN'T SEEN ANYBODY LIK THAT. IF I DO, I'LL LET YOU KNOW, OFFICER.
THANKS.
WHEW... THAT WAS CLOSE.

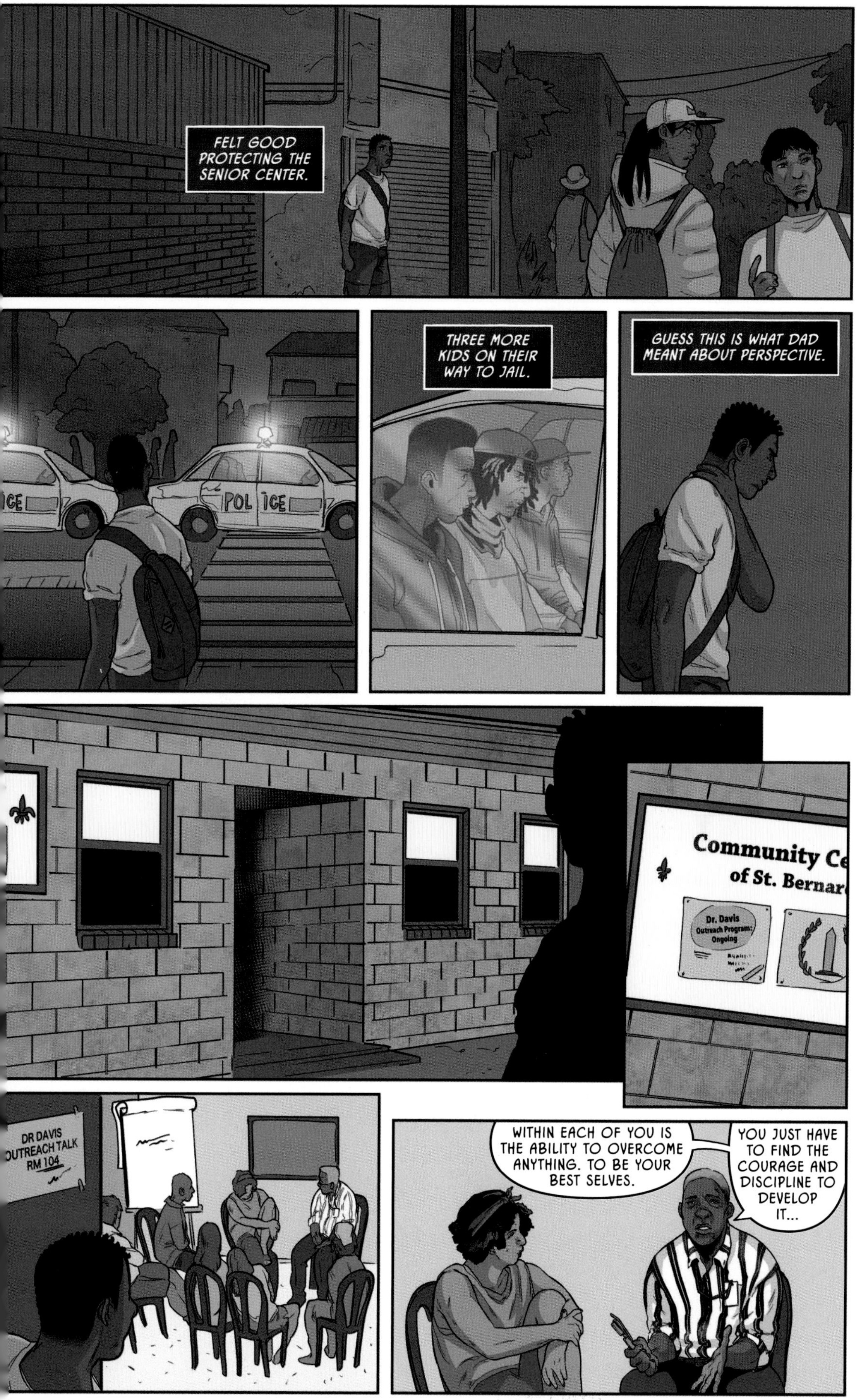
FELT GOOD PROTECTING THE SENIOR CENTER.
POL ICE
THREE MORE KIDS ON THEIR WAY TO JAIL.
GUESS THIS IS WHAT DAD MEANT ABOUT PERSPECTIVE.
Community Ce
of St. Bernar
Dr. Davis Outreach Program: Ongoing
DR DAVIS OUTREACH TALK RM 104
WITHIN EACH OF YOU IS THE ABILITY TO OVERCOME ANYTHING. TO BE YOUR BEST SELVES.
YOU JUST HAVE TO FIND THE COURAGE AND DISCIPLINE TO DEVELOP IT...

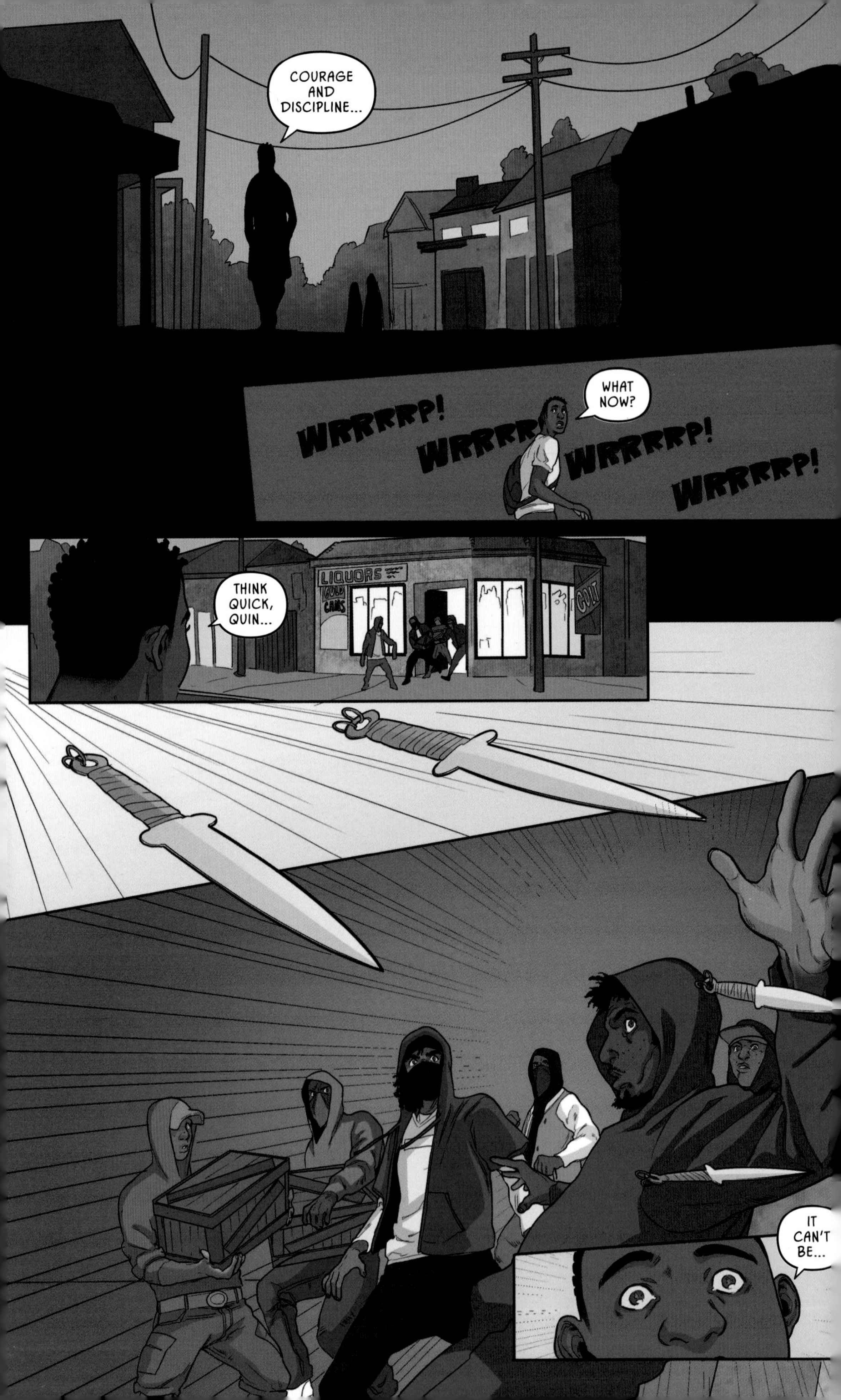
COURAGE AND DISCIPLINE...
WRRRRP!
WRRRRP!
WRRRRP!
WRRRRP!
WHAT NOW?
LIQUORS
COLD CANS
COLT
THINK QUICK, QUIN...
IT CAN'T BE...

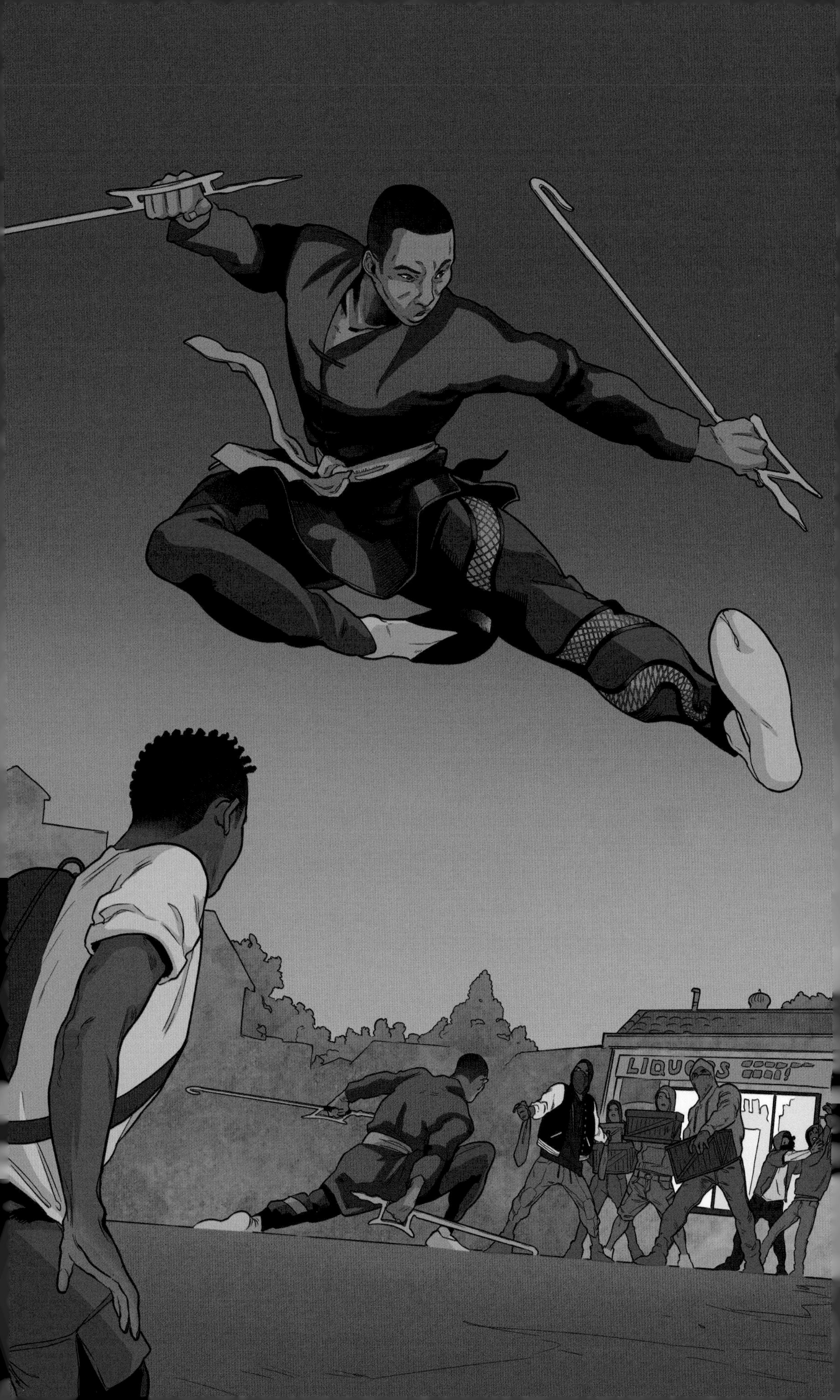

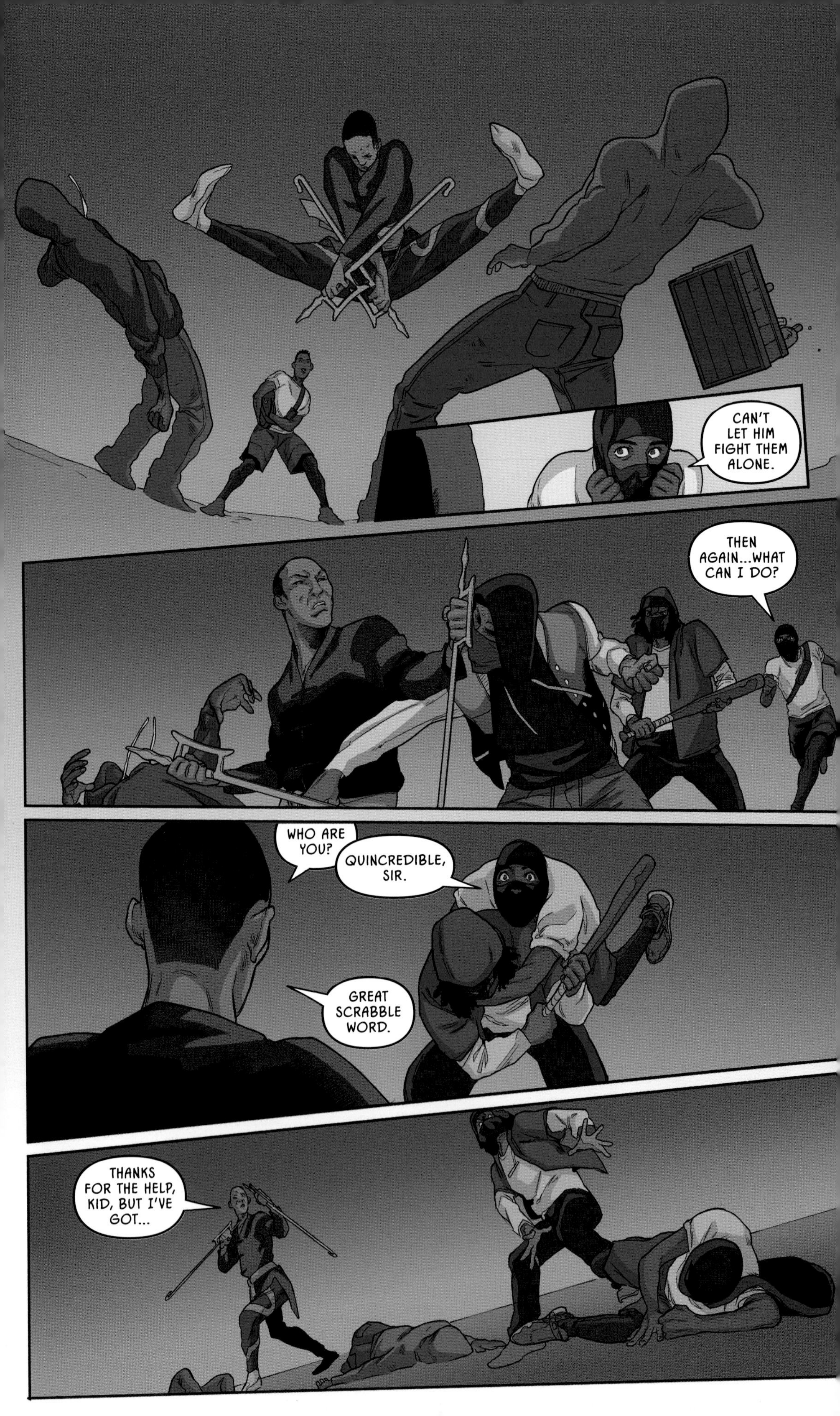
CAN'T LET HIM FIGHT THEM ALONE.
THEN AGAIN...WHAT CAN I DO?
WHO ARE YOU?
QUINCREDIBLE, SIR.
GREAT SCRABBLE WORD.
THANKS FOR THE HELP, KID, BUT I'VE GOT...

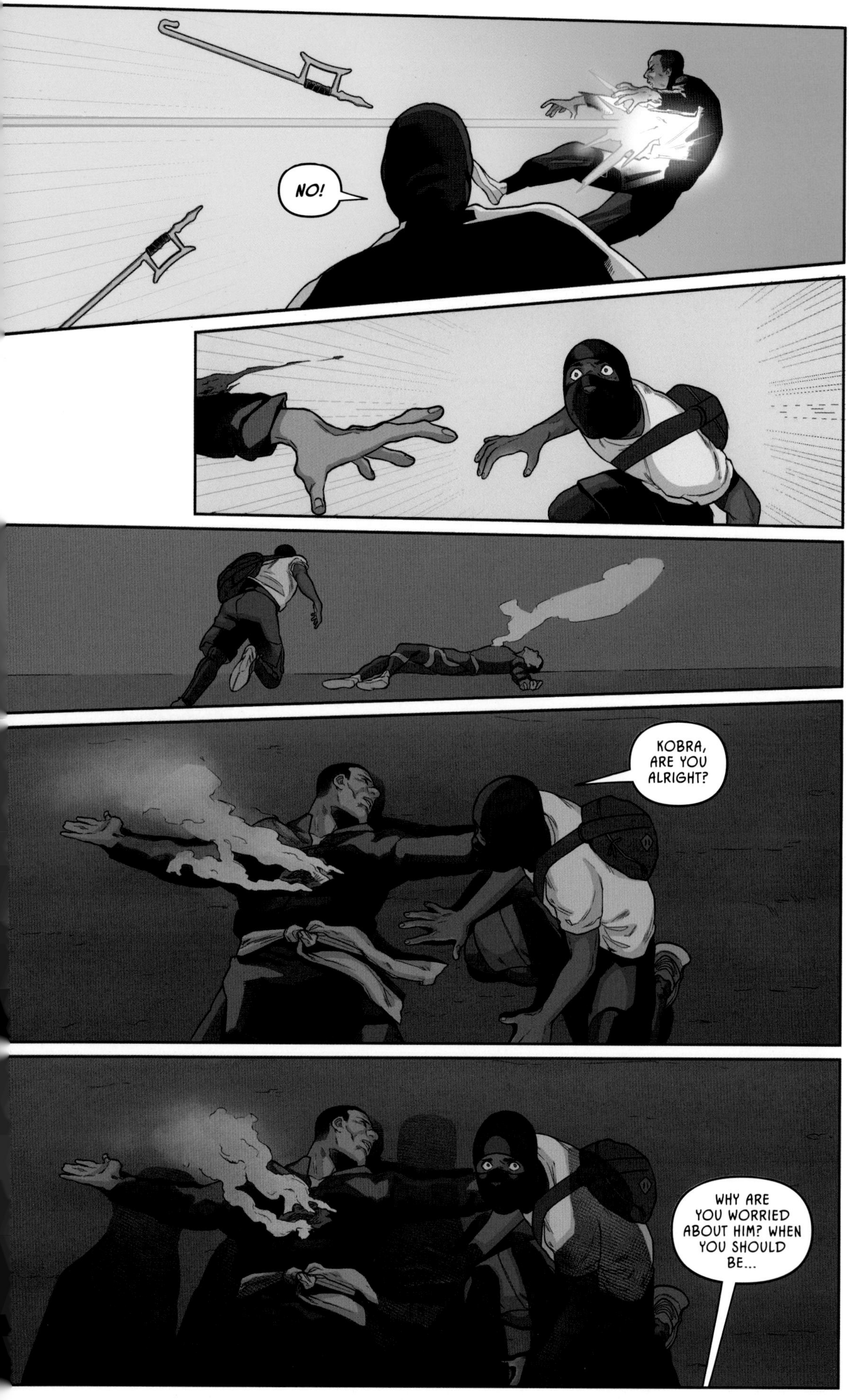
NO!
KOBRA, ARE YOU ALRIGHT?
WHY ARE YOU WORRIED ABOUT HIM? WHEN YOU SHOULD BE...

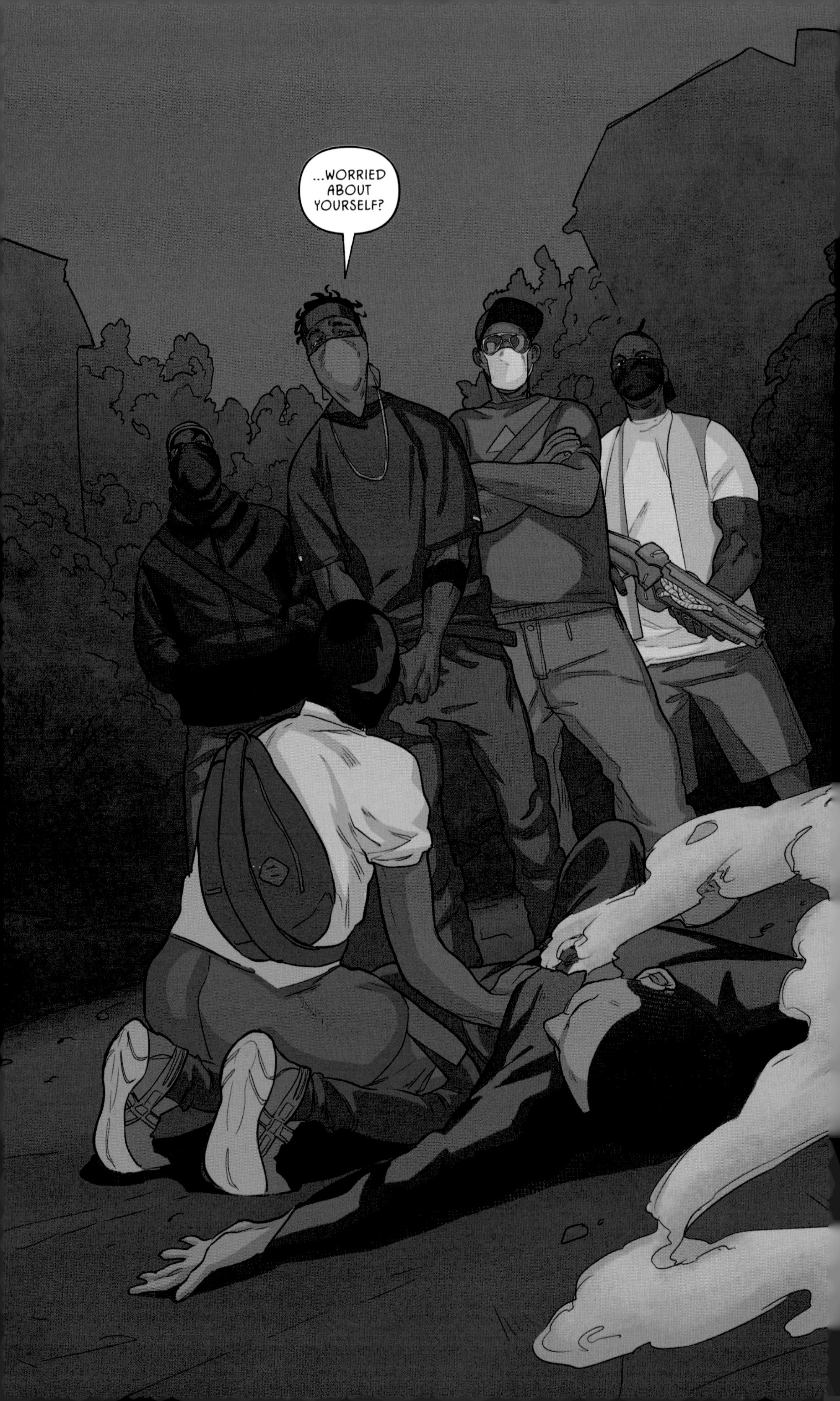
...WORRIED ABOUT YOURSELF?

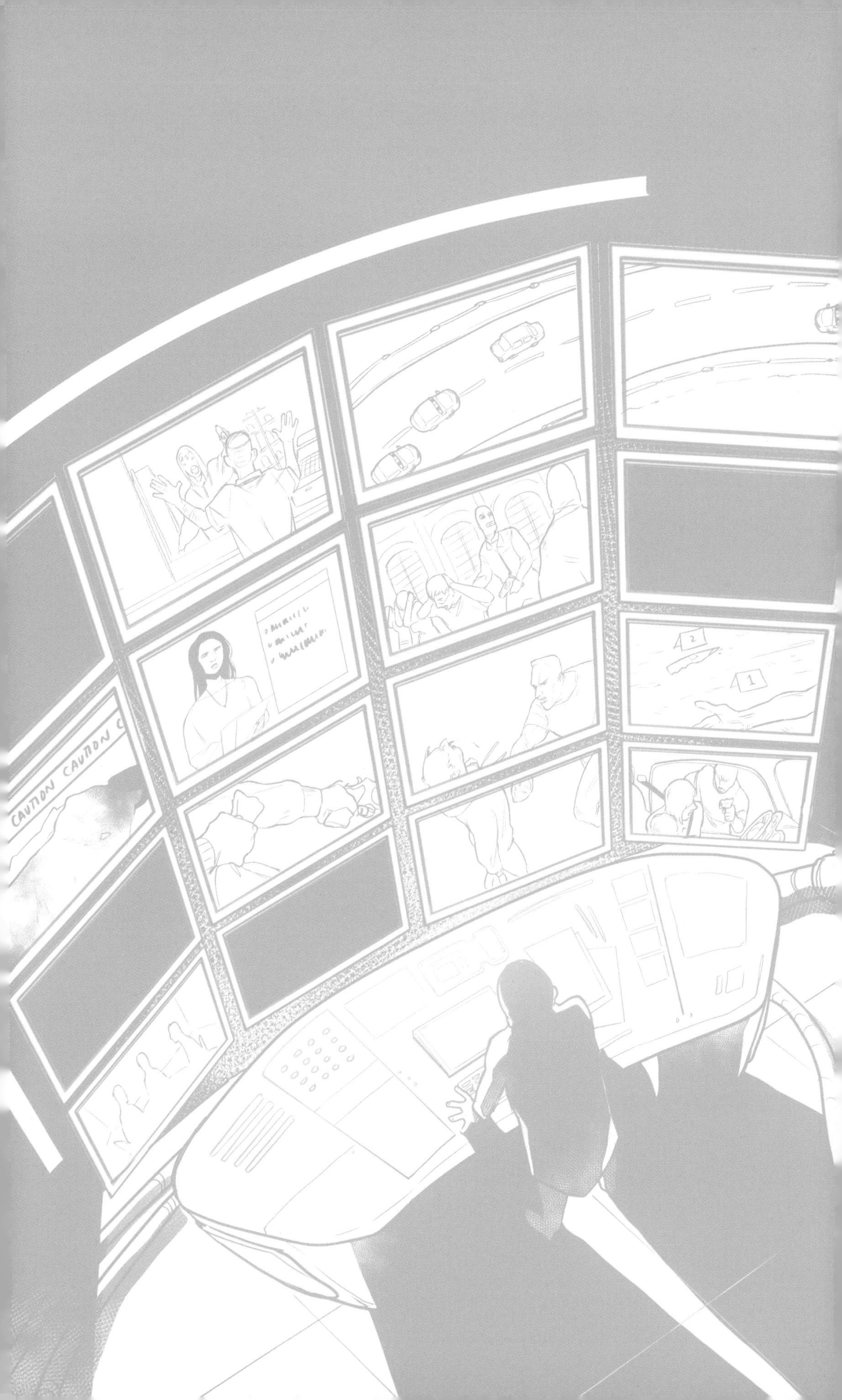
CAUTION CAUTION
2
1

CHAPTER THREE

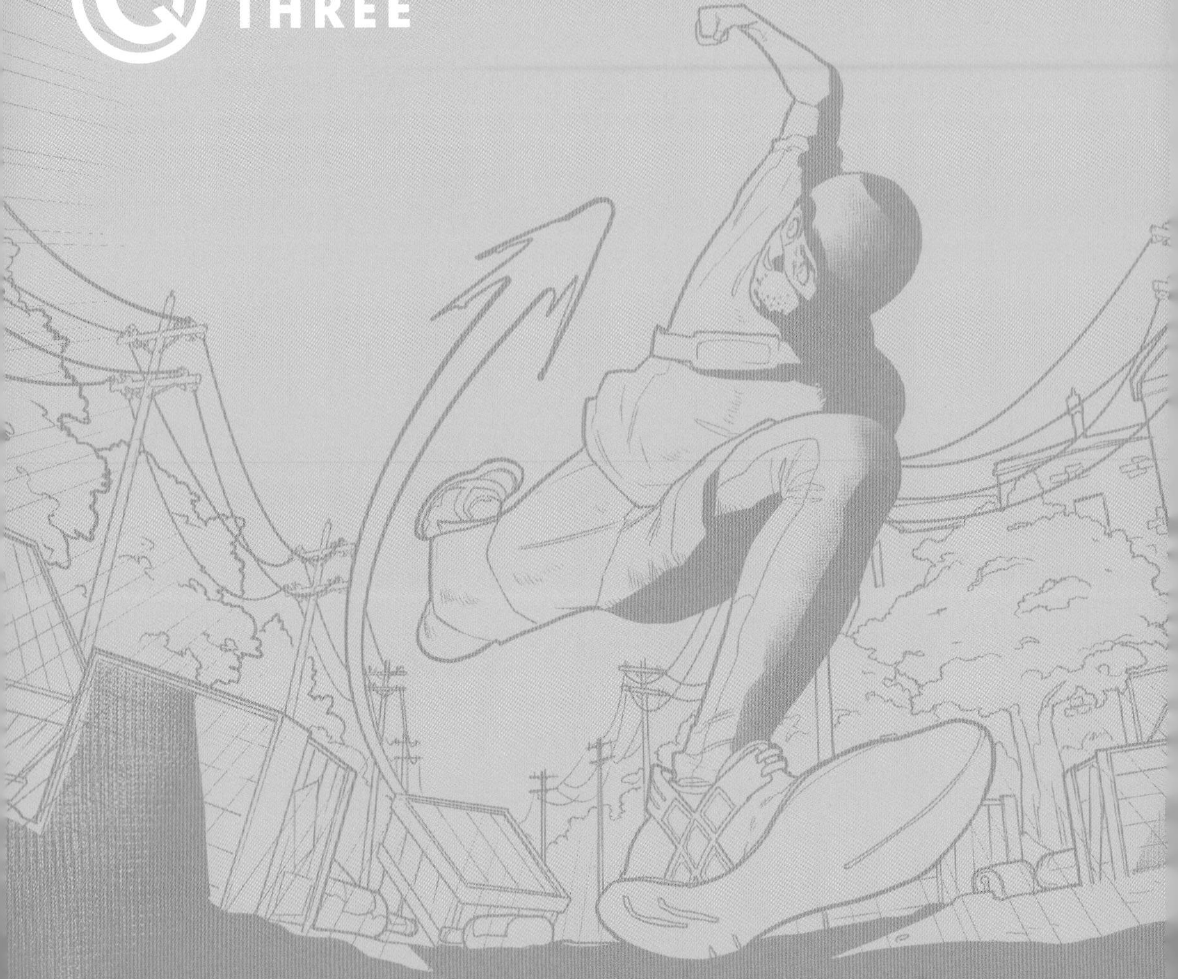

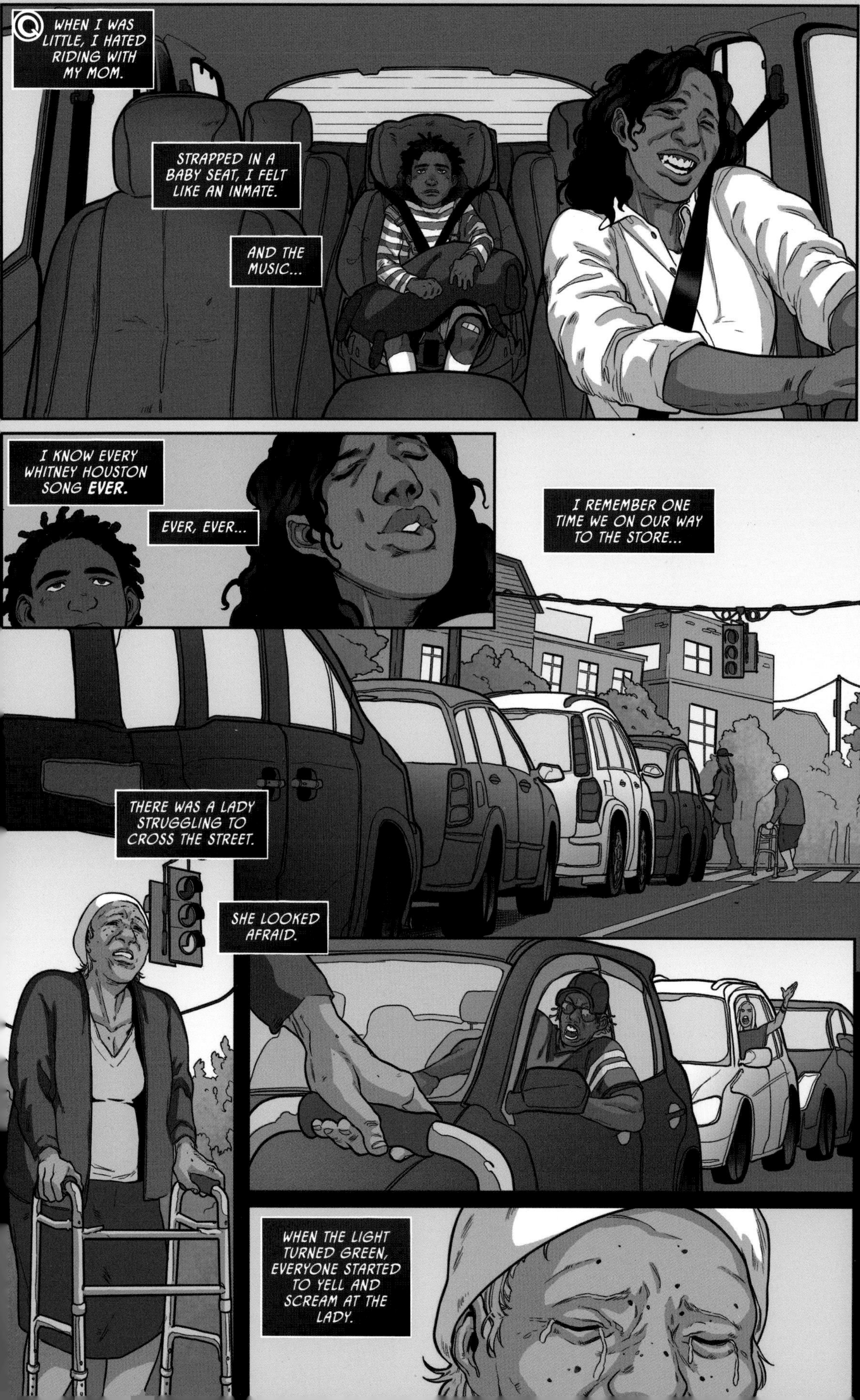
WHEN I WAS LITTLE, I HATED RIDING WITH MY MOM.
STRAPPED IN A BABY SEAT, I FELT LIKE AN INMATE.
AND THE MUSIC...
I KNOW EVERY WHITNEY HOUSTON SONG **EVER.**
EVER, EVER...
I REMEMBER ONE TIME WE ON OUR WAY TO THE STORE...
THERE WAS A LADY STRUGGLING TO CROSS THE STREET.
SHE LOOKED AFRAID.
WHEN THE LIGHT TURNED GREEN, EVERYONE STARTED TO YELL AND SCREAM AT THE LADY.

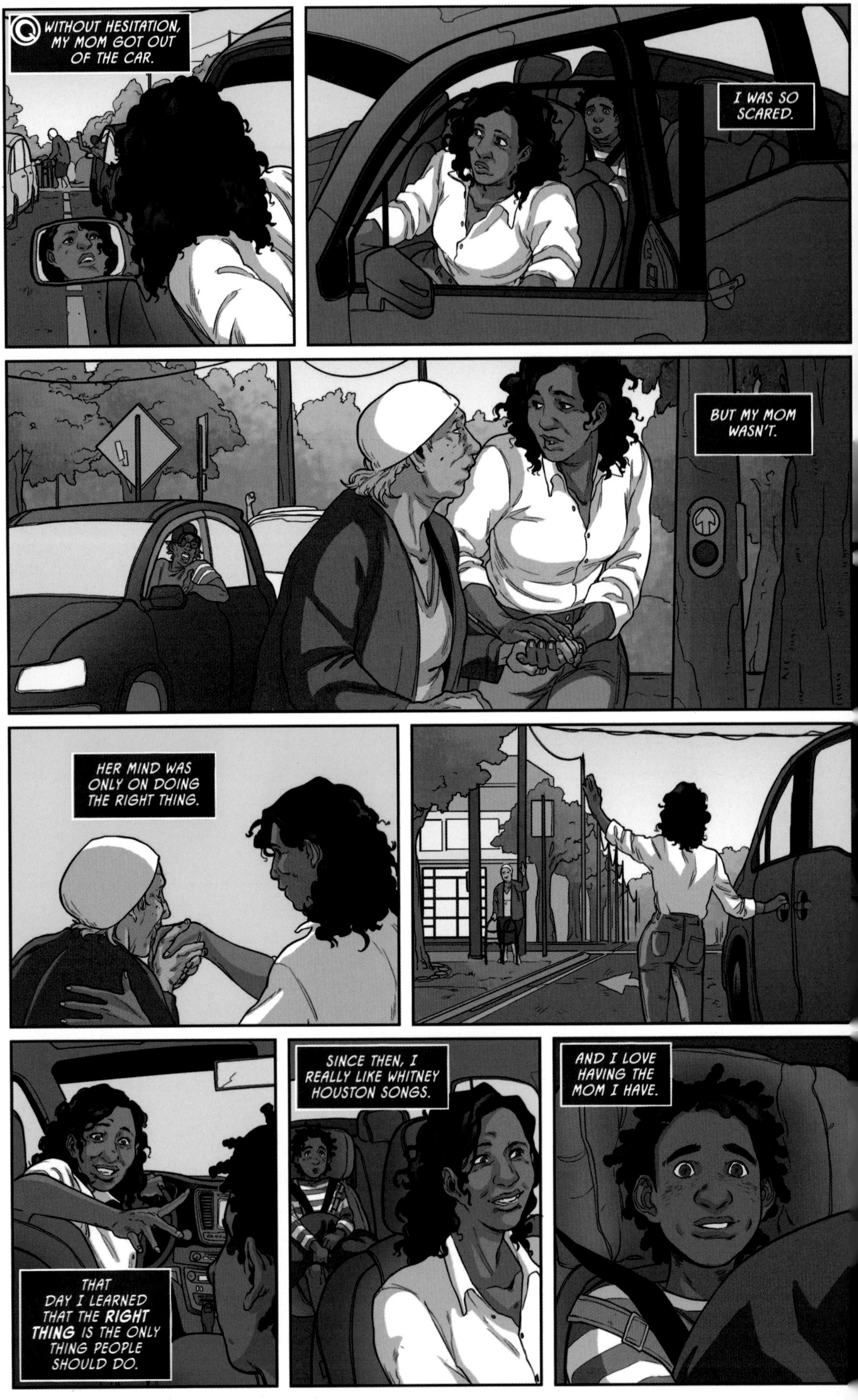
WITHOUT HESITATION, MY MOM GOT OUT OF THE CAR.
I WAS SO SCARED.
BUT MY MOM WASN'T.
HER MIND WAS ONLY ON DOING THE RIGHT THING.
THAT DAY I LEARNED THAT THE RIGHT THING IS THE ONLY THING PEOPLE SHOULD DO.
SINCE THEN, I REALLY LIKE WHITNEY HOUSTON SONGS.
AND I LOVE HAVING THE MOM I HAVE.

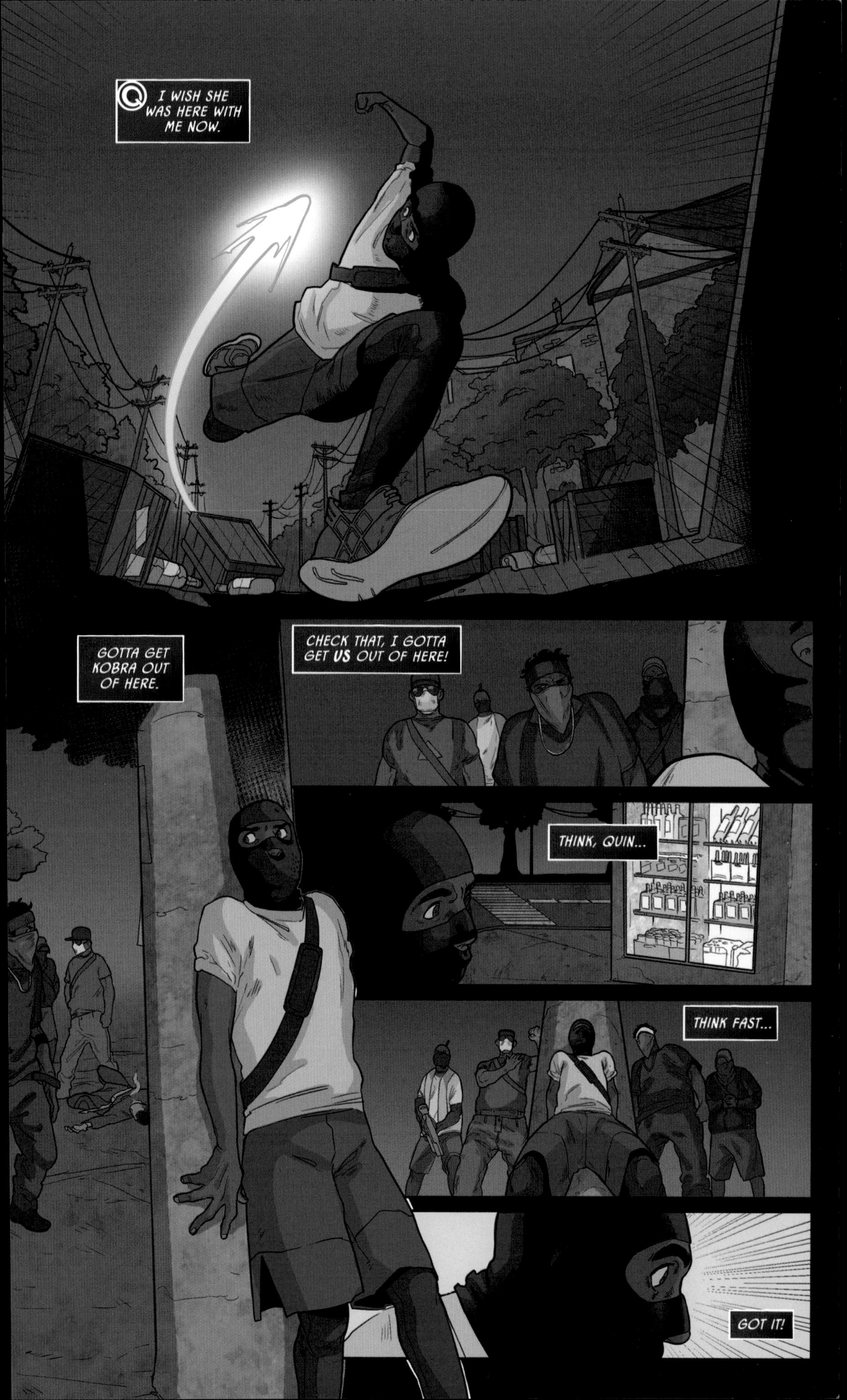
I WISH SHE WAS HERE WITH ME NOW.
GOTTA GET KOBRA OUT OF HERE.
CHECK THAT, I GOTTA GET US OUT OF HERE!
THINK, QUIN...
THINK FAST...
GOT IT!

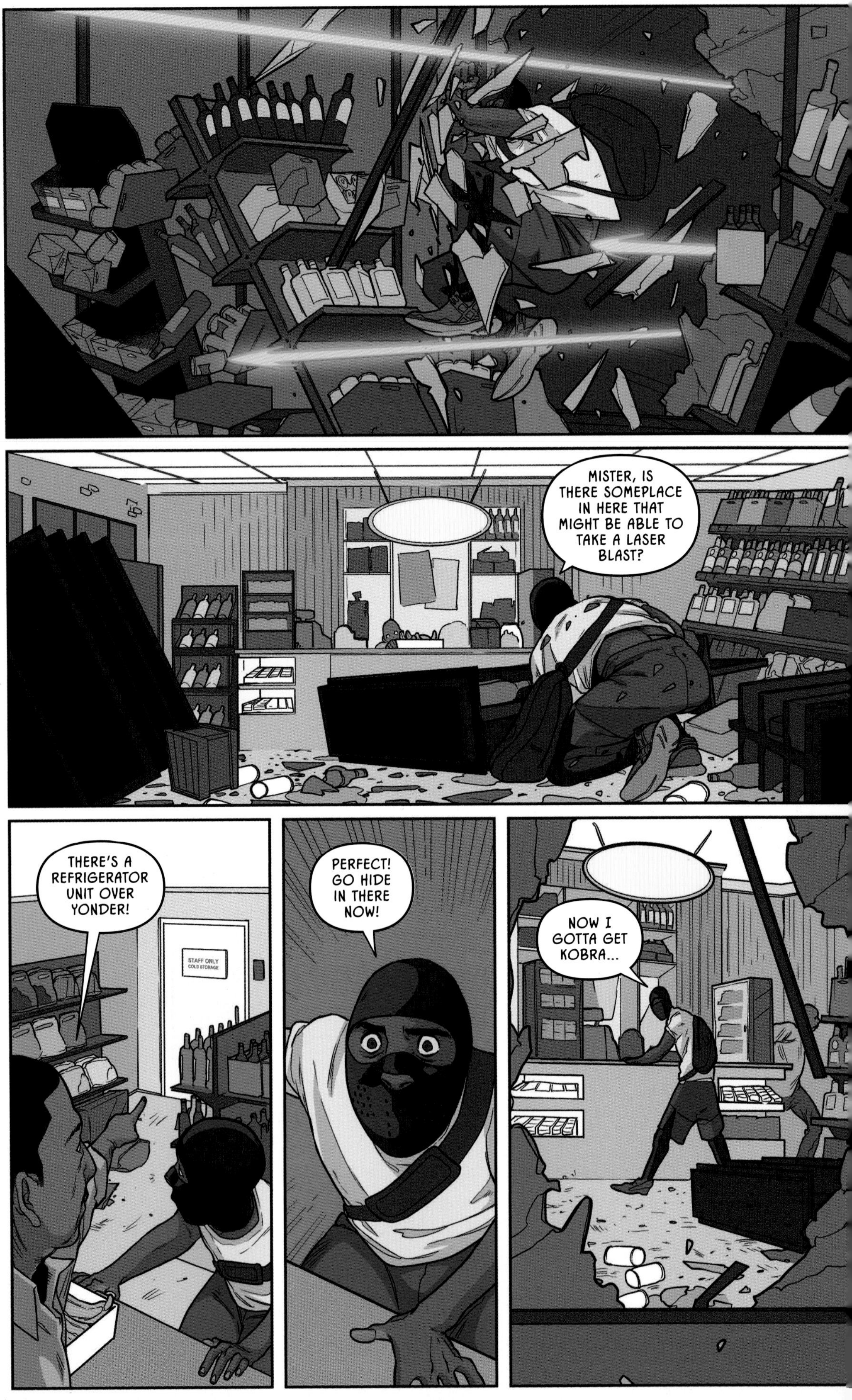
MISTER, IS THERE SOMEPLACE IN HERE THAT MIGHT BE ABLE TO TAKE A LASER BLAST?
THERE'S A REFRIGERATOR UNIT OVER YONDER!
STAFF ONLY
COLD STORAGE
PERFECT! GO HIDE IN THERE NOW!
NOW I GOTTA GET KOBRA...

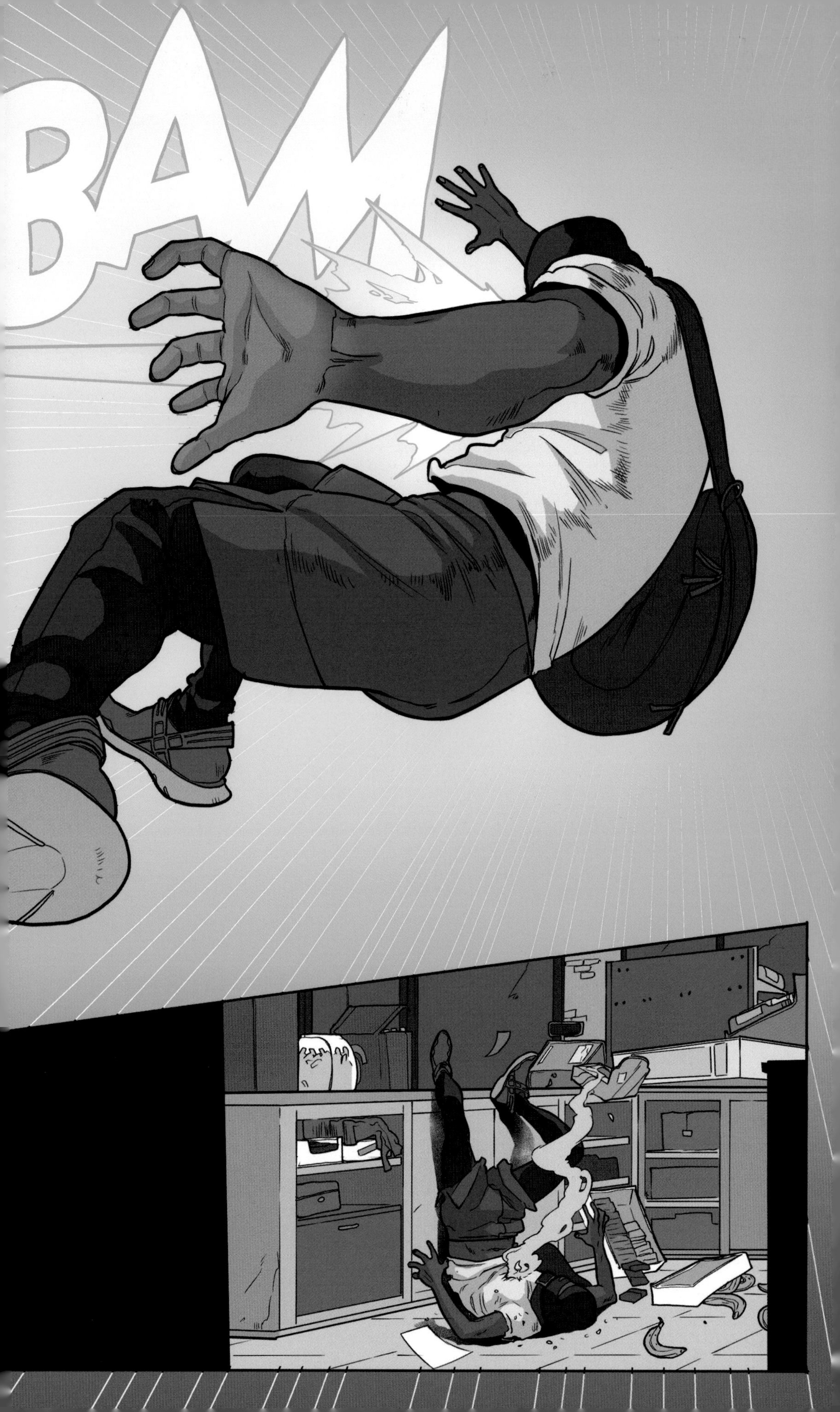
BAM

WOW.

WELL, QUIN, YOU CAN TAKE A LASER BLAST HEAD ON. THAT'S GOOD NEWS FOR ME.

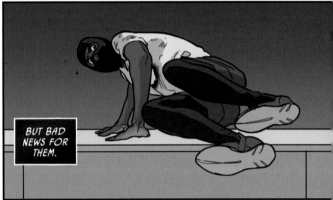

BUT BAD NEWS FOR THEM.

THAT FOOL IS COMING THIS WAY!

BLAST HIM AGAIN!

CLOSE, FELLAS, BUT I'M SURE YOU CAN DO BETTER THAN THAT...

IF YOU *REALLY* WANT ME...

LIQUORS

YOU'RE GOING TO HAVE TO COME IN HERE AND GET ME!

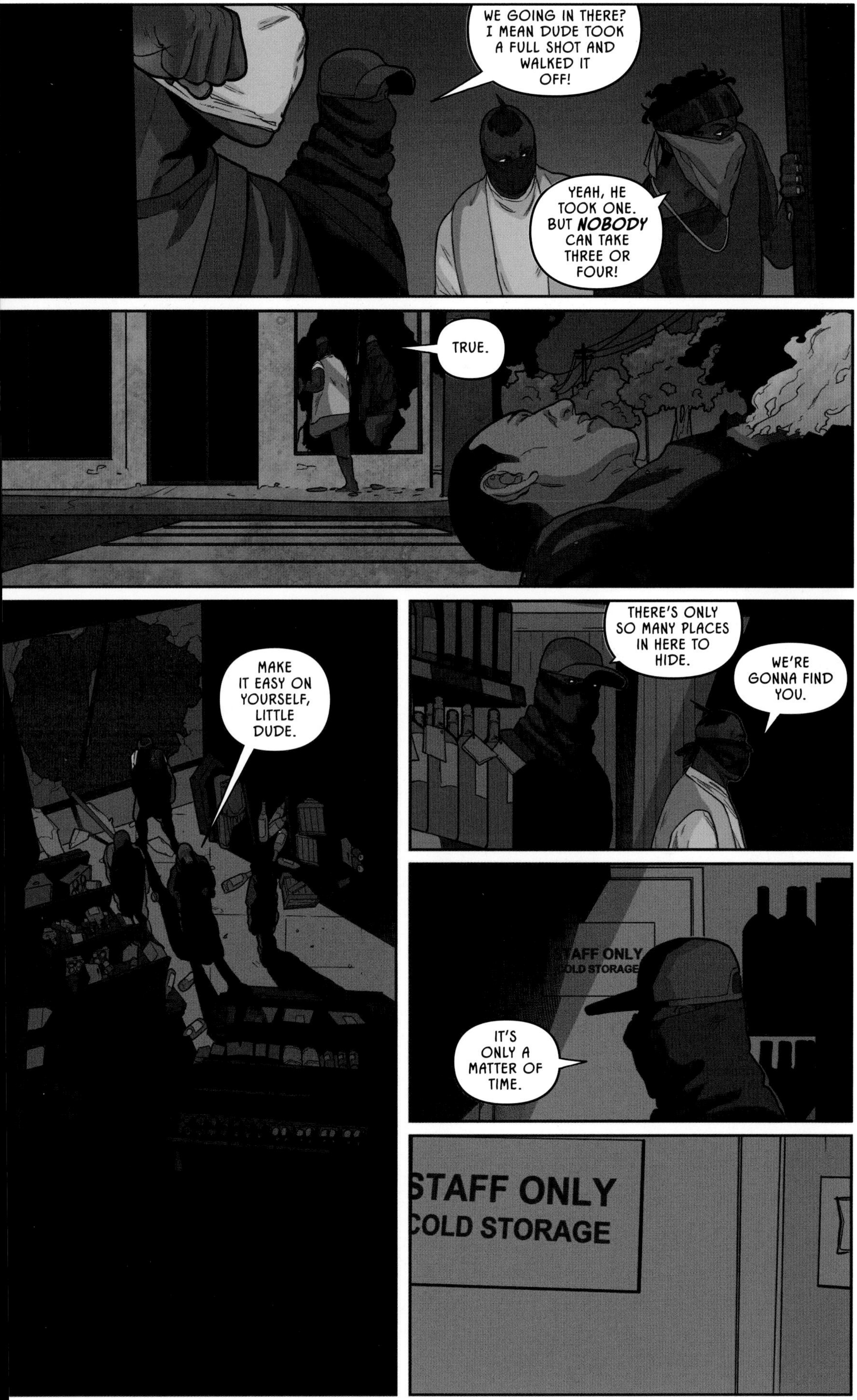
WE GOING IN THERE? I MEAN DUDE TOOK A FULL SHOT AND WALKED IT OFF!
YEAH, HE TOOK ONE. BUT NOBODY CAN TAKE THREE OR FOUR!
TRUE.
MAKE IT EASY ON YOURSELF, LITTLE DUDE.
THERE'S ONLY SO MANY PLACES IN HERE TO HIDE.
WE'RE GONNA FIND YOU.
STAFF ONLY
COLD STORAGE
IT'S ONLY A MATTER OF TIME.
STAFF ONLY
COLD STORAGE

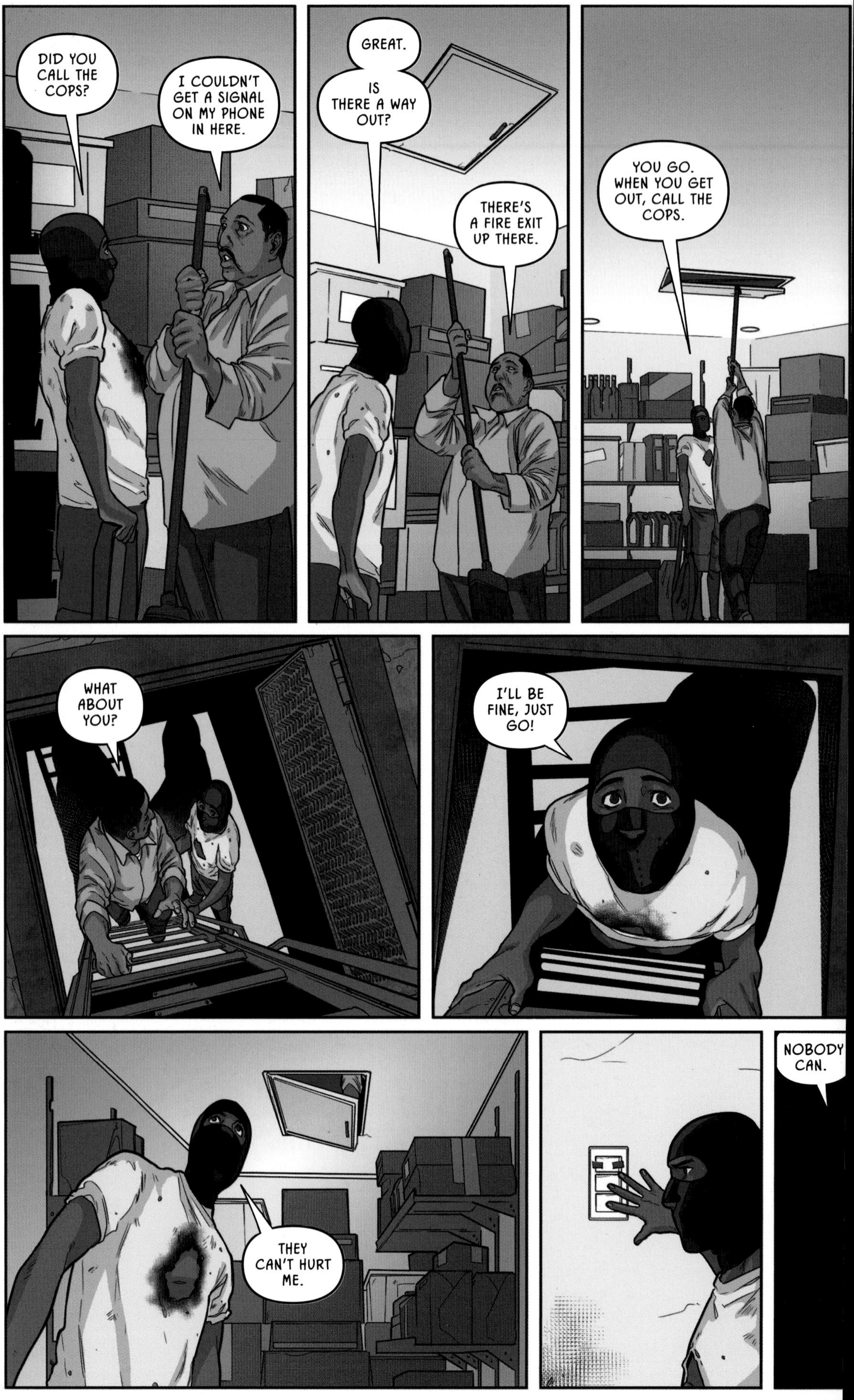
DID YOU CALL THE COPS?
I COULDN'T GET A SIGNAL ON MY PHONE IN HERE.
GREAT.
IS THERE A WAY OUT?
THERE'S A FIRE EXIT UP THERE.
YOU GO. WHEN YOU GET OUT, CALL THE COPS.
WHAT ABOUT YOU?
I'LL BE FINE, JUST GO!
THEY CAN'T HURT ME.
NOBODY CAN.

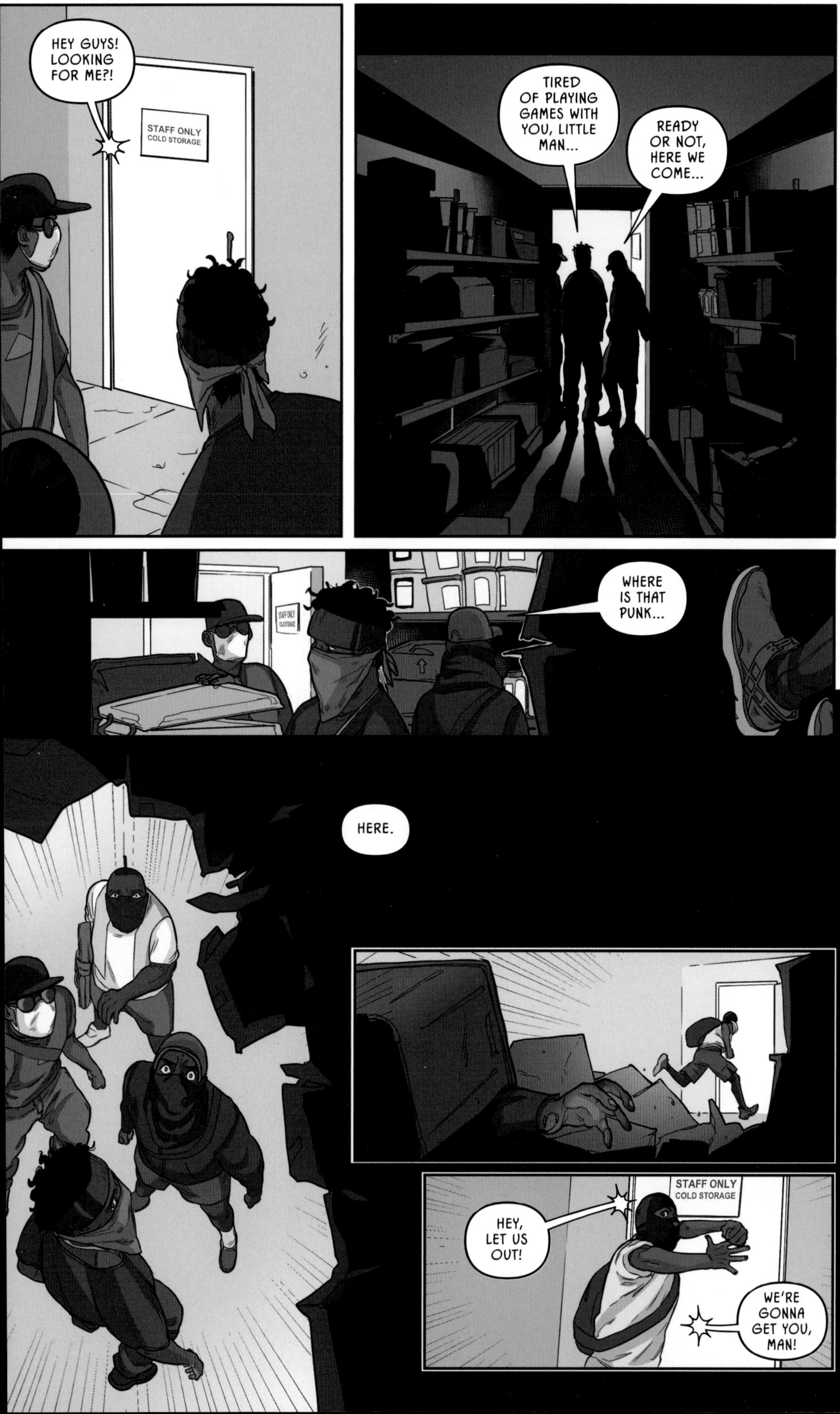
HEY GUYS! LOOKING FOR ME?!
STAFF ONLY COLD STORAGE
TIRED OF PLAYING GAMES WITH YOU, LITTLE MAN...
READY OR NOT, HERE WE COME...
WHERE IS THAT PUNK...
HERE.
STAFF ONLY COLD STORAGE
HEY, LET US OUT!
WE'RE GONNA GET YOU, MAN!

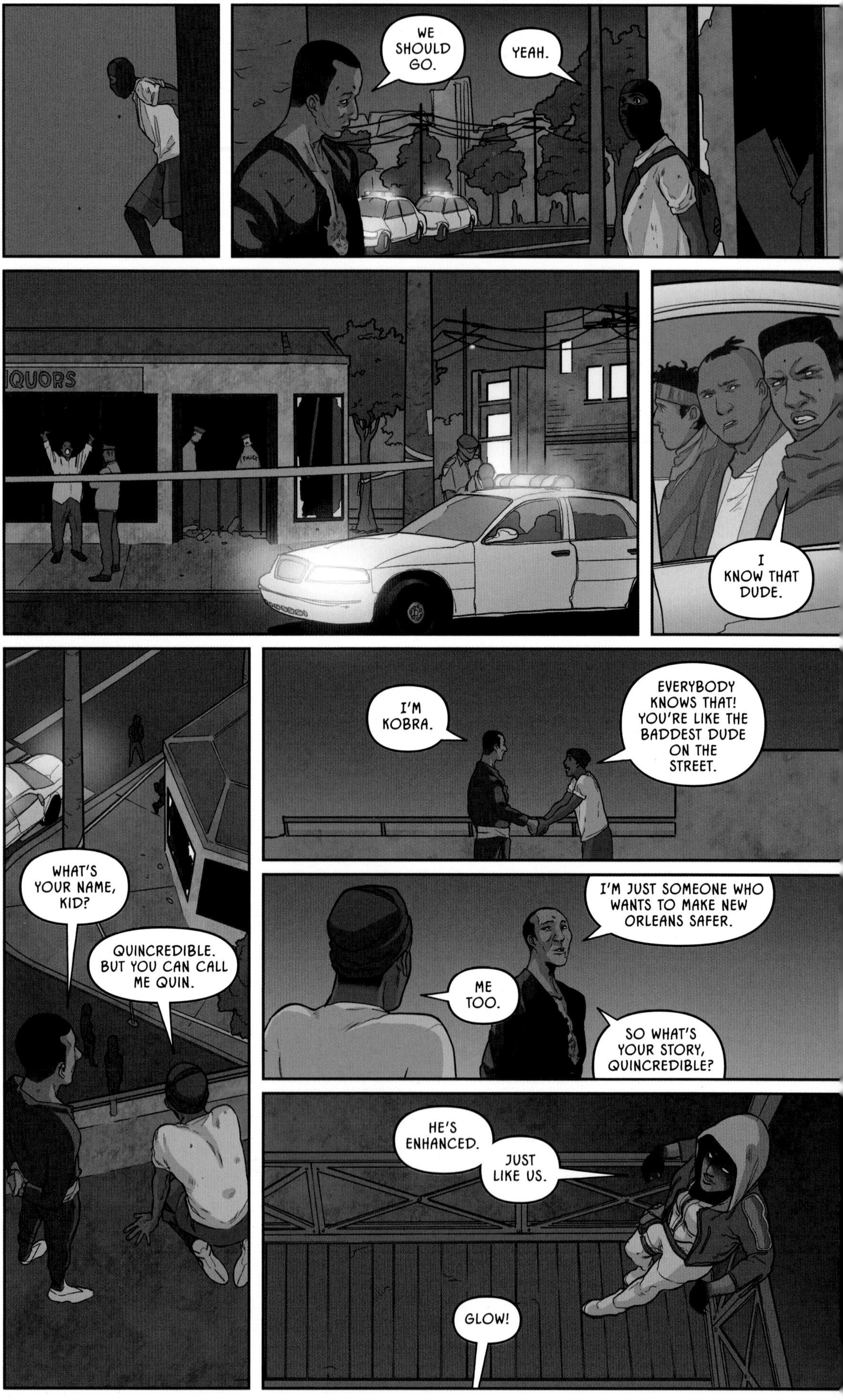

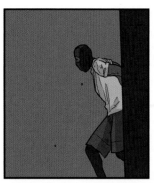

WE SHOULD GO.
YEAH.
IQUORS
I KNOW THAT DUDE.
I'M KOBRA.
EVERYBODY KNOWS THAT! YOU'RE LIKE THE BADDEST DUDE ON THE STREET.
WHAT'S YOUR NAME, KID?
QUINCREDIBLE. BUT YOU CAN CALL ME QUIN.
I'M JUST SOMEONE WHO WANTS TO MAKE NEW ORLEANS SAFER.
ME TOO.
SO WHAT'S YOUR STORY, QUINCREDIBLE?
HE'S ENHANCED.
JUST LIKE US.
GLOW!

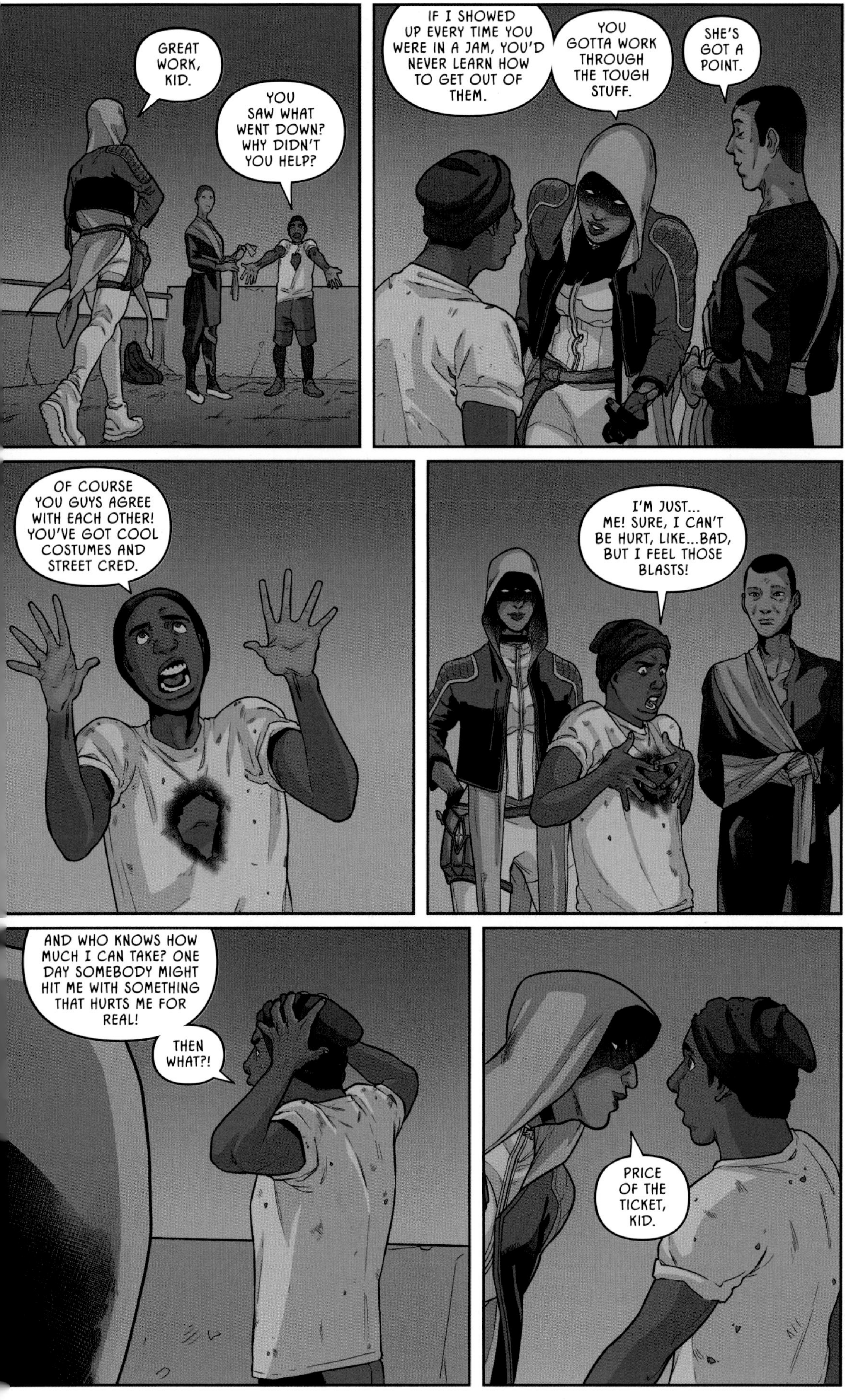
GREAT WORK, KID.
YOU SAW WHAT WENT DOWN? WHY DIDN'T YOU HELP?
IF I SHOWED UP EVERY TIME YOU WERE IN A JAM, YOU'D NEVER LEARN HOW TO GET OUT OF THEM.
YOU GOTTA WORK THROUGH THE TOUGH STUFF.
SHE'S GOT A POINT.
OF COURSE YOU GUYS AGREE WITH EACH OTHER! YOU'VE GOT COOL COSTUMES AND STREET CRED.
I'M JUST... ME! SURE, I CAN'T BE HURT, LIKE...BAD, BUT I FEEL THOSE BLASTS!
AND WHO KNOWS HOW MUCH I CAN TAKE? ONE DAY SOMEBODY MIGHT HIT ME WITH SOMETHING THAT HURTS ME FOR REAL!
THEN WHAT?!
PRICE OF THE TICKET, KID.

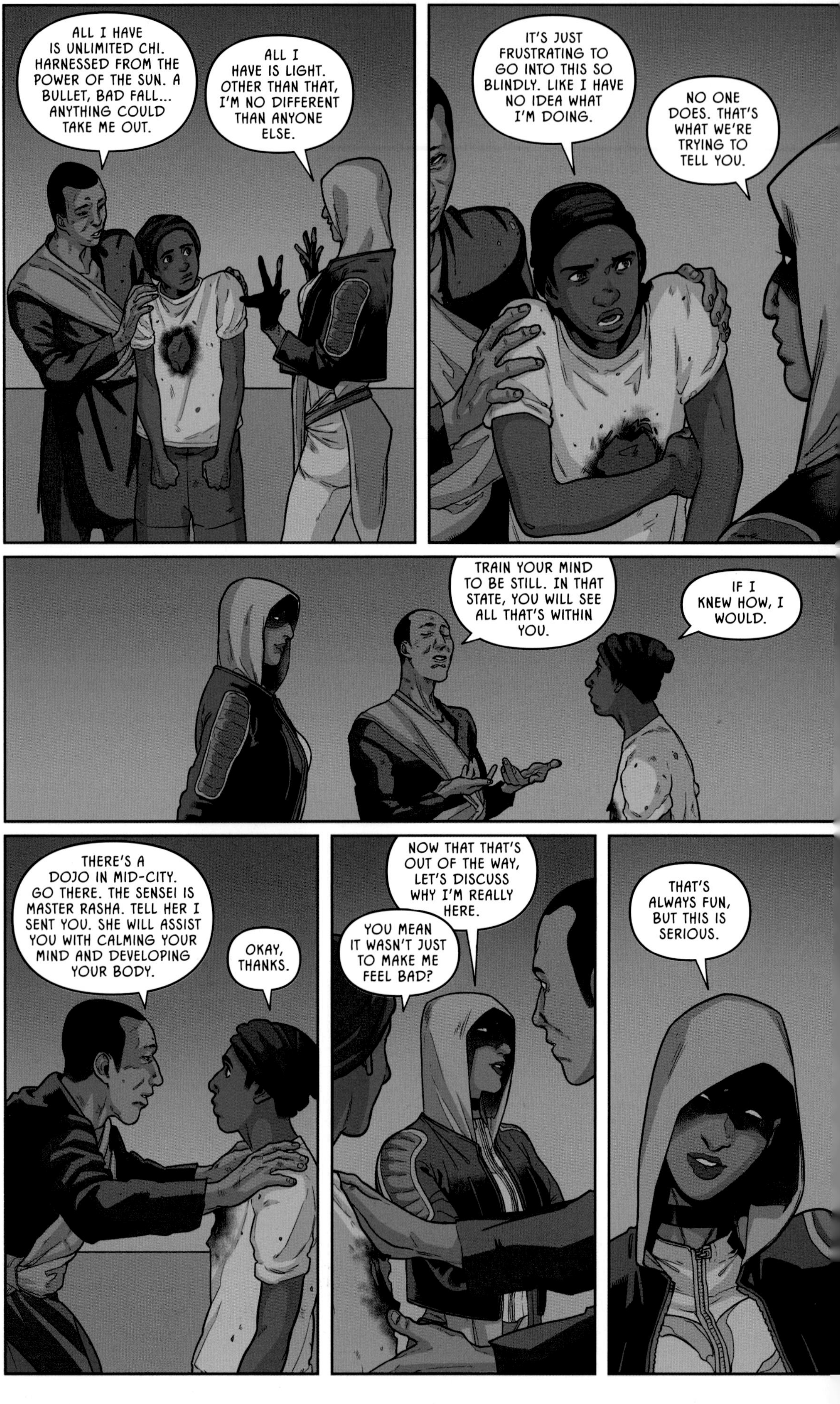
ALL I HAVE IS UNLIMITED CHI. HARNESSED FROM THE POWER OF THE SUN. A BULLET, BAD FALL... ANYTHING COULD TAKE ME OUT.
ALL I HAVE IS LIGHT. OTHER THAN THAT, I'M NO DIFFERENT THAN ANYONE ELSE.
IT'S JUST FRUSTRATING TO GO INTO THIS SO BLINDLY. LIKE I HAVE NO IDEA WHAT I'M DOING.
NO ONE DOES. THAT'S WHAT WE'RE TRYING TO TELL YOU.
TRAIN YOUR MIND TO BE STILL. IN THAT STATE, YOU WILL SEE ALL THAT'S WITHIN YOU.
IF I KNEW HOW, I WOULD.
THERE'S A DOJO IN MID-CITY. GO THERE. THE SENSEI IS MASTER RASHA. TELL HER I SENT YOU. SHE WILL ASSIST YOU WITH CALMING YOUR MIND AND DEVELOPING YOUR BODY.
OKAY, THANKS.
NOW THAT THAT'S OUT OF THE WAY, LET'S DISCUSS WHY I'M REALLY HERE.
YOU MEAN IT WASN'T JUST TO MAKE ME FEEL BAD?
THAT'S ALWAYS FUN, BUT THIS IS SERIOUS.

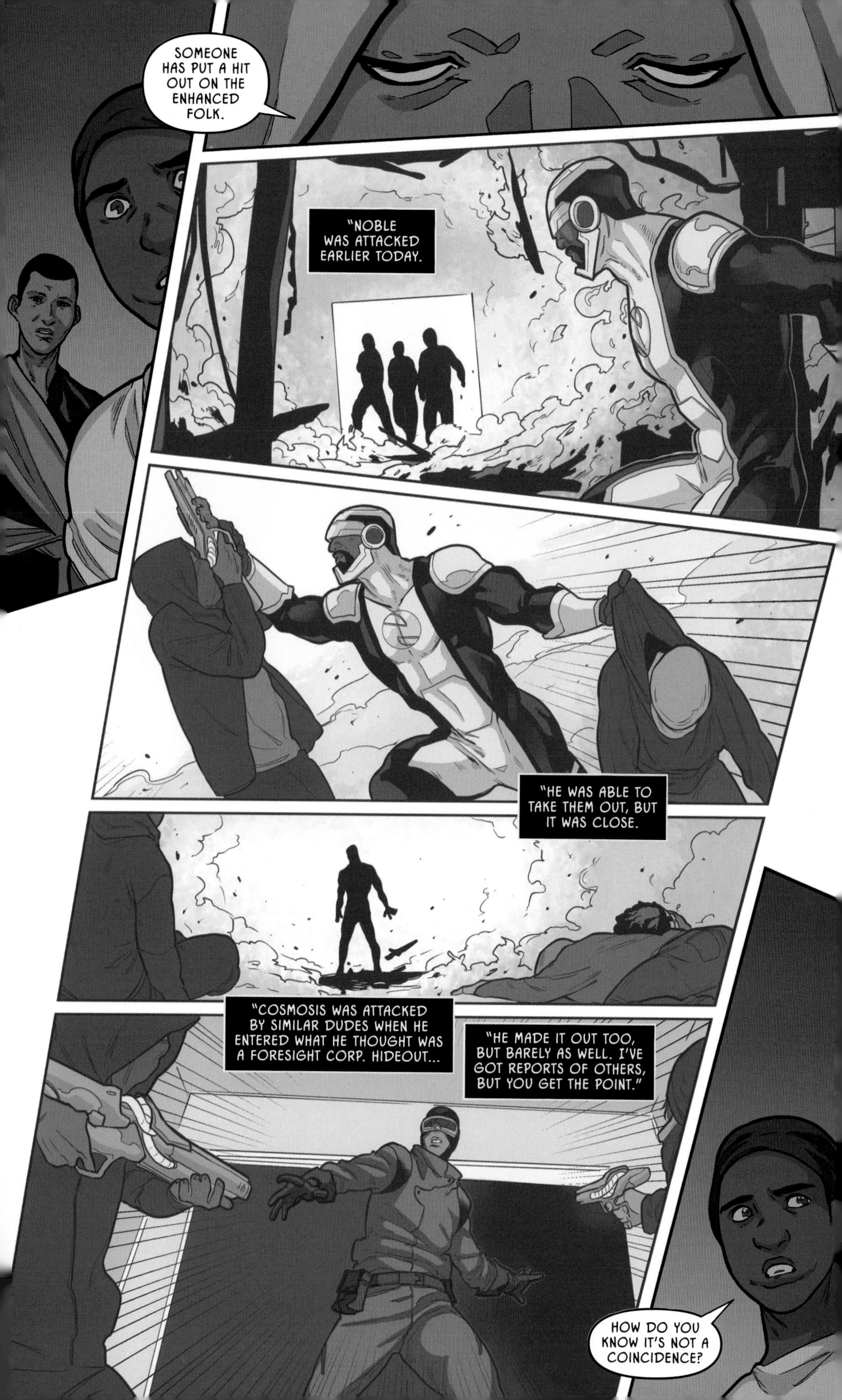
SOMEONE HAS PUT A HIT OUT ON THE ENHANCED FOLK.
"NOBLE WAS ATTACKED EARLIER TODAY.
"HE WAS ABLE TO TAKE THEM OUT, BUT IT WAS CLOSE.
"COSMOSIS WAS ATTACKED BY SIMILAR DUDES WHEN HE ENTERED WHAT HE THOUGHT WAS A FORESIGHT CORP. HIDEOUT...
"HE MADE IT OUT TOO, BUT BARELY AS WELL. I'VE GOT REPORTS OF OTHERS, BUT YOU GET THE POINT."
HOW DO YOU KNOW IT'S NOT A COINCIDENCE?

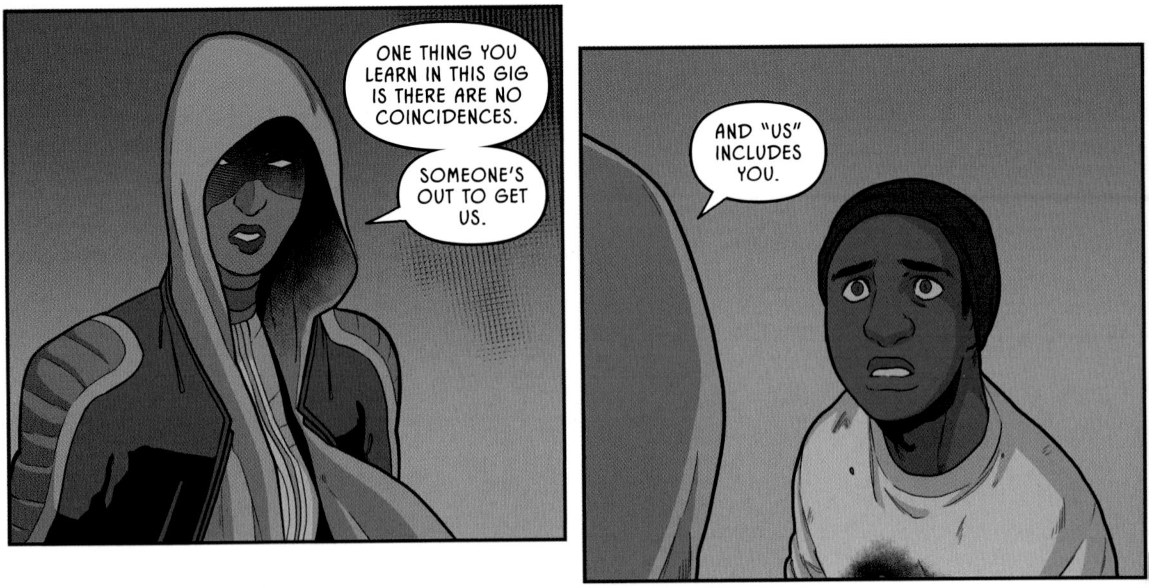
ONE THING YOU LEARN IN THIS GIG IS THERE ARE NO COINCIDENCES.
SOMEONE'S OUT TO GET US.
AND "US" INCLUDES YOU.

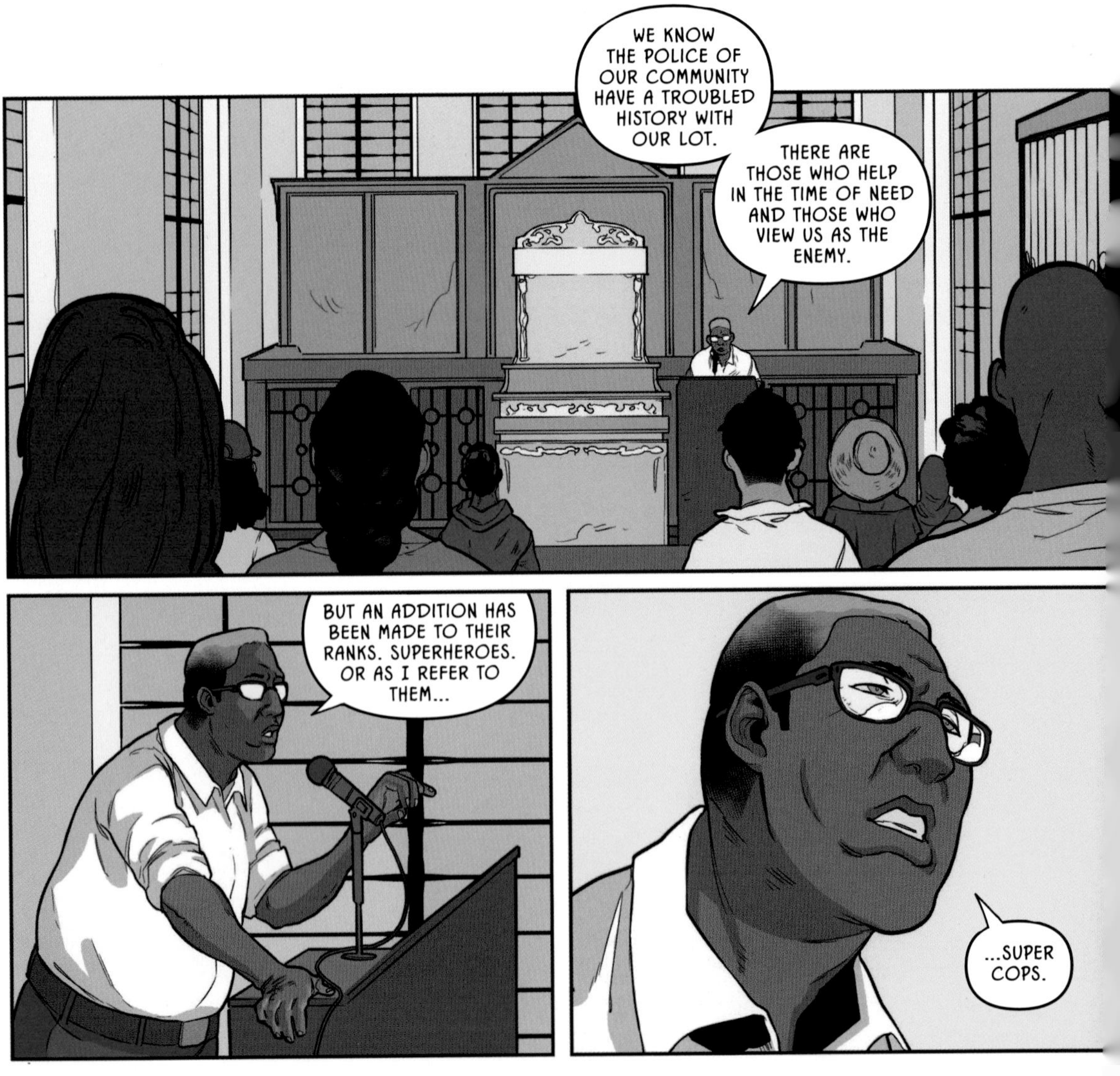
WE KNOW THE POLICE OF OUR COMMUNITY HAVE A TROUBLED HISTORY WITH OUR LOT.
THERE ARE THOSE WHO HELP IN THE TIME OF NEED AND THOSE WHO VIEW US AS THE ENEMY.
BUT AN ADDITION HAS BEEN MADE TO THEIR RANKS. SUPERHEROES. OR AS I REFER TO THEM...
...SUPER COPS.

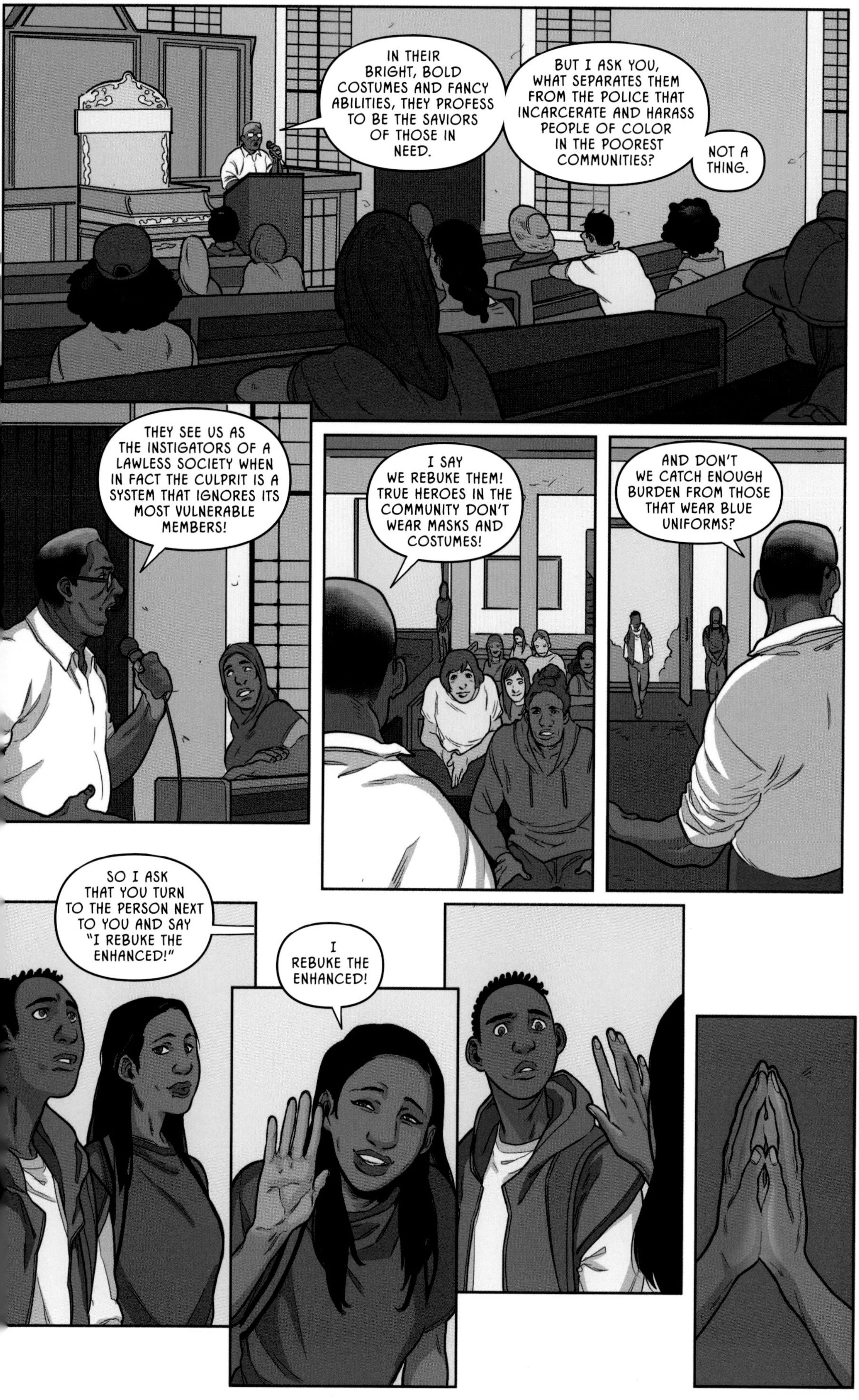
IN THEIR BRIGHT, BOLD COSTUMES AND FANCY ABILITIES, THEY PROFESS TO BE THE SAVIORS OF THOSE IN NEED.
BUT I ASK YOU, WHAT SEPARATES THEM FROM THE POLICE THAT INCARCERATE AND HARASS PEOPLE OF COLOR IN THE POOREST COMMUNITIES?
NOT A THING.
THEY SEE US AS THE INSTIGATORS OF A LAWLESS SOCIETY WHEN IN FACT THE CULPRIT IS A SYSTEM THAT IGNORES ITS MOST VULNERABLE MEMBERS!
I SAY WE REBUKE THEM! TRUE HEROES IN THE COMMUNITY DON'T WEAR MASKS AND COSTUMES!
AND DON'T WE CATCH ENOUGH BURDEN FROM THOSE THAT WEAR BLUE UNIFORMS?
SO I ASK THAT YOU TURN TO THE PERSON NEXT TO YOU AND SAY "I REBUKE THE ENHANCED!"
I REBUKE THE ENHANCED!

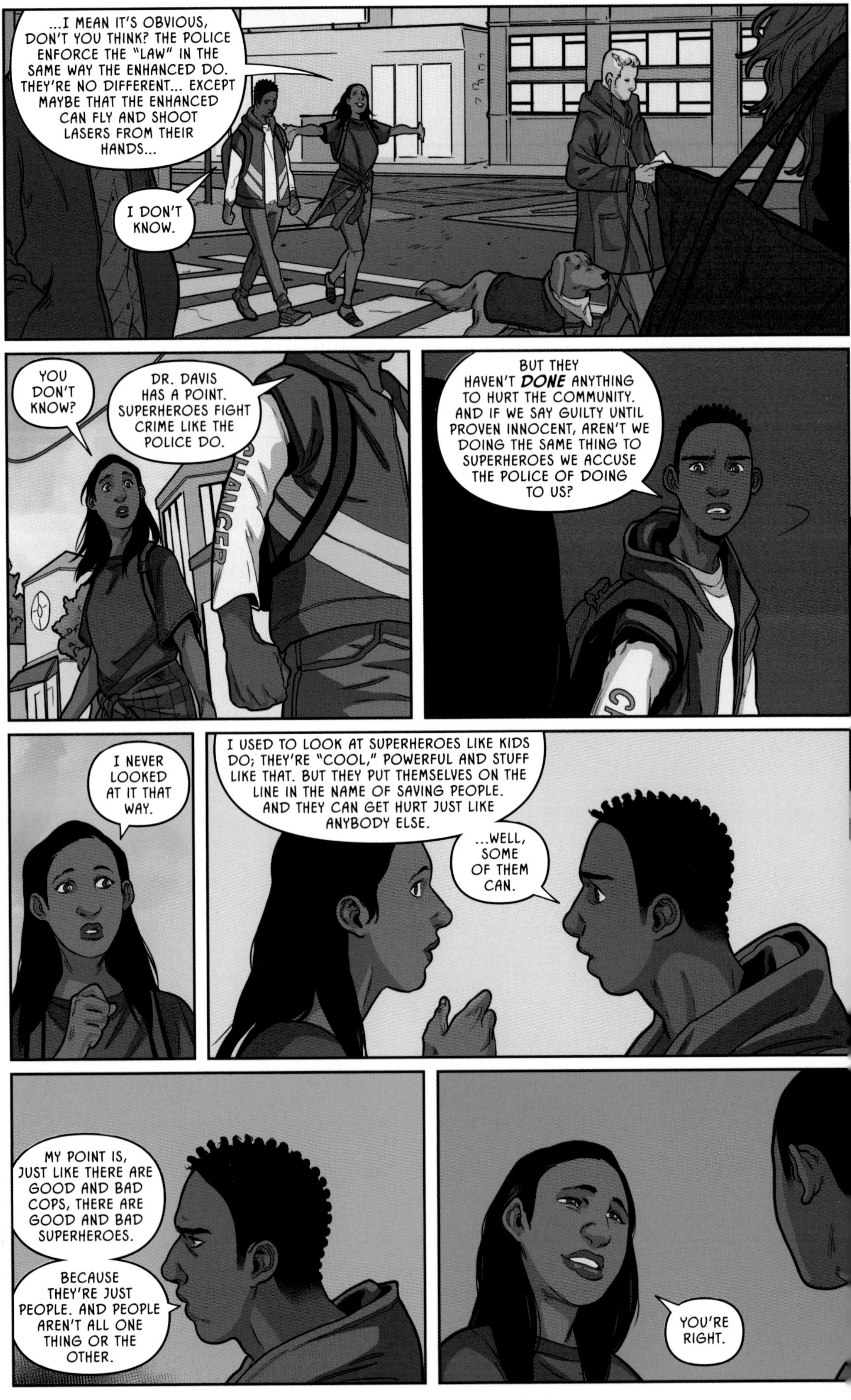
...I MEAN IT'S OBVIOUS, DON'T YOU THINK? THE POLICE ENFORCE THE "LAW" IN THE SAME WAY THE ENHANCED DO. THEY'RE NO DIFFERENT... EXCEPT MAYBE THAT THE ENHANCED CAN FLY AND SHOOT LASERS FROM THEIR HANDS...
I DON'T KNOW.
YOU DON'T KNOW?
DR. DAVIS HAS A POINT. SUPERHEROES FIGHT CRIME LIKE THE POLICE DO.
BUT THEY HAVEN'T ***DONE*** ANYTHING TO HURT THE COMMUNITY. AND IF WE SAY GUILTY UNTIL PROVEN INNOCENT, AREN'T WE DOING THE SAME THING TO SUPERHEROES WE ACCUSE THE POLICE OF DOING TO US?
I NEVER LOOKED AT IT THAT WAY.
I USED TO LOOK AT SUPERHEROES LIKE KIDS DO; THEY'RE "COOL," POWERFUL AND STUFF LIKE THAT. BUT THEY PUT THEMSELVES ON THE LINE IN THE NAME OF SAVING PEOPLE. AND THEY CAN GET HURT JUST LIKE ANYBODY ELSE.
...WELL, SOME OF THEM CAN.
MY POINT IS, JUST LIKE THERE ARE GOOD AND BAD COPS, THERE ARE GOOD AND BAD SUPERHEROES.
BECAUSE THEY'RE JUST PEOPLE. AND PEOPLE AREN'T ALL ONE THING OR THE OTHER.
YOU'RE RIGHT.

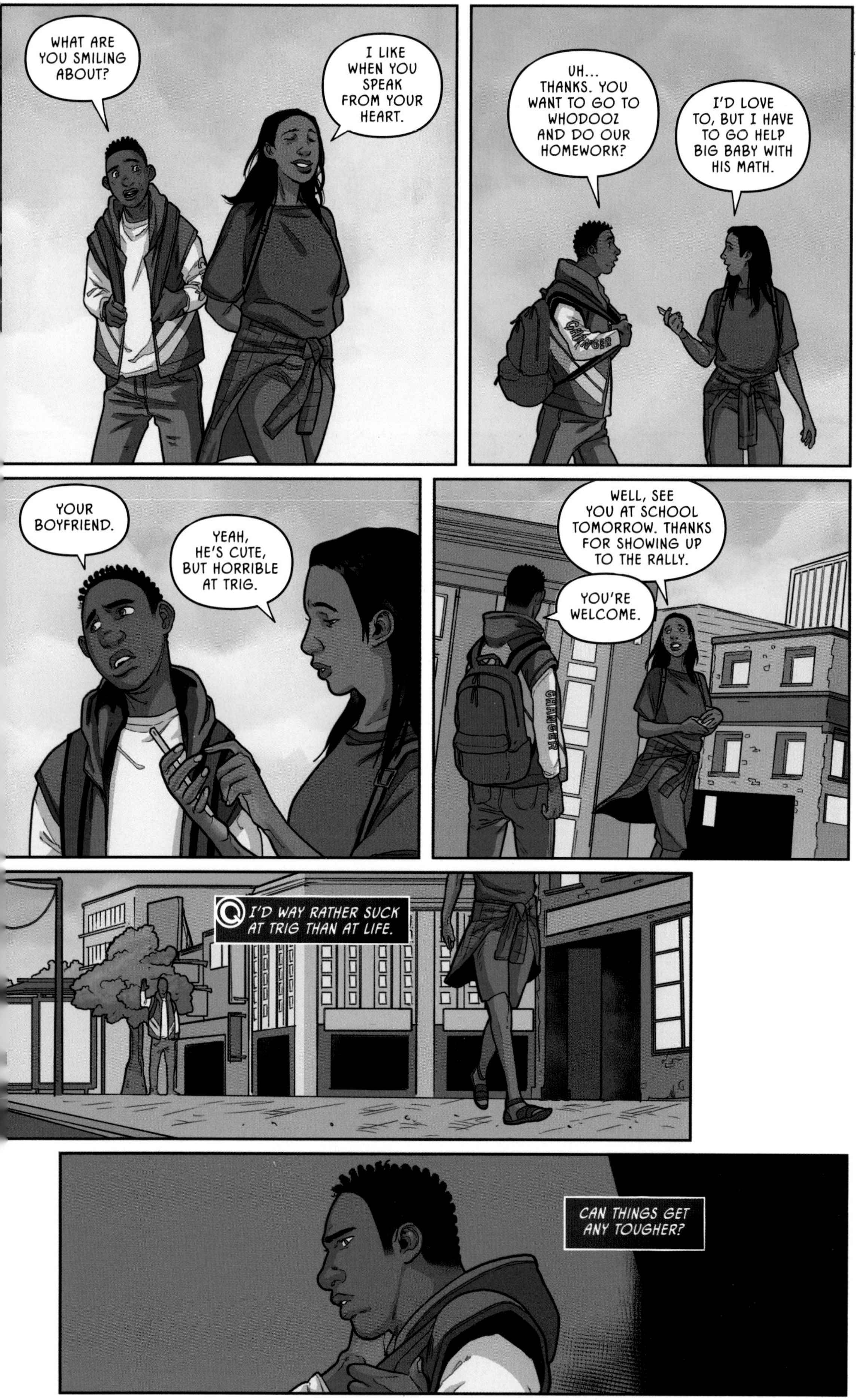

WHAT ARE YOU SMILING ABOUT?
I LIKE WHEN YOU SPEAK FROM YOUR HEART.
UH... THANKS. YOU WANT TO GO TO WHODOOZ AND DO OUR HOMEWORK?
I'D LOVE TO, BUT I HAVE TO GO HELP BIG BABY WITH HIS MATH.
CHANGER
YOUR BOYFRIEND.
YEAH, HE'S CUTE, BUT HORRIBLE AT TRIG.
WELL, SEE YOU AT SCHOOL TOMORROW. THANKS FOR SHOWING UP TO THE RALLY.
YOU'RE WELCOME.
CHANGER
I'D WAY RATHER SUCK AT TRIG THAN AT LIFE.
CAN THINGS GET ANY TOUGHER?

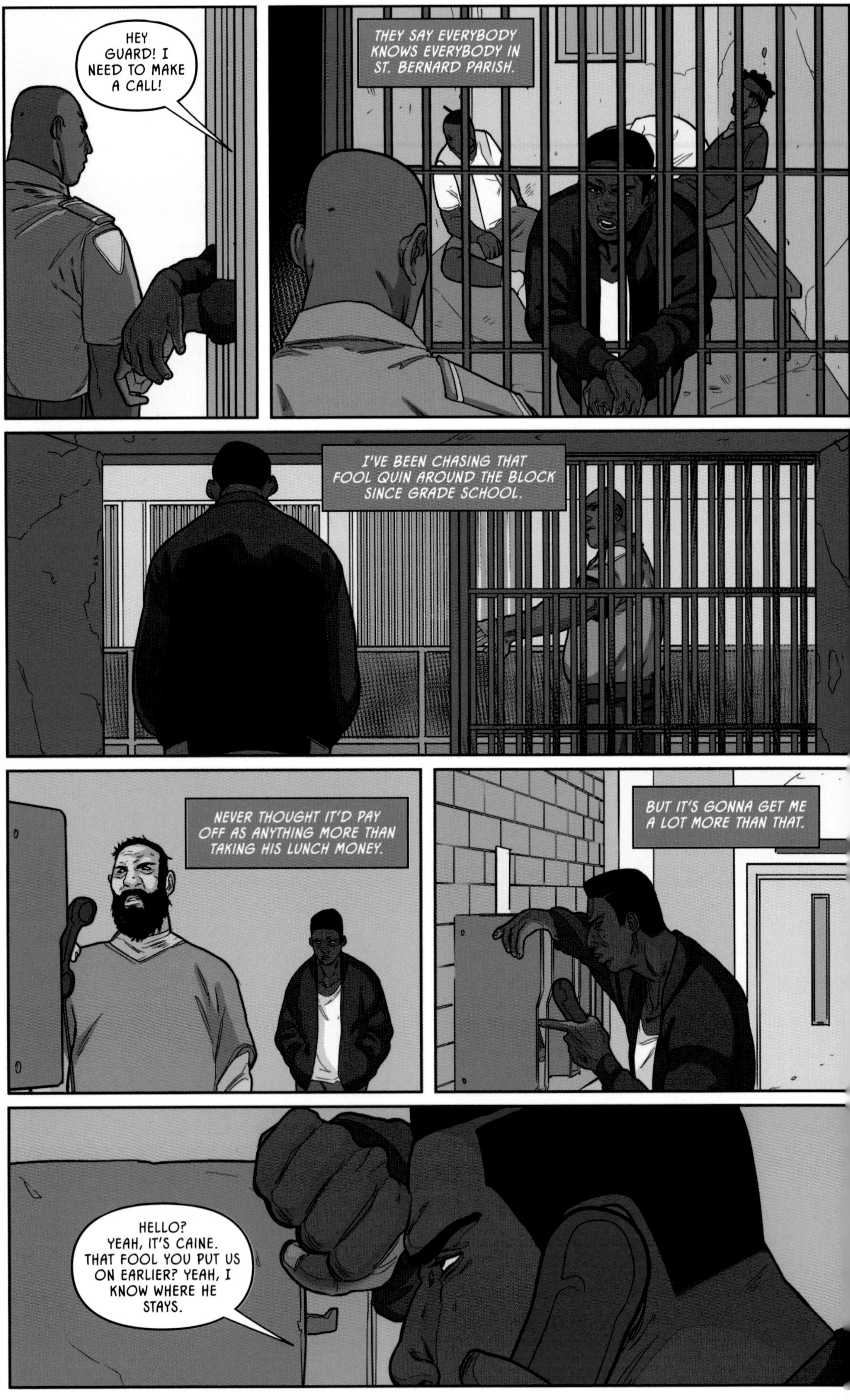
HEY GUARD! I NEED TO MAKE A CALL!
THEY SAY EVERYBODY KNOWS EVERYBODY IN ST. BERNARD PARISH.
I'VE BEEN CHASING THAT FOOL QUIN AROUND THE BLOCK SINCE GRADE SCHOOL.
NEVER THOUGHT IT'D PAY OFF AS ANYTHING MORE THAN TAKING HIS LUNCH MONEY.
BUT IT'S GONNA GET ME A LOT MORE THAN THAT.
HELLO? YEAH, IT'S CAINE. THAT FOOL YOU PUT US ON EARLIER? YEAH, I KNOW WHERE HE STAYS.

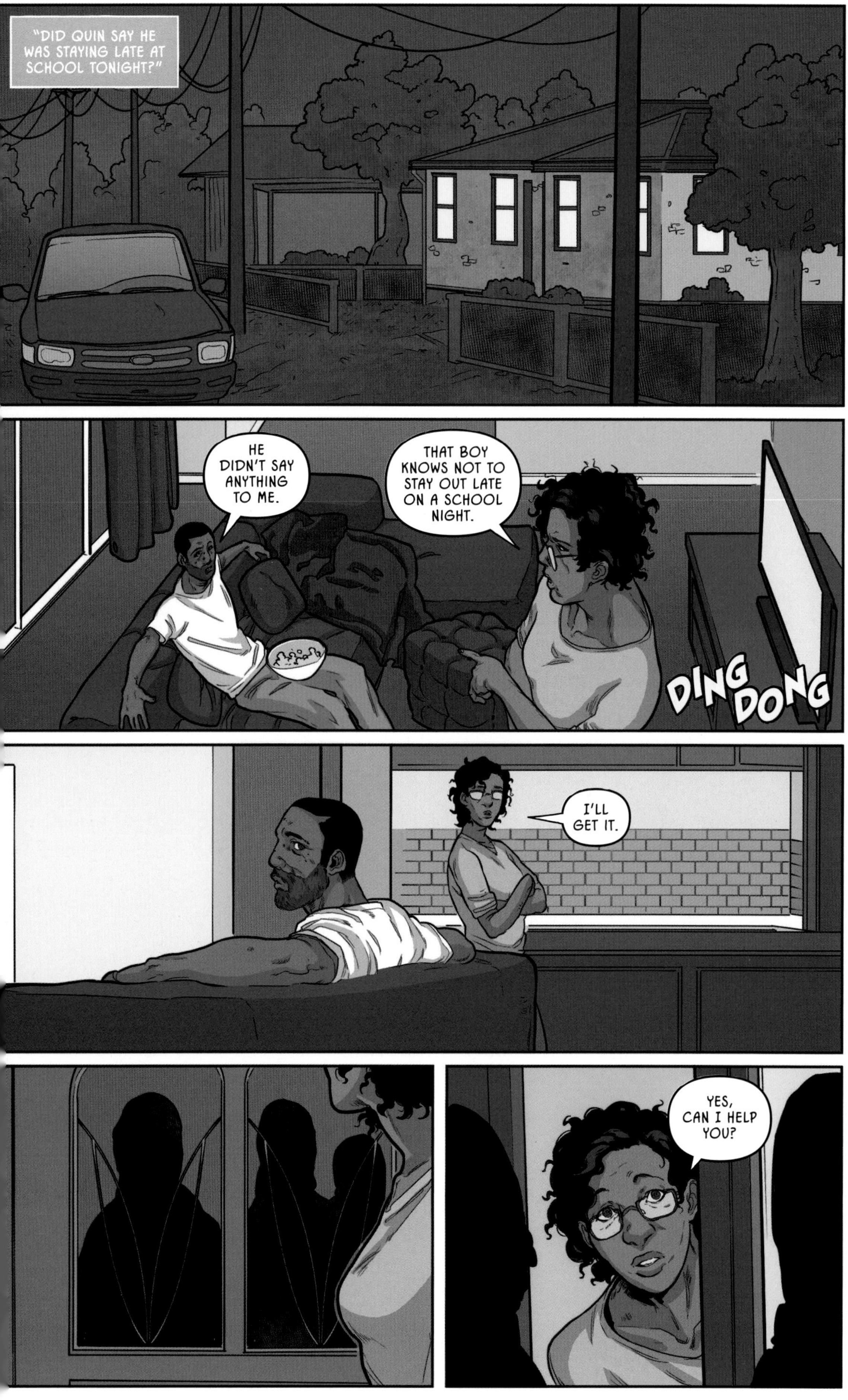
"DID QUIN SAY HE WAS STAYING LATE AT SCHOOL TONIGHT?"
HE DIDN'T SAY ANYTHING TO ME.
THAT BOY KNOWS NOT TO STAY OUT LATE ON A SCHOOL NIGHT.
DING DONG
I'LL GET IT.
YES, CAN I HELP YOU?

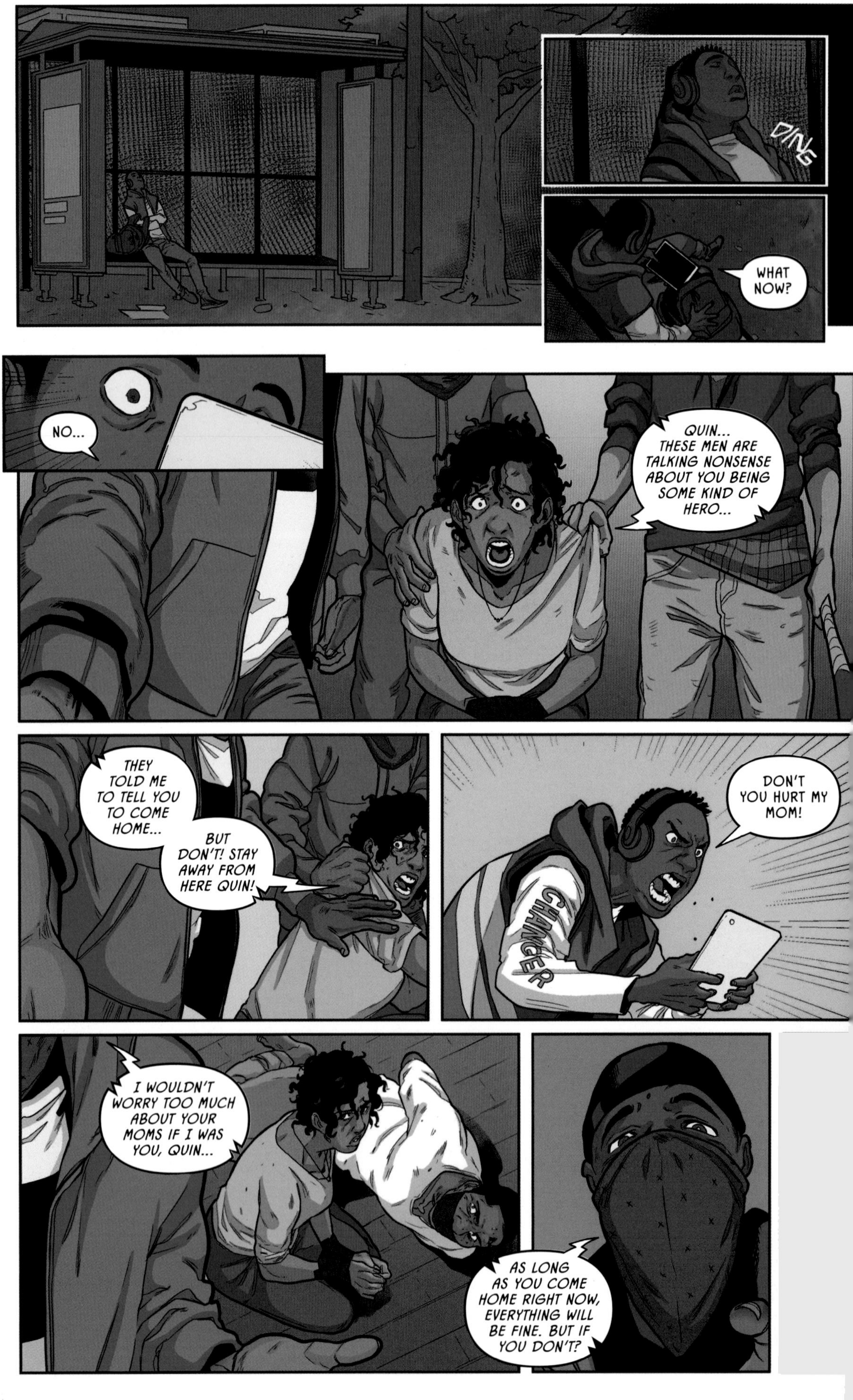
DING
WHAT NOW?
NO...
QUIN... THESE MEN ARE TALKING NONSENSE ABOUT YOU BEING SOME KIND OF HERO...
THEY TOLD ME TO TELL YOU TO COME HOME...
BUT DON'T! STAY AWAY FROM HERE QUIN!
DON'T YOU HURT MY MOM!
CHANGER
I WOULDN'T WORRY TOO MUCH ABOUT YOUR MOMS IF I WAS YOU, QUIN...
AS LONG AS YOU COME HOME RIGHT NOW, EVERYTHING WILL BE FINE. BUT IF YOU DON'T?

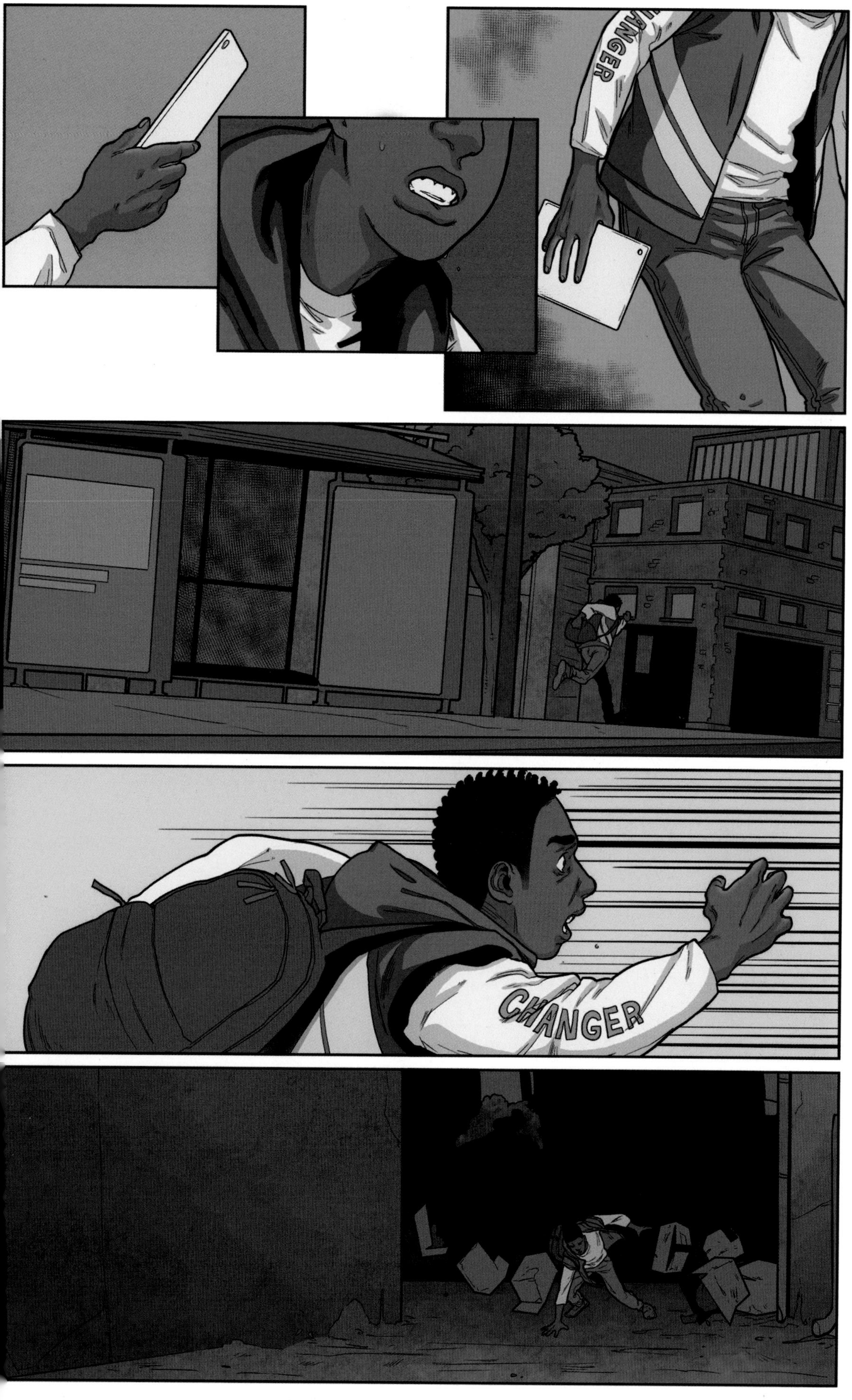
CHANGER

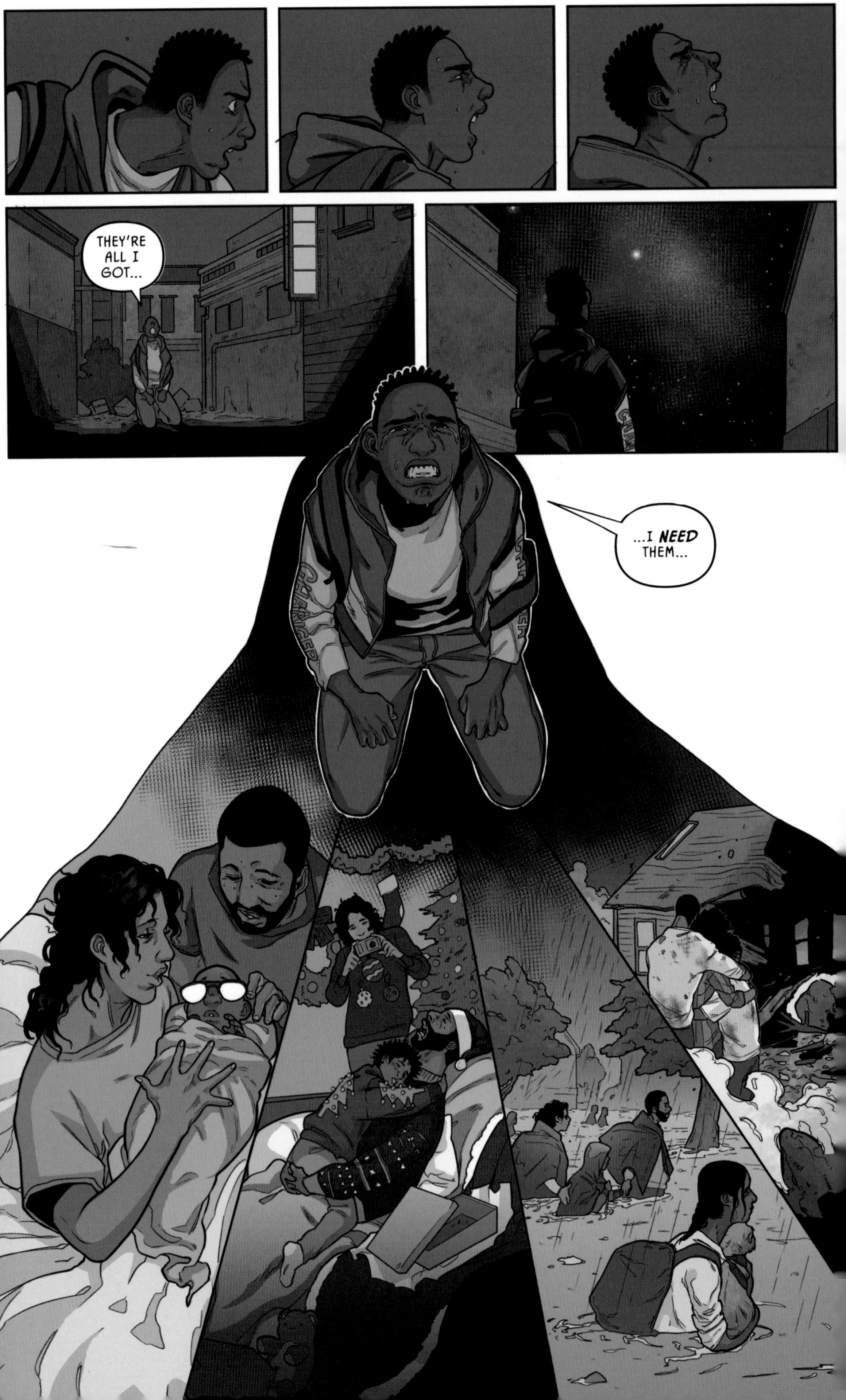
THEY'RE ALL I GOT...
...I NEED THEM...

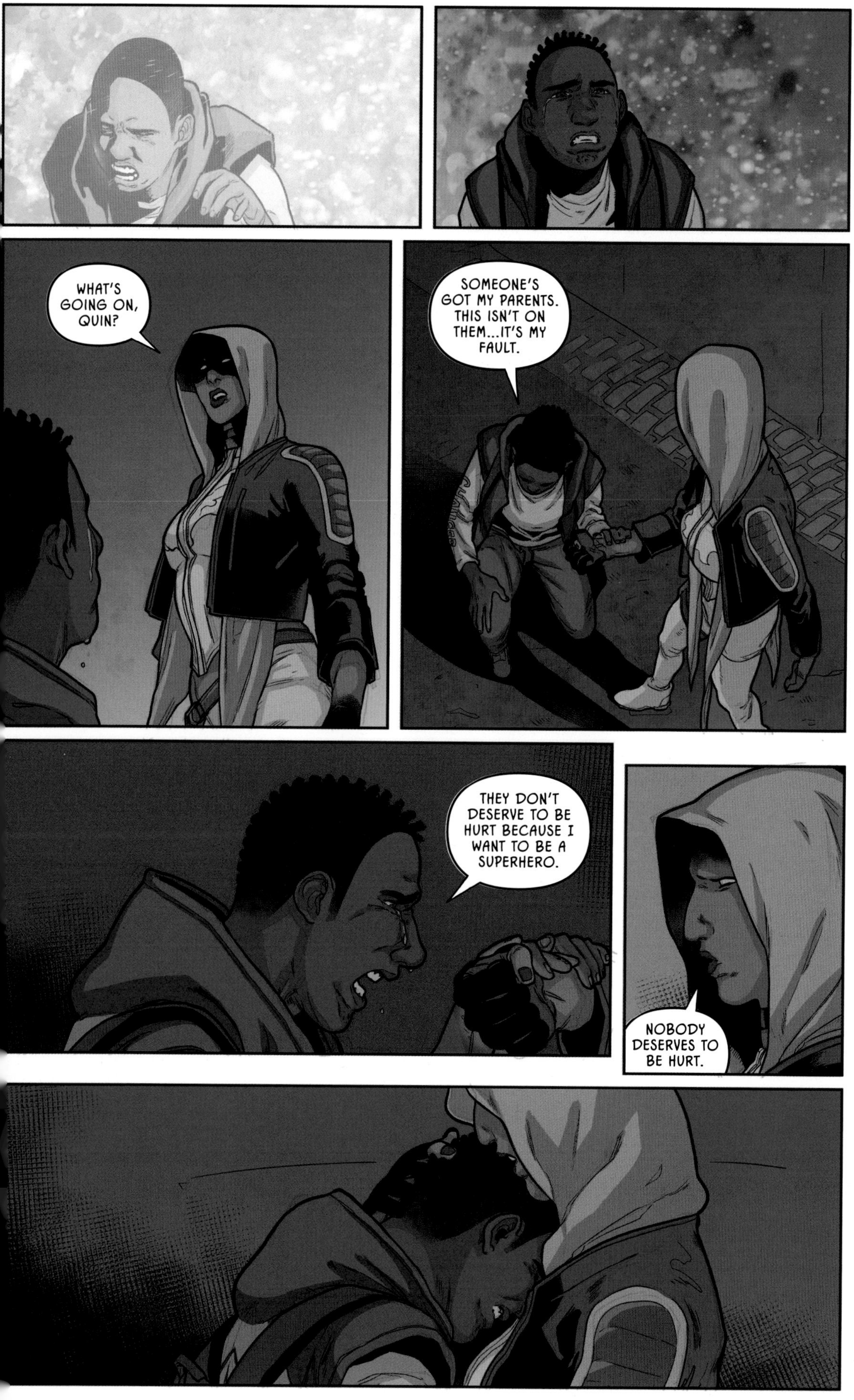
WHAT'S GOING ON, QUIN?
SOMEONE'S GOT MY PARENTS. THIS ISN'T ON THEM...IT'S MY FAULT.
THEY DON'T DESERVE TO BE HURT BECAUSE I WANT TO BE A SUPERHERO.
NOBODY DESERVES TO BE HURT.

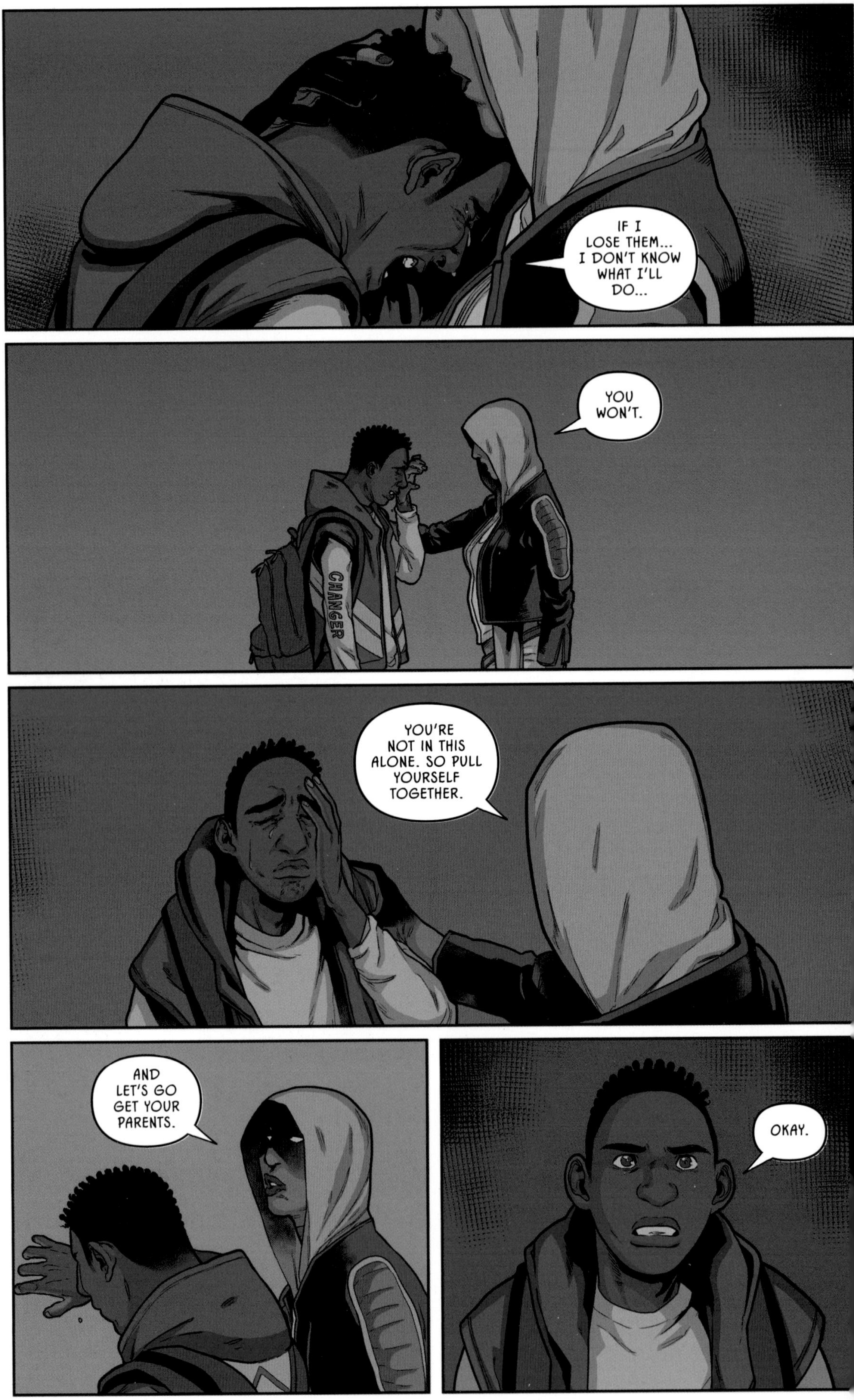
IF I LOSE THEM... I DON'T KNOW WHAT I'LL DO...
YOU WON'T.
CHANGER
YOU'RE NOT IN THIS ALONE. SO PULL YOURSELF TOGETHER.
AND LET'S GO GET YOUR PARENTS.
OKAY.

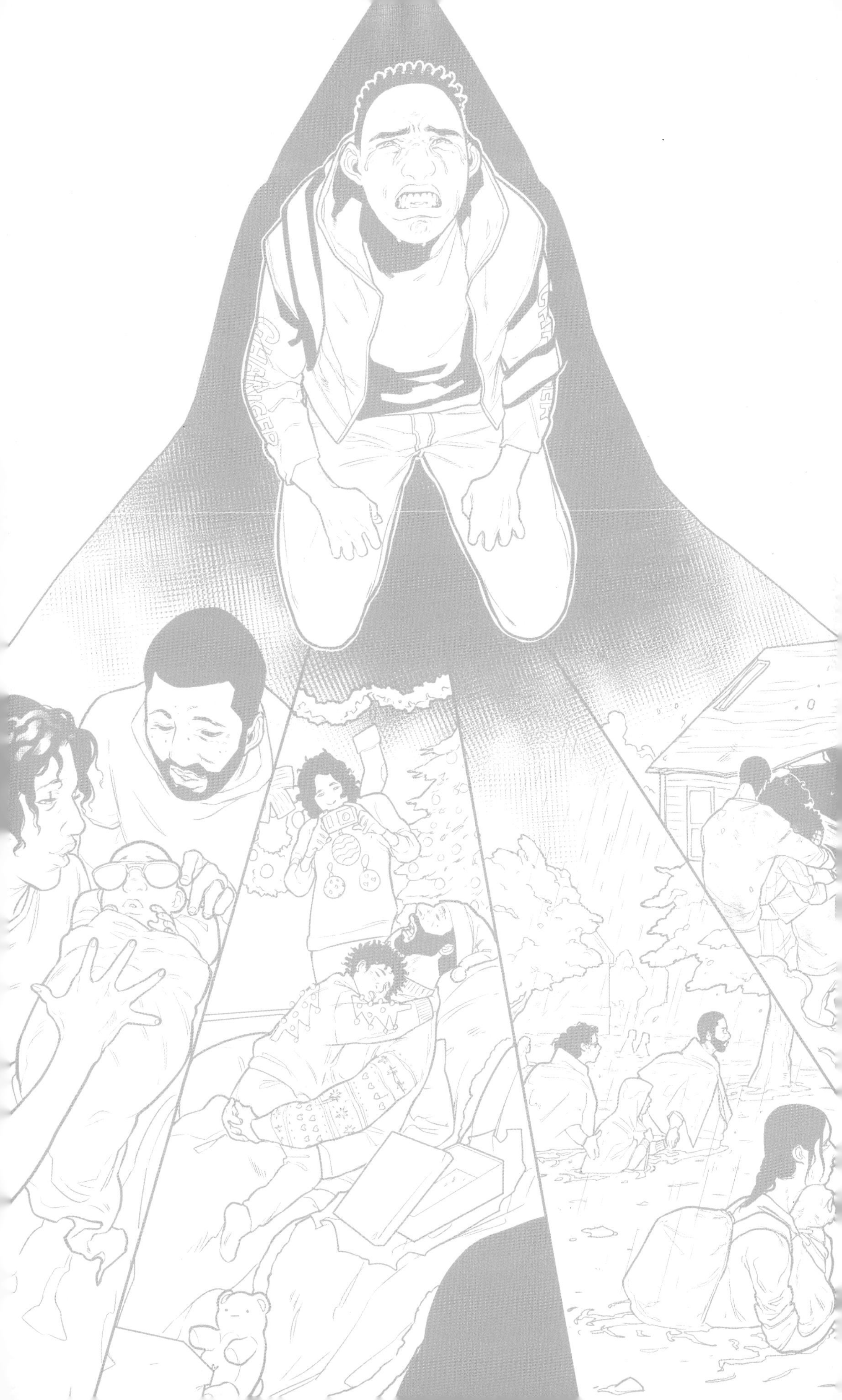

CHAPTER FOUR

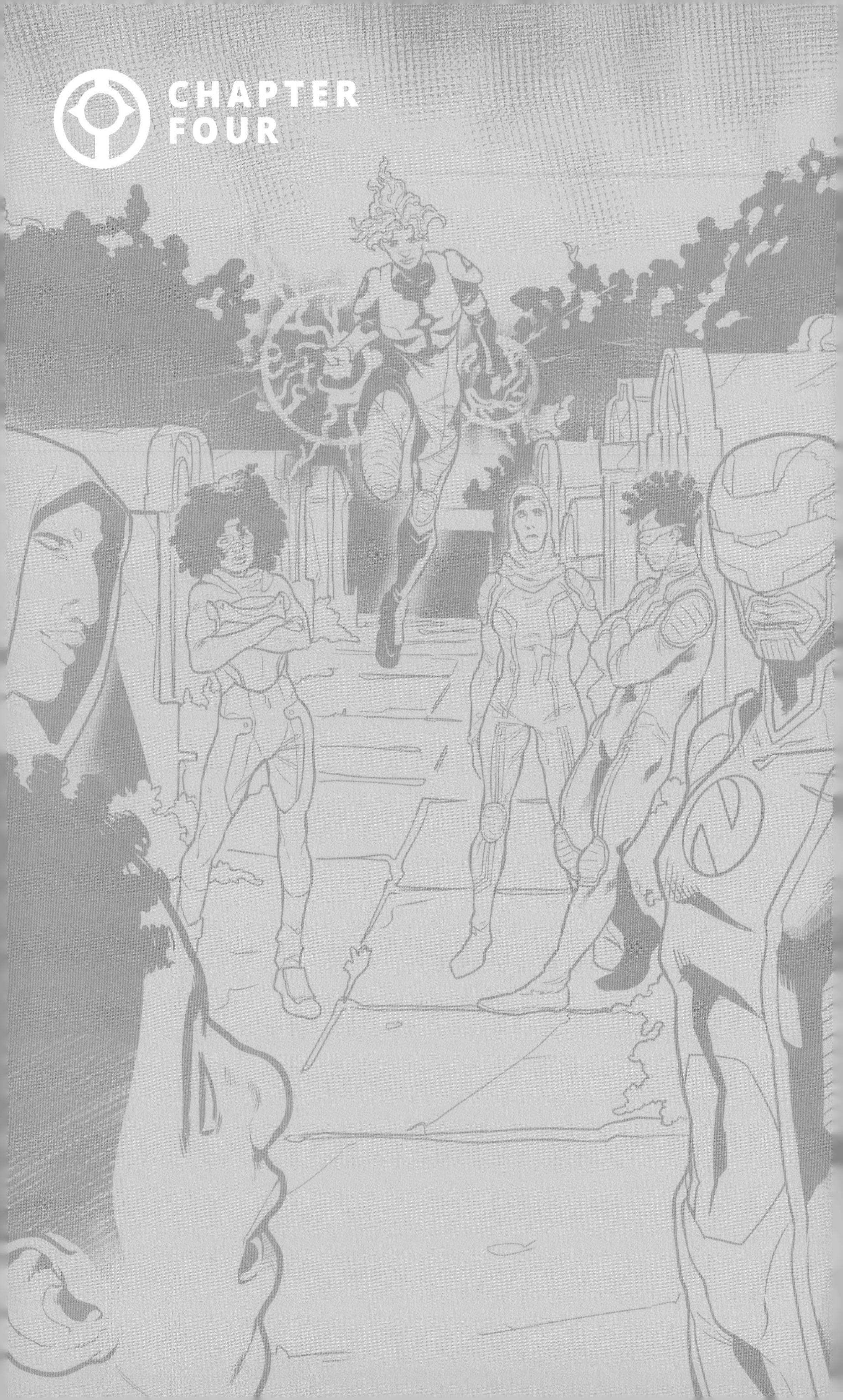

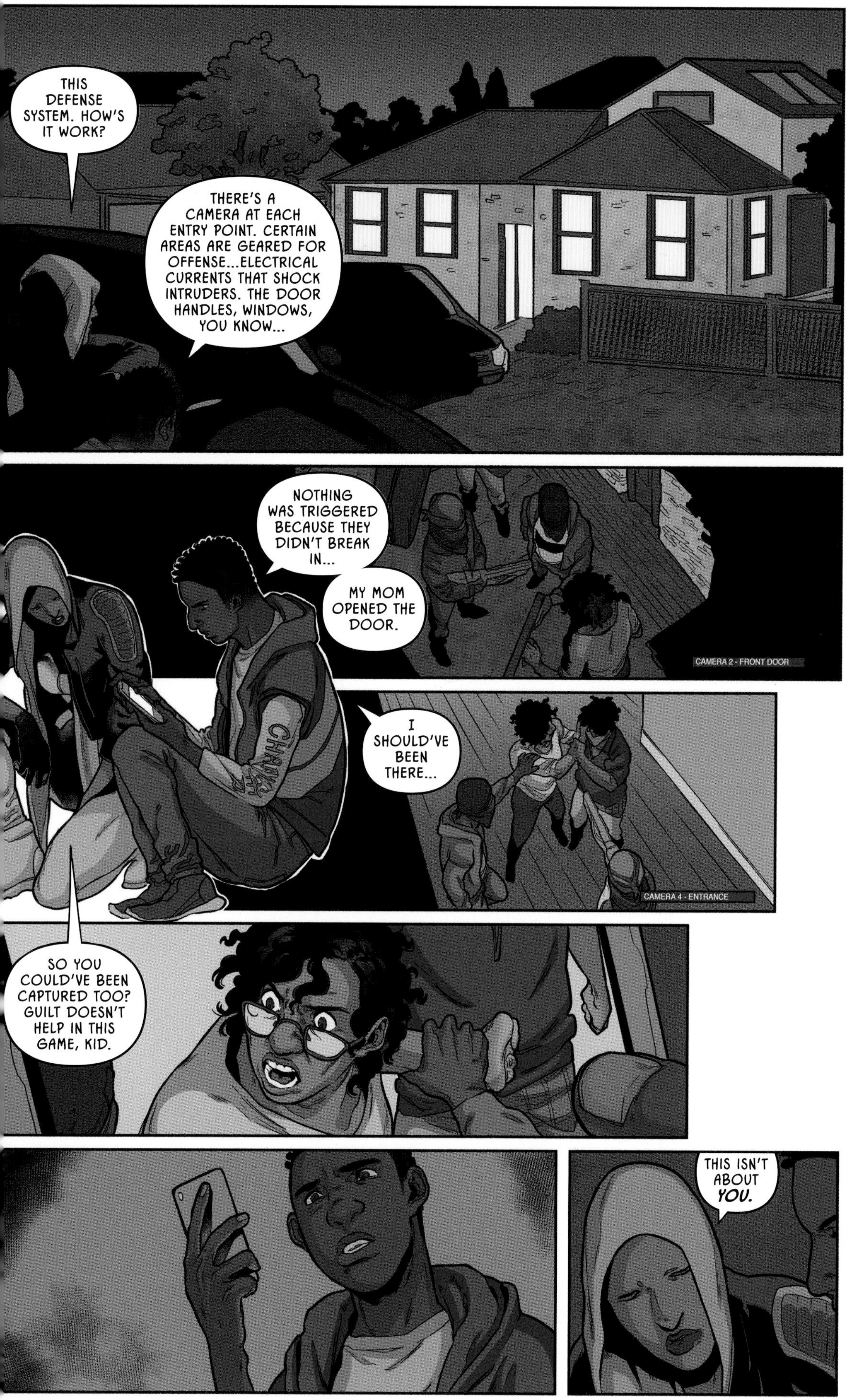
THIS DEFENSE SYSTEM. HOW'S IT WORK?
THERE'S A CAMERA AT EACH ENTRY POINT. CERTAIN AREAS ARE GEARED FOR OFFENSE...ELECTRICAL CURRENTS THAT SHOCK INTRUDERS. THE DOOR HANDLES, WINDOWS, YOU KNOW...
NOTHING WAS TRIGGERED BECAUSE THEY DIDN'T BREAK IN...
MY MOM OPENED THE DOOR.
CAMERA 2 - FRONT DOOR
I SHOULD'VE BEEN THERE...
CAMERA 4 - ENTRANCE
SO YOU COULD'VE BEEN CAPTURED TOO? GUILT DOESN'T HELP IN THIS GAME, KID.
THIS ISN'T ABOUT *YOU.*

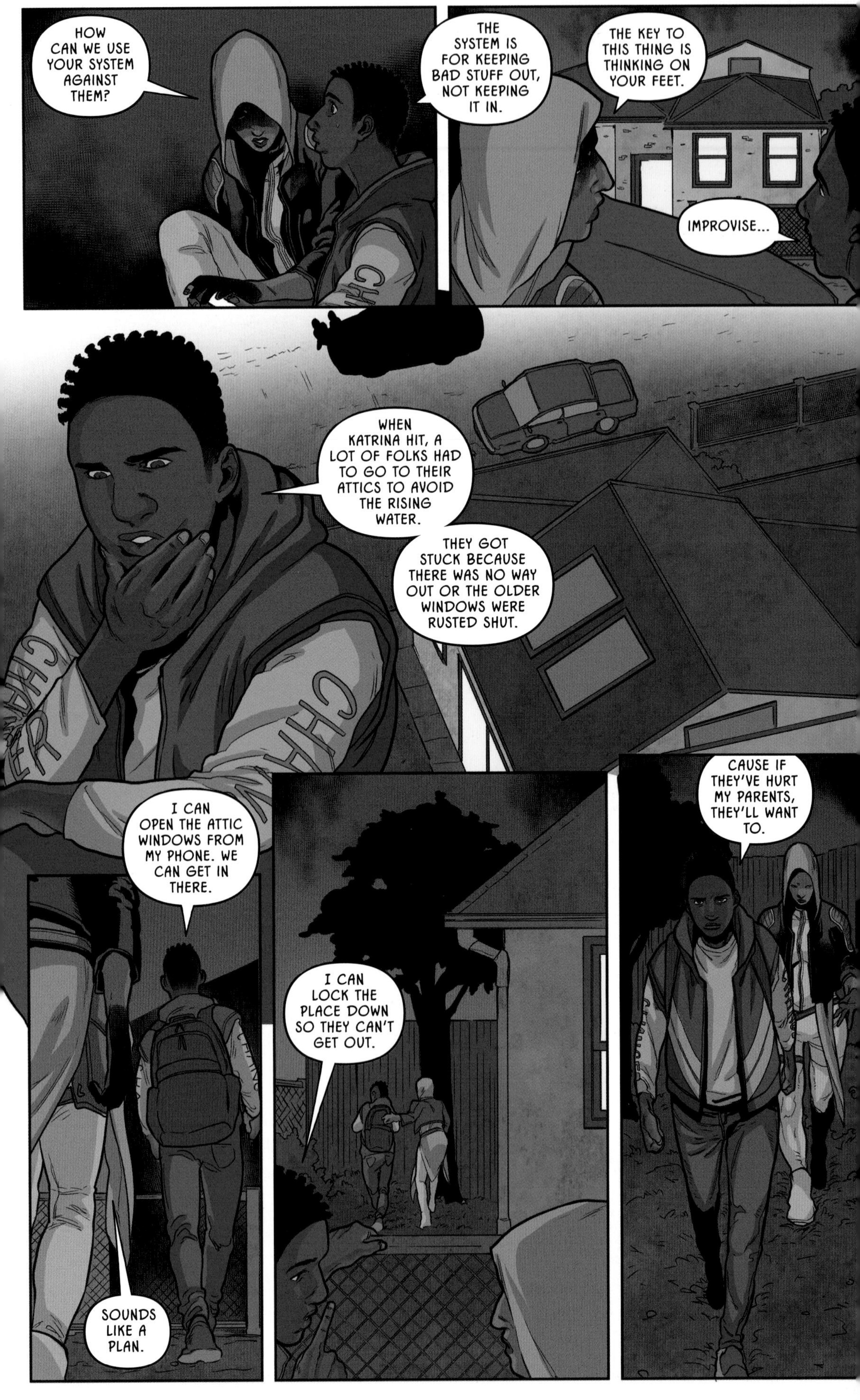
HOW CAN WE USE YOUR SYSTEM AGAINST THEM?
THE SYSTEM IS FOR KEEPING BAD STUFF OUT, NOT KEEPING IT IN.
THE KEY TO THIS THING IS THINKING ON YOUR FEET.
IMPROVISE...
WHEN KATRINA HIT, A LOT OF FOLKS HAD TO GO TO THEIR ATTICS TO AVOID THE RISING WATER.
THEY GOT STUCK BECAUSE THERE WAS NO WAY OUT OR THE OLDER WINDOWS WERE RUSTED SHUT.
I CAN OPEN THE ATTIC WINDOWS FROM MY PHONE. WE CAN GET IN THERE.
SOUNDS LIKE A PLAN.
I CAN LOCK THE PLACE DOWN SO THEY CAN'T GET OUT.
CAUSE IF THEY'VE HURT MY PARENTS, THEY'LL WANT TO.

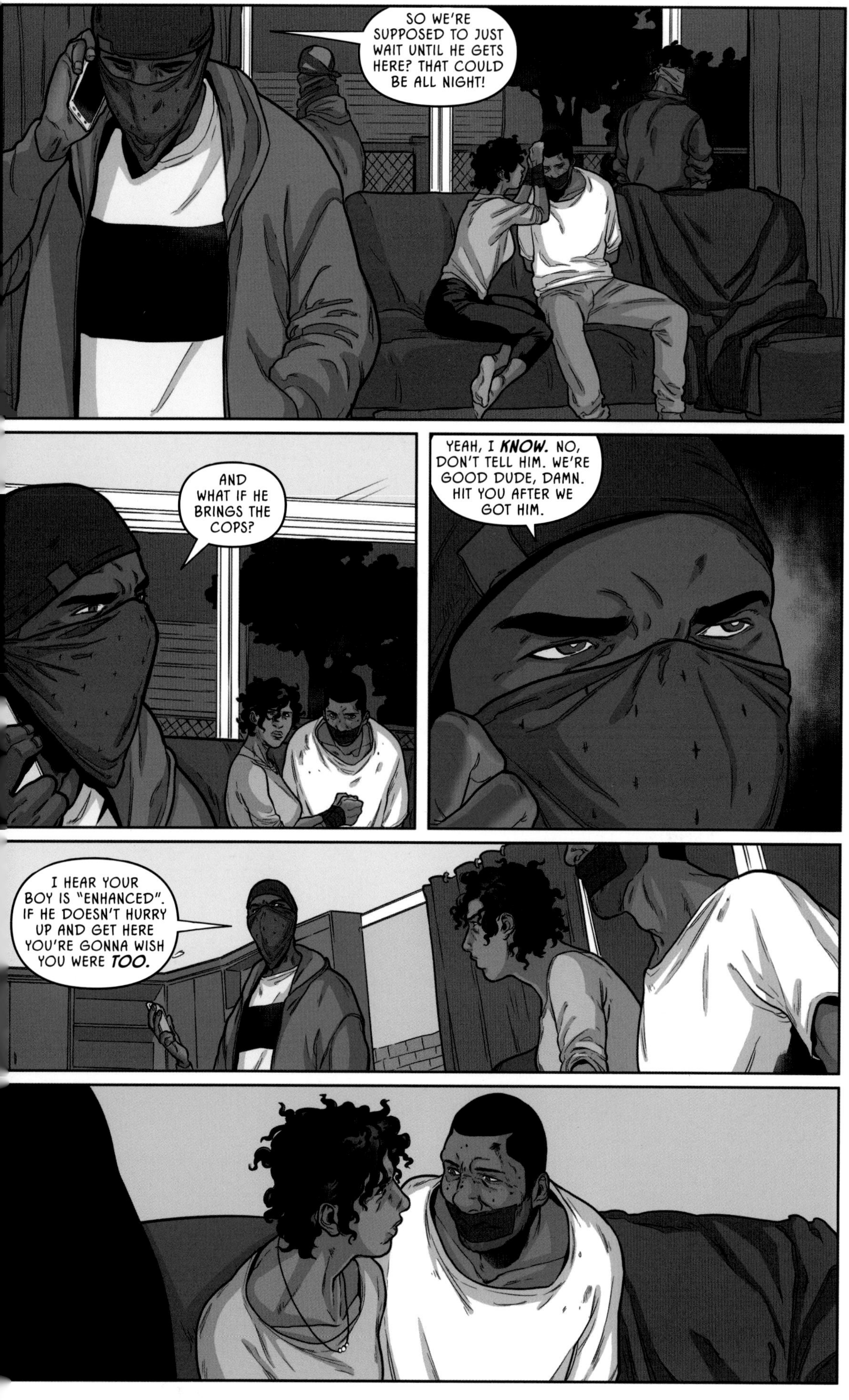
SO WE'RE SUPPOSED TO JUST WAIT UNTIL HE GETS HERE? THAT COULD BE ALL NIGHT!
AND WHAT IF HE BRINGS THE COPS?
YEAH, I ***KNOW.*** NO, DON'T TELL HIM. WE'RE GOOD DUDE, DAMN. HIT YOU AFTER WE GOT HIM.
I HEAR YOUR BOY IS "ENHANCED". IF HE DOESN'T HURRY UP AND GET HERE YOU'RE GONNA WISH YOU WERE ***TOO.***

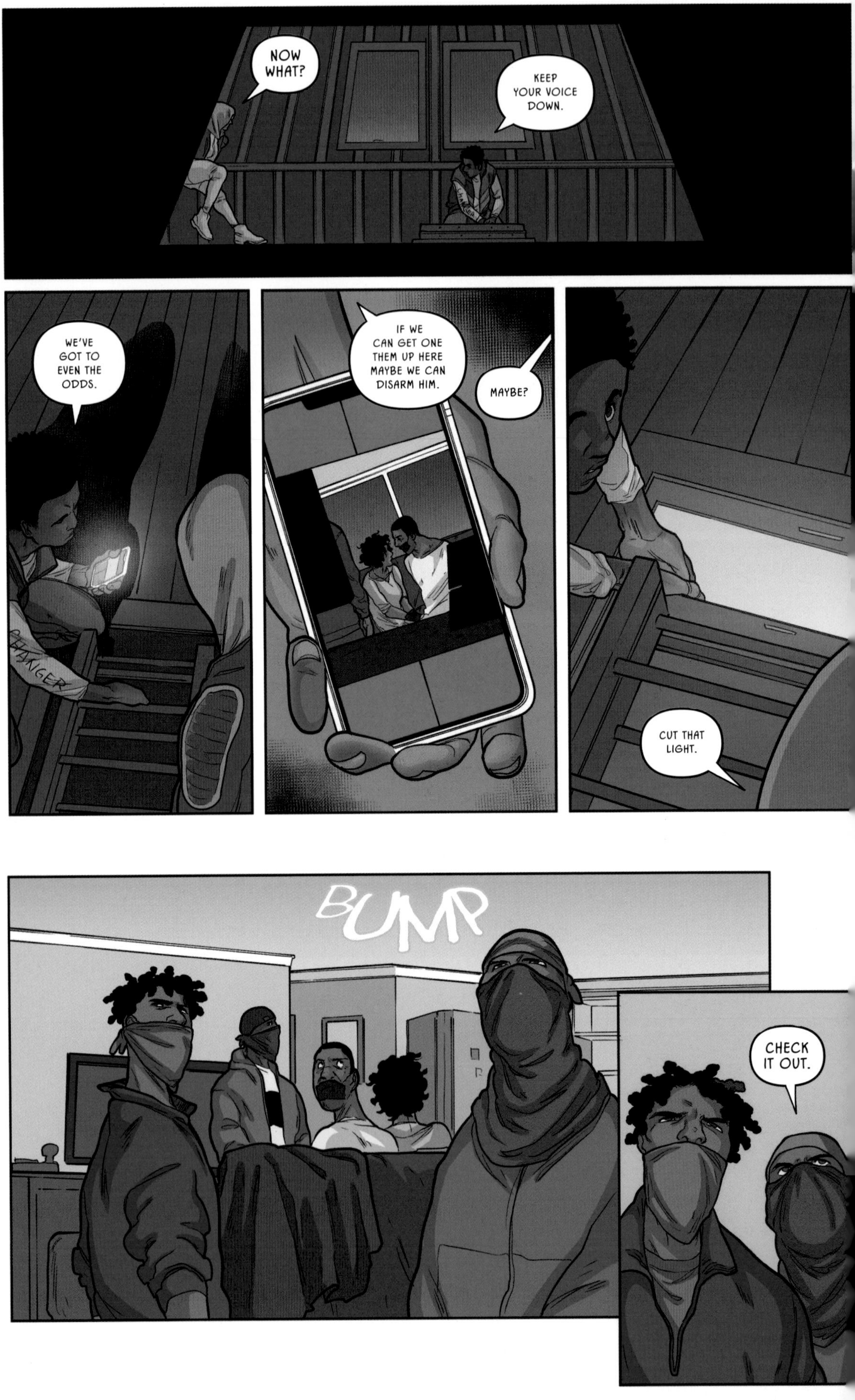

NOW WHAT?
KEEP YOUR VOICE DOWN.
CHARGER
WE'VE GOT TO EVEN THE ODDS.
CHARGER
IF WE CAN GET ONE THEM UP HERE MAYBE WE CAN DISARM HIM.
MAYBE?
CUT THAT LIGHT.
BUMP
CHECK IT OUT.

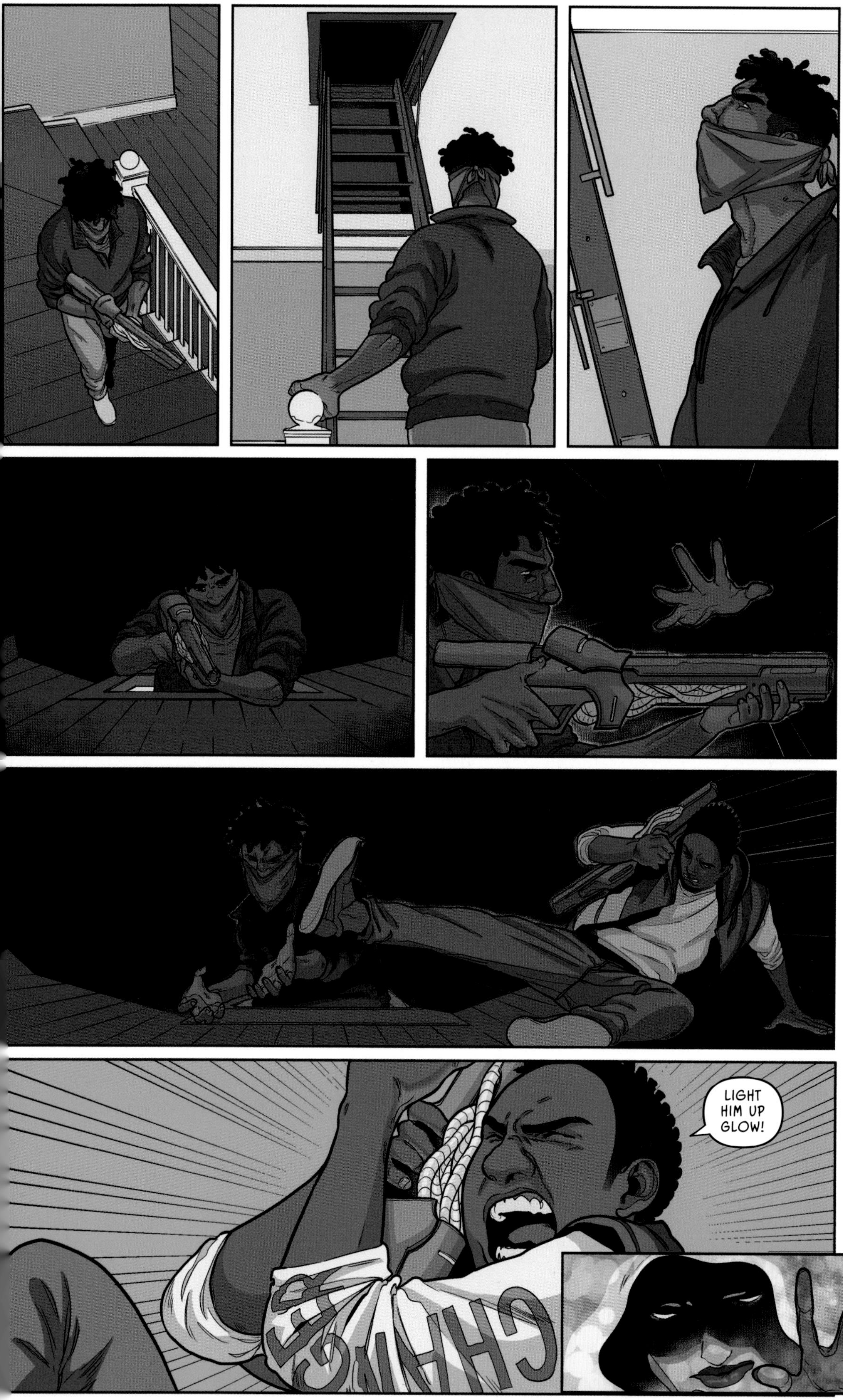
LIGHT
HIM UP
GLOW!

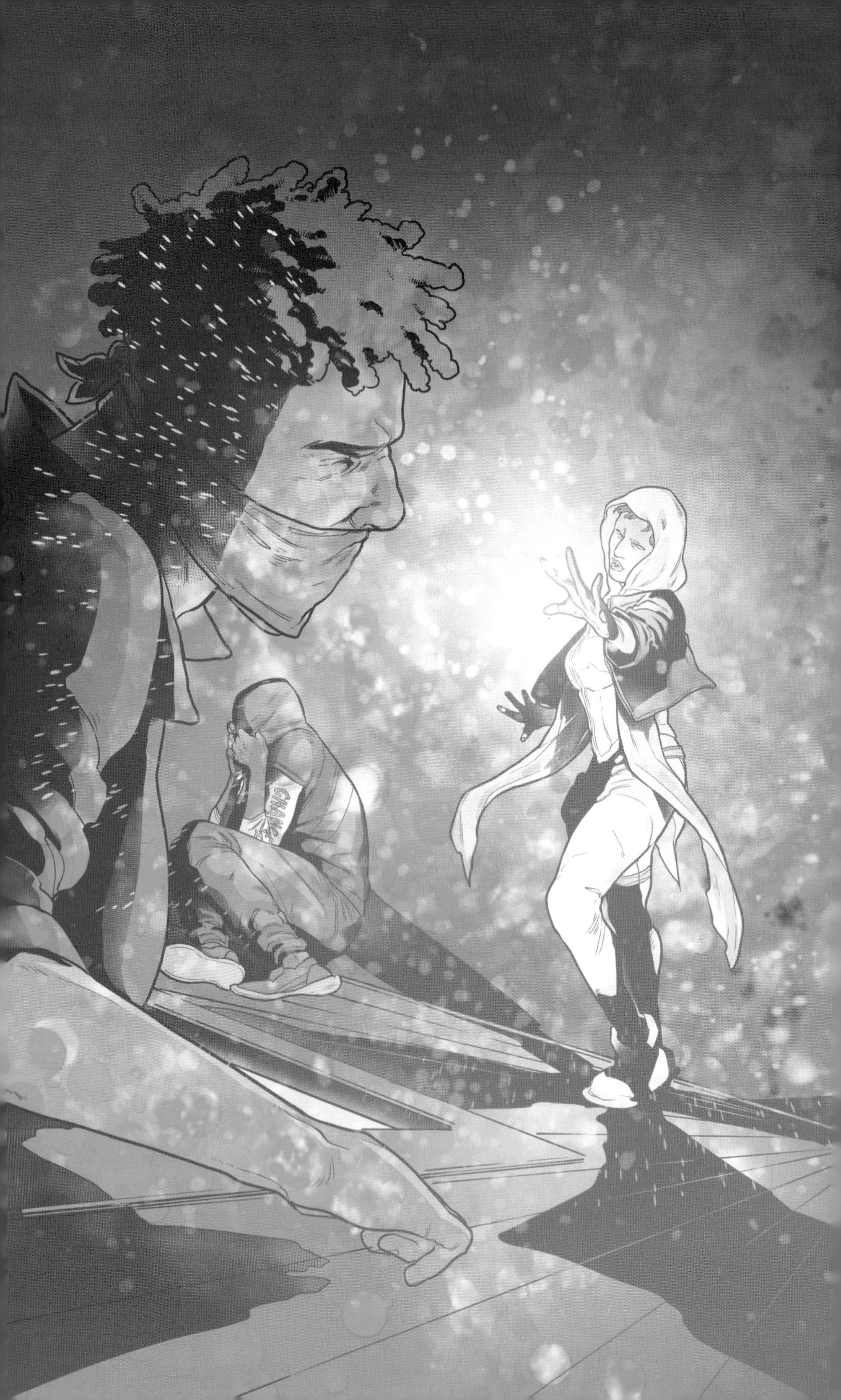

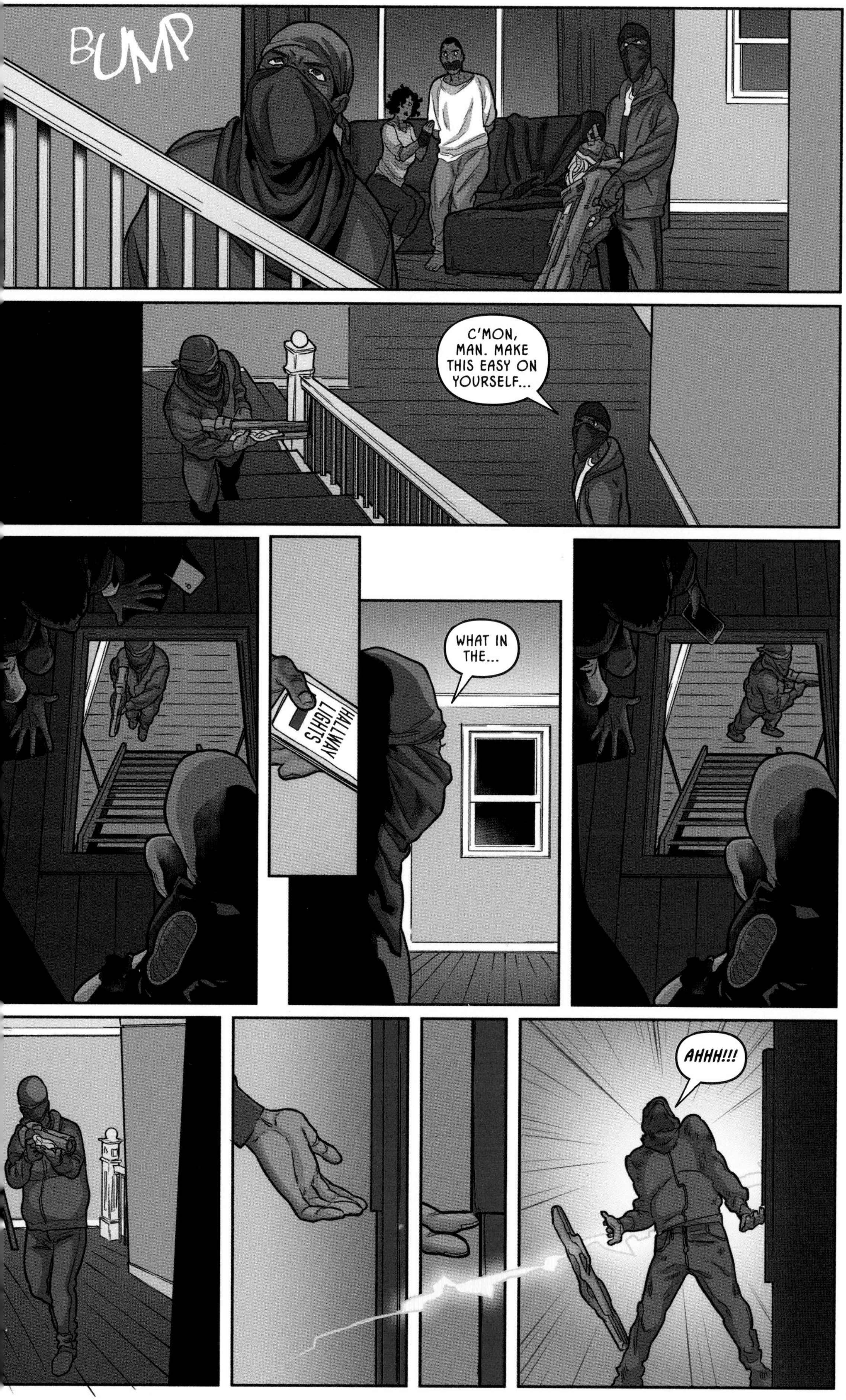
BUMP
C'MON, MAN. MAKE THIS EASY ON YOURSELF...
HALLWAY LIGHTS
WHAT IN THE...
AHHH!!!

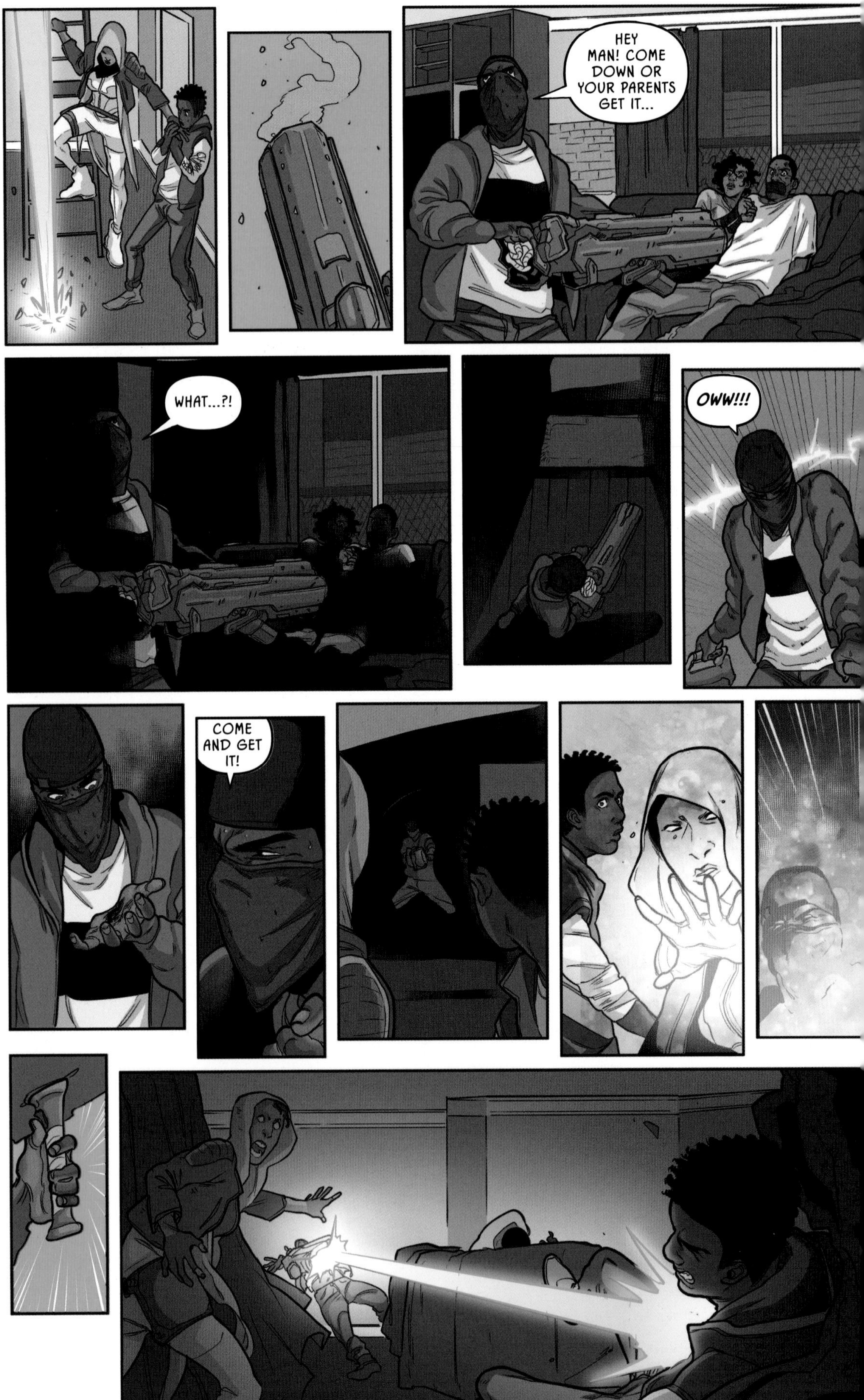
HEY MAN! COME DOWN OR YOUR PARENTS GET IT...
WHAT...?!
OWW!!!
COME AND GET IT!

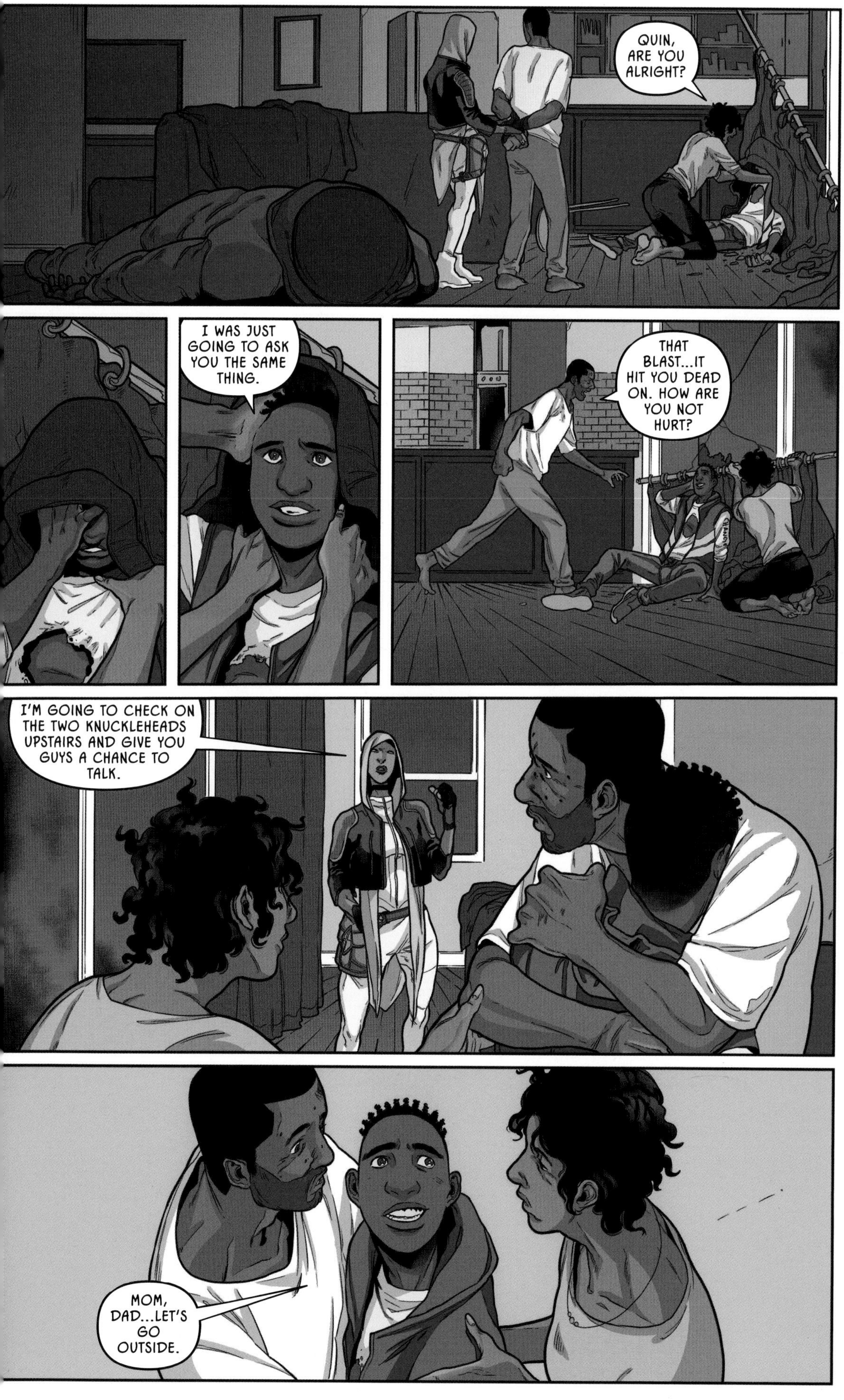
QUIN, ARE YOU ALRIGHT?
I WAS JUST GOING TO ASK YOU THE SAME THING.
THAT BLAST...IT HIT YOU DEAD ON. HOW ARE YOU NOT HURT?
I'M GOING TO CHECK ON THE TWO KNUCKLEHEADS UPSTAIRS AND GIVE YOU GUYS A CHANCE TO TALK.
MOM, DAD...LET'S GO OUTSIDE.

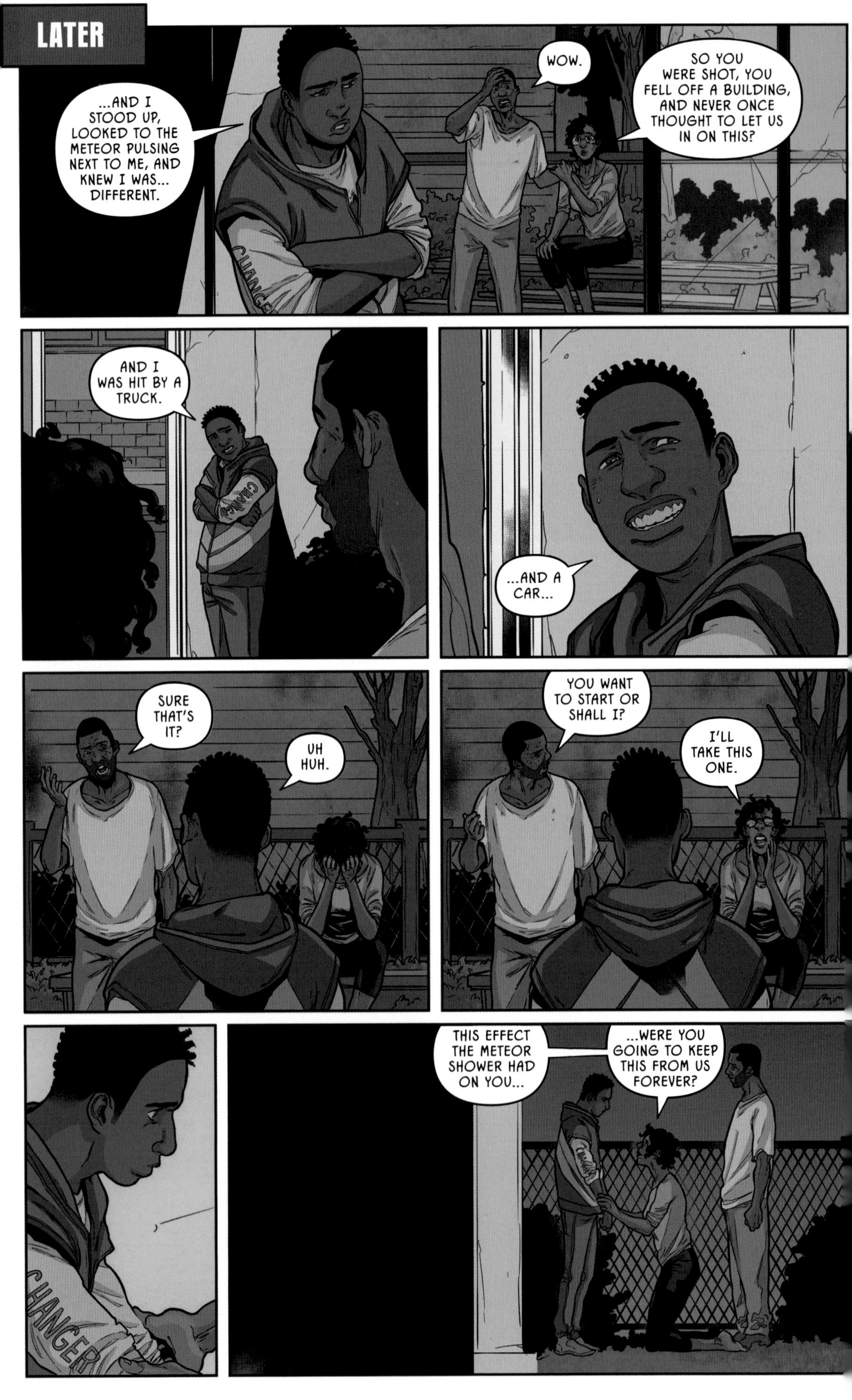
LATER
...AND I STOOD UP, LOOKED TO THE METEOR PULSING NEXT TO ME, AND KNEW I WAS... DIFFERENT.
WOW.
SO YOU WERE SHOT, YOU FELL OFF A BUILDING, AND NEVER ONCE THOUGHT TO LET US IN ON THIS?
AND I WAS HIT BY A TRUCK.
...AND A CAR...
SURE THAT'S IT?
UH HUH.
YOU WANT TO START OR SHALL I?
I'LL TAKE THIS ONE.
THIS EFFECT THE METEOR SHOWER HAD ON YOU...
...WERE YOU GOING TO KEEP THIS FROM US FOREVER?

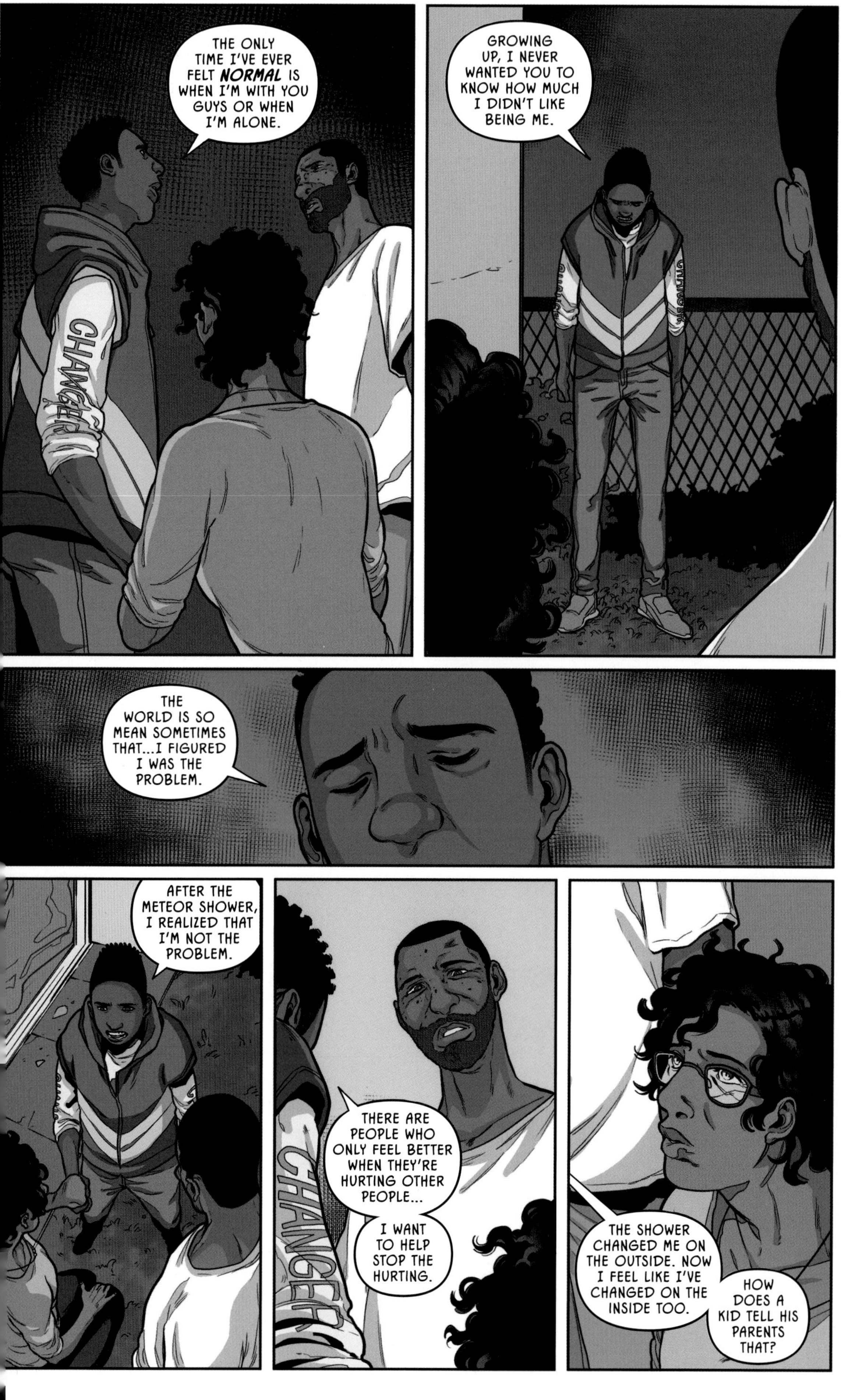

THE ONLY TIME I'VE EVER FELT **NORMAL** IS WHEN I'M WITH YOU GUYS OR WHEN I'M ALONE.
CHANGER
GROWING UP, I NEVER WANTED YOU TO KNOW HOW MUCH I DIDN'T LIKE BEING ME.
THE WORLD IS SO MEAN SOMETIMES THAT...I FIGURED I WAS THE PROBLEM.
AFTER THE METEOR SHOWER, I REALIZED THAT I'M NOT THE PROBLEM.
THERE ARE PEOPLE WHO ONLY FEEL BETTER WHEN THEY'RE HURTING OTHER PEOPLE...
I WANT TO HELP STOP THE HURTING.
CHANGER
THE SHOWER CHANGED ME ON THE OUTSIDE. NOW I FEEL LIKE I'VE CHANGED ON THE INSIDE TOO.
HOW DOES A KID TELL HIS PARENTS THAT?

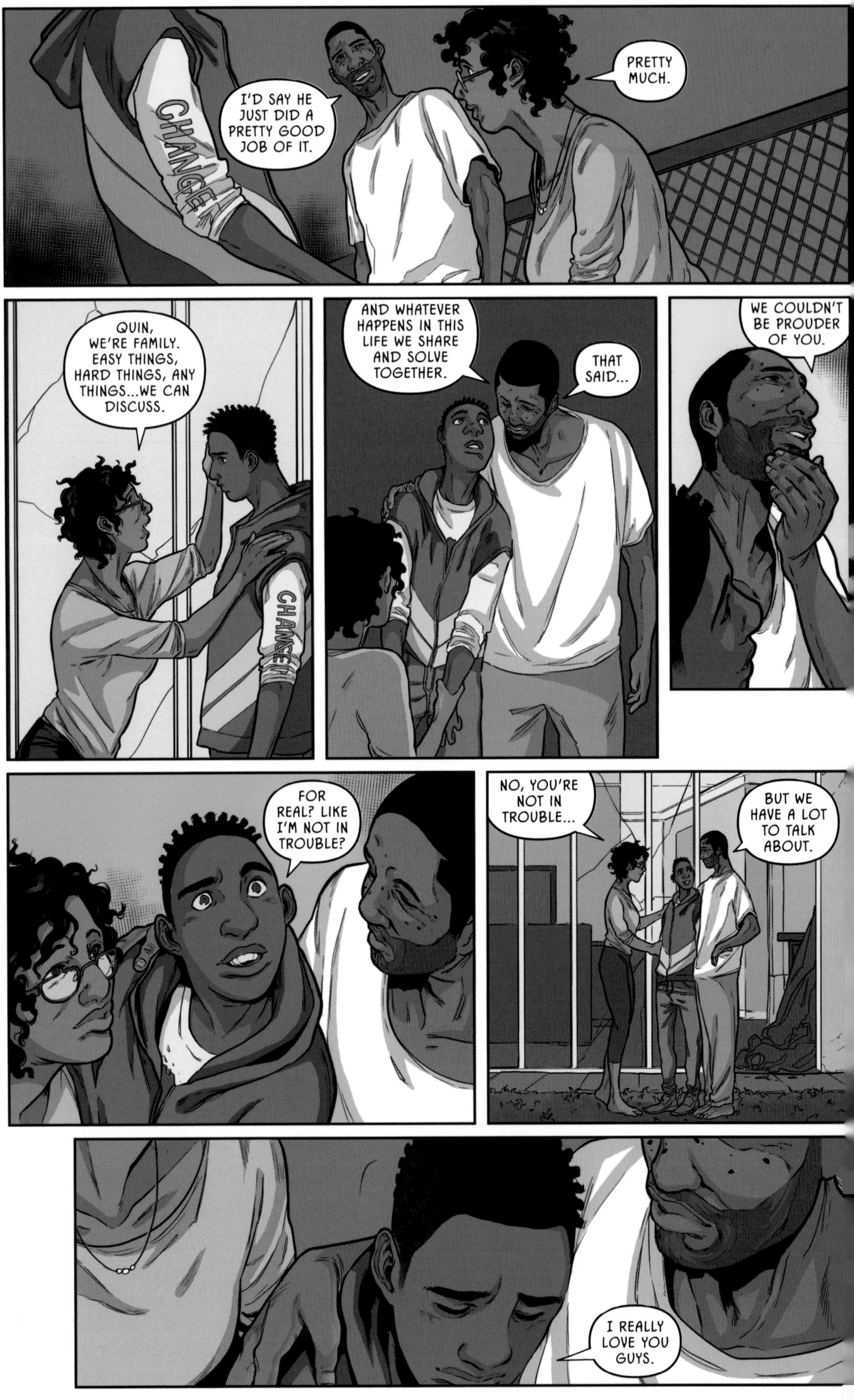
CHANGE
I'D SAY HE JUST DID A PRETTY GOOD JOB OF IT.
PRETTY MUCH.
QUIN, WE'RE FAMILY. EASY THINGS, HARD THINGS, ANY THINGS...WE CAN DISCUSS.
CHANGE
AND WHATEVER HAPPENS IN THIS LIFE WE SHARE AND SOLVE TOGETHER.
THAT SAID...
WE COULDN'T BE PROUDER OF YOU.
FOR REAL? LIKE I'M NOT IN TROUBLE?
NO, YOU'RE NOT IN TROUBLE...
BUT WE HAVE A LOT TO TALK ABOUT.
I REALLY LOVE YOU GUYS.

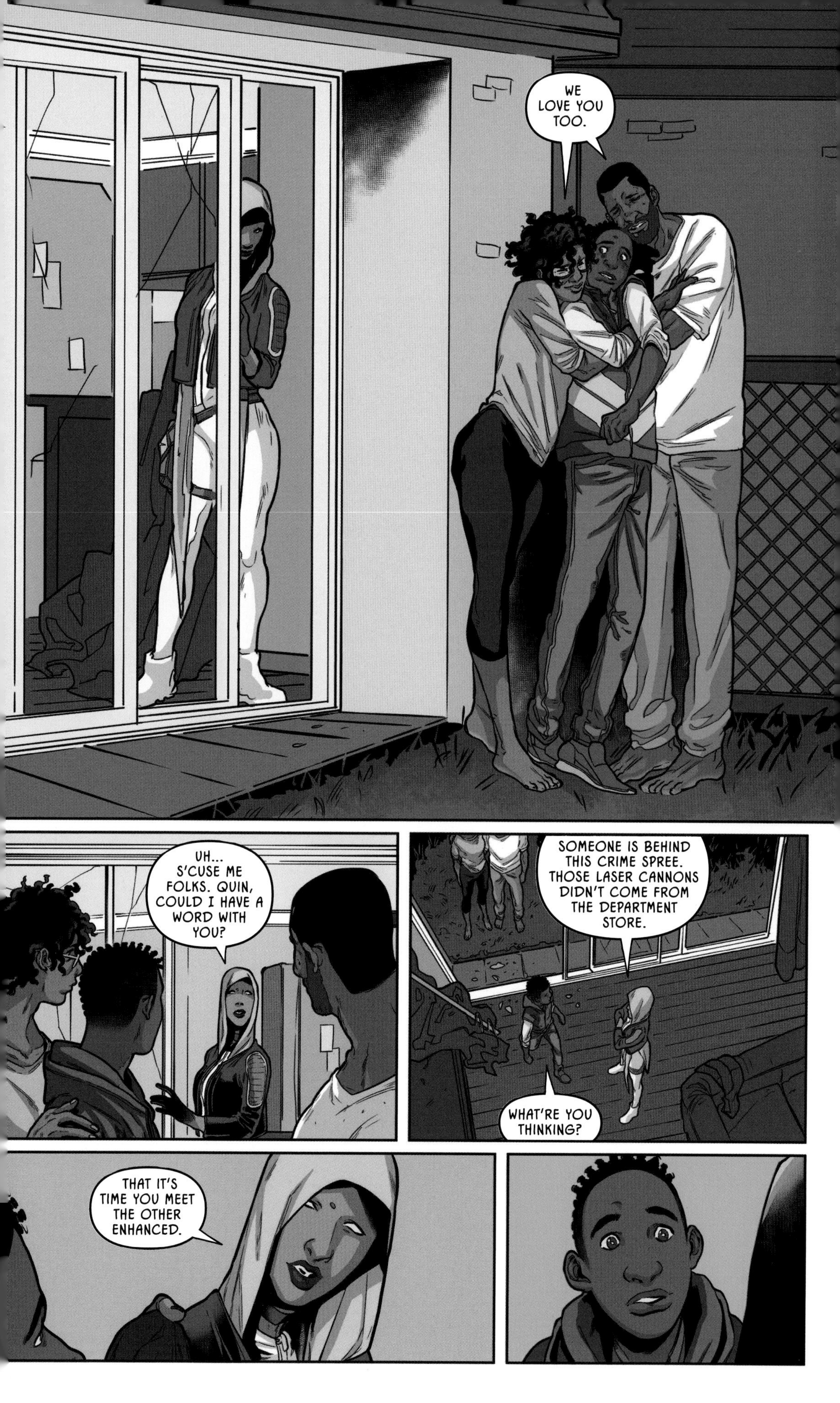
WE LOVE YOU TOO.
UH... S'CUSE ME FOLKS. QUIN, COULD I HAVE A WORD WITH YOU?
SOMEONE IS BEHIND THIS CRIME SPREE. THOSE LASER CANNONS DIDN'T COME FROM THE DEPARTMENT STORE.
WHAT'RE YOU THINKING?
THAT IT'S TIME YOU MEET THE OTHER ENHANCED.

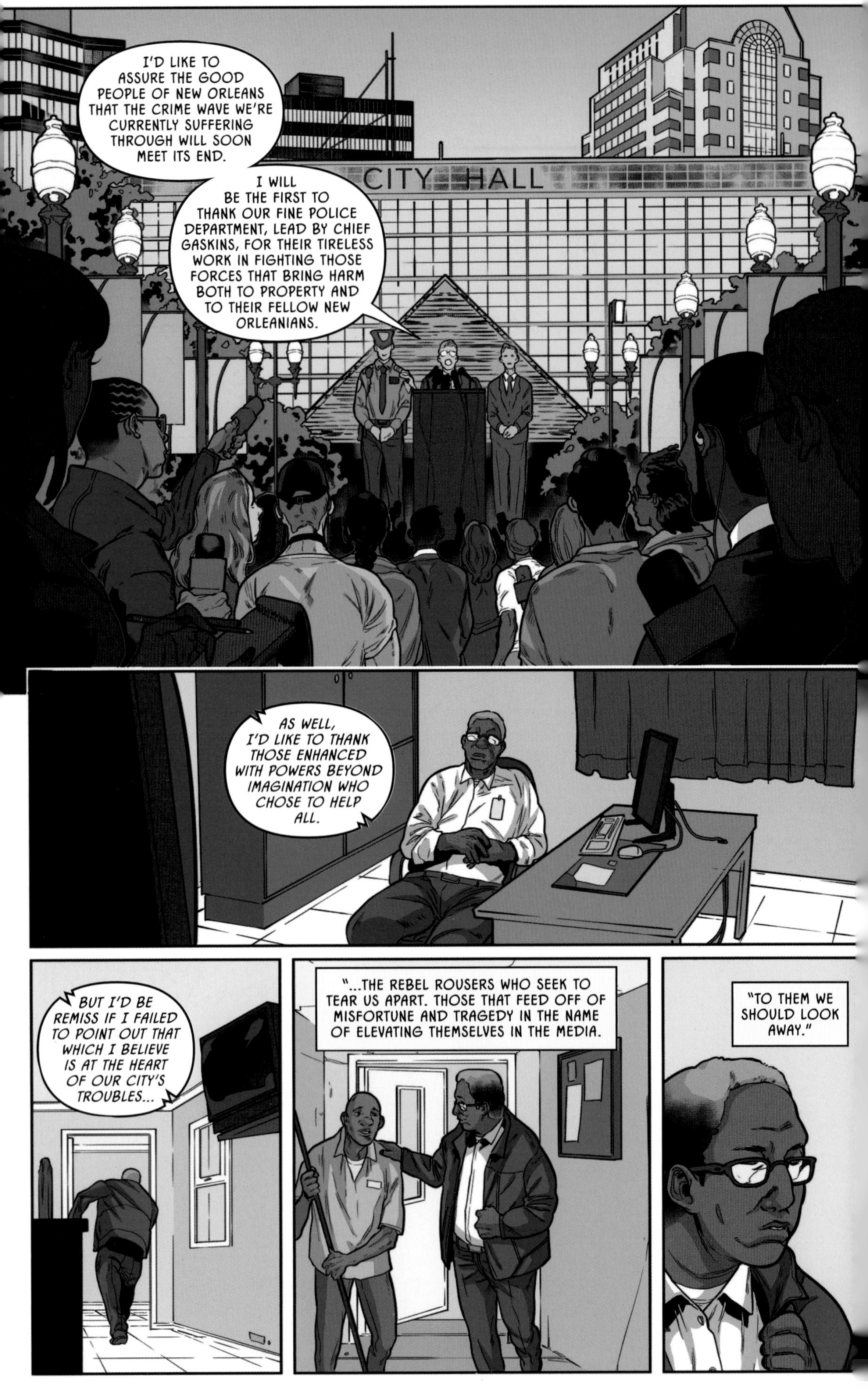
I'D LIKE TO ASSURE THE GOOD PEOPLE OF NEW ORLEANS THAT THE CRIME WAVE WE'RE CURRENTLY SUFFERING THROUGH WILL SOON MEET ITS END.
I WILL BE THE FIRST TO THANK OUR FINE POLICE DEPARTMENT, LEAD BY CHIEF GASKINS, FOR THEIR TIRELESS WORK IN FIGHTING THOSE FORCES THAT BRING HARM BOTH TO PROPERTY AND TO THEIR FELLOW NEW ORLEANIANS.
CITY HALL
AS WELL, I'D LIKE TO THANK THOSE ENHANCED WITH POWERS BEYOND IMAGINATION WHO CHOSE TO HELP ALL.
BUT I'D BE REMISS IF I FAILED TO POINT OUT THAT WHICH I BELIEVE IS AT THE HEART OF OUR CITY'S TROUBLES...
"...THE REBEL ROUSERS WHO SEEK TO TEAR US APART. THOSE THAT FEED OFF OF MISFORTUNE AND TRAGEDY IN THE NAME OF ELEVATING THEMSELVES IN THE MEDIA.
"TO THEM WE SHOULD LOOK AWAY."

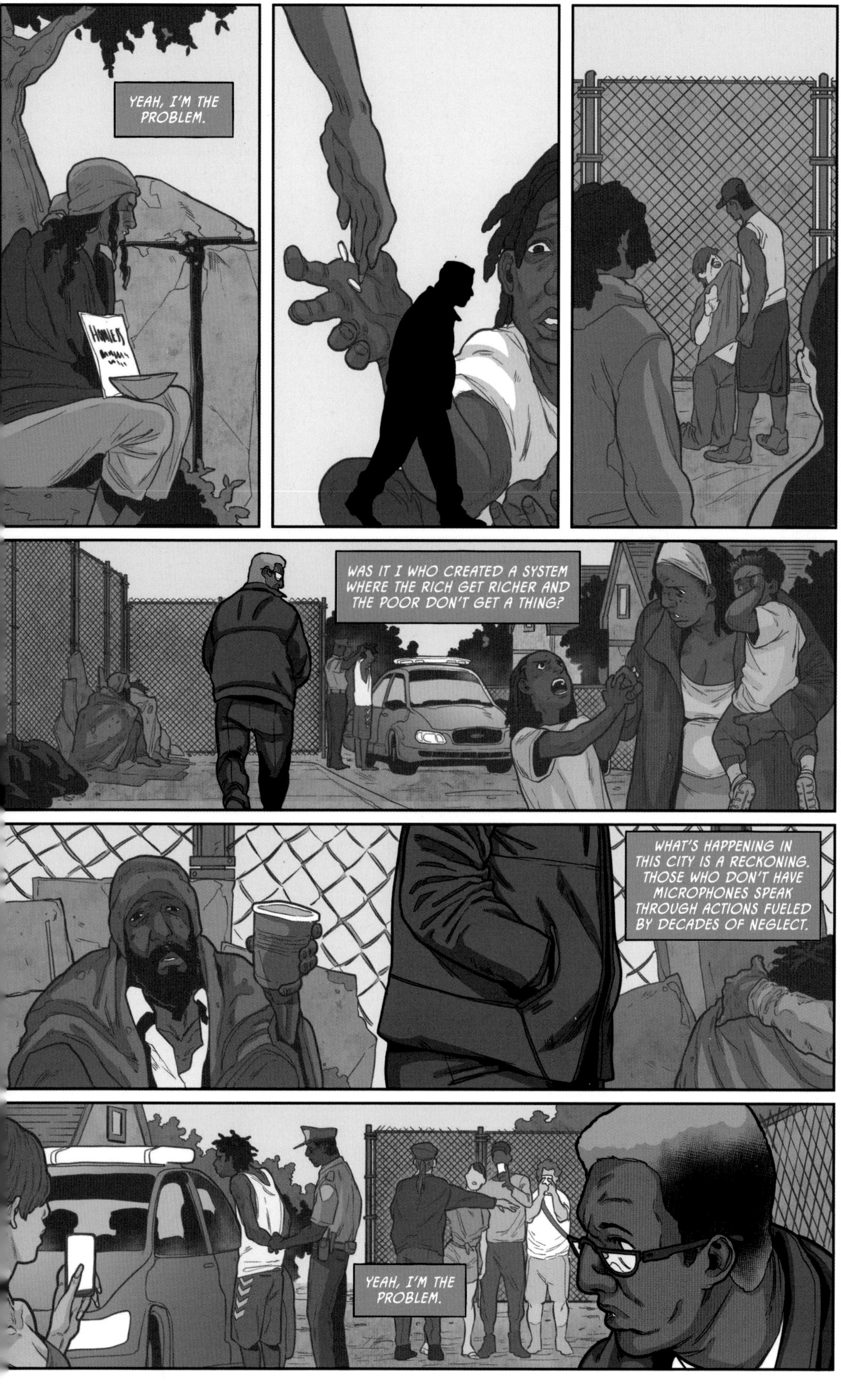

YEAH, I'M THE PROBLEM.
WAS IT I WHO CREATED A SYSTEM WHERE THE RICH GET RICHER AND THE POOR DON'T GET A THING?
WHAT'S HAPPENING IN THIS CITY IS A RECKONING. THOSE WHO DON'T HAVE MICROPHONES SPEAK THROUGH ACTIONS FUELED BY DECADES OF NEGLECT.
YEAH, I'M THE PROBLEM.

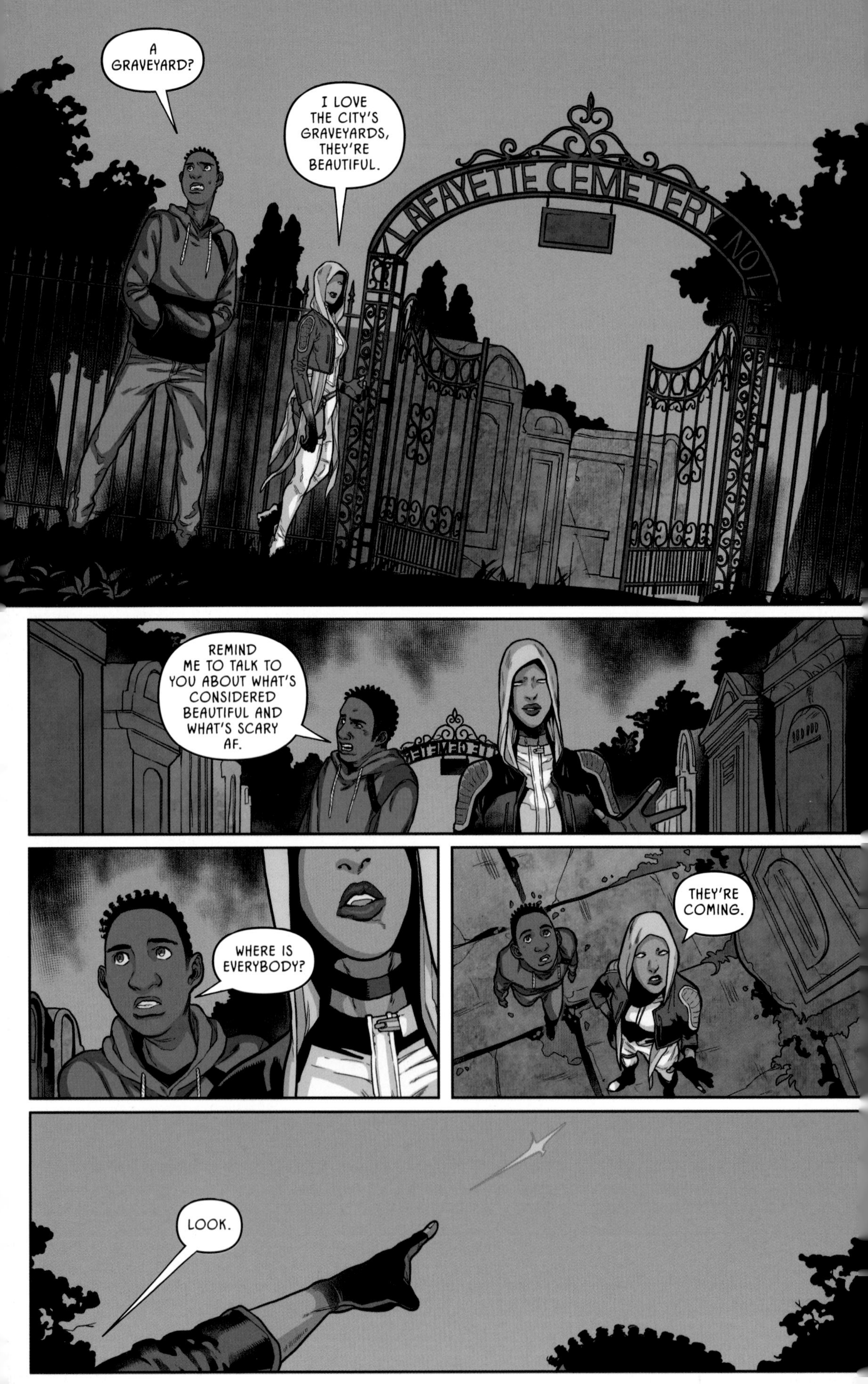
A GRAVEYARD?
I LOVE THE CITY'S GRAVEYARDS, THEY'RE BEAUTIFUL.
LAFAYETTE CEMETERY NO. 1
REMIND ME TO TALK TO YOU ABOUT WHAT'S CONSIDERED BEAUTIFUL AND WHAT'S SCARY AF.
WHERE IS EVERYBODY?
THEY'RE COMING.
LOOK.

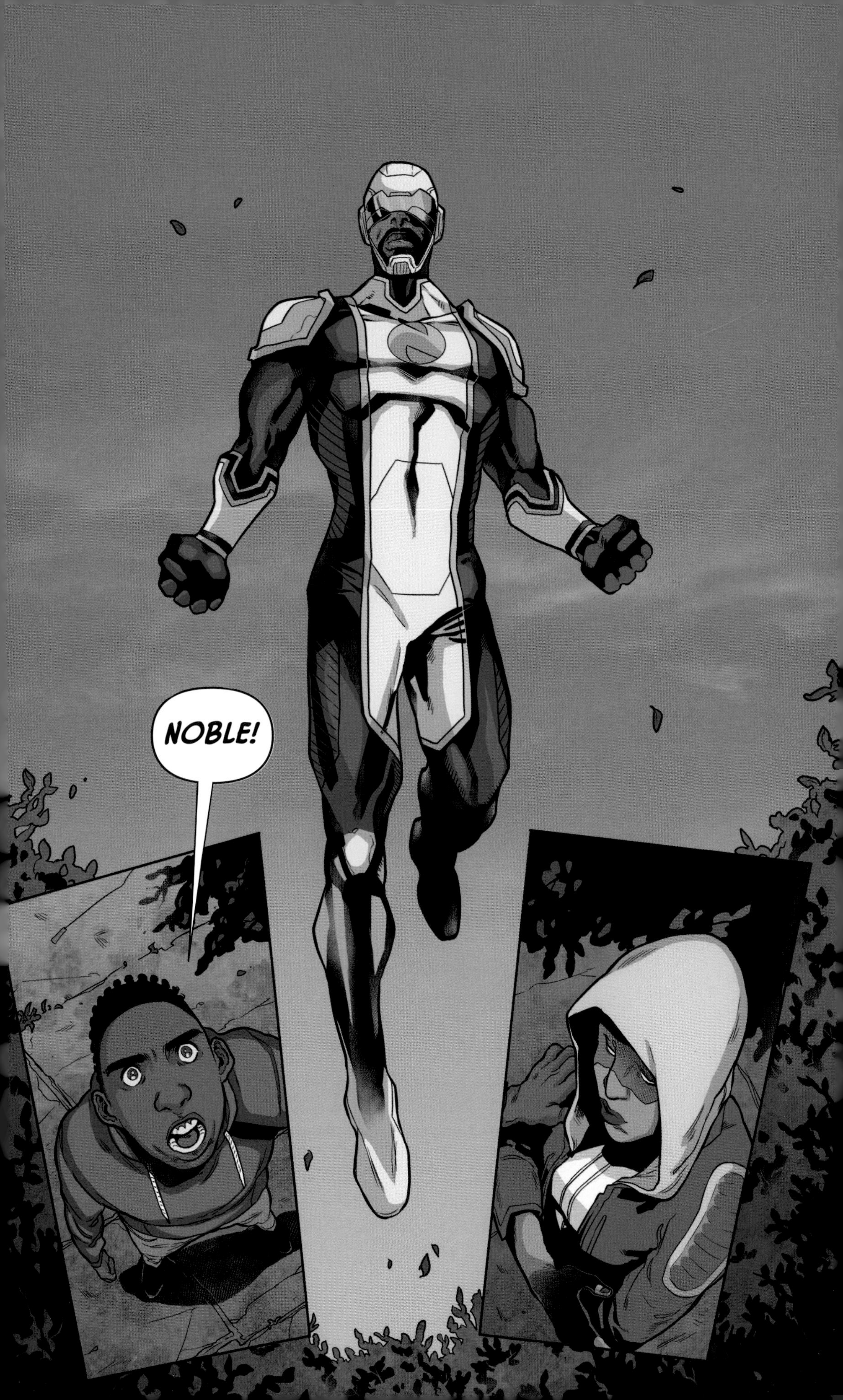
NOBLE!

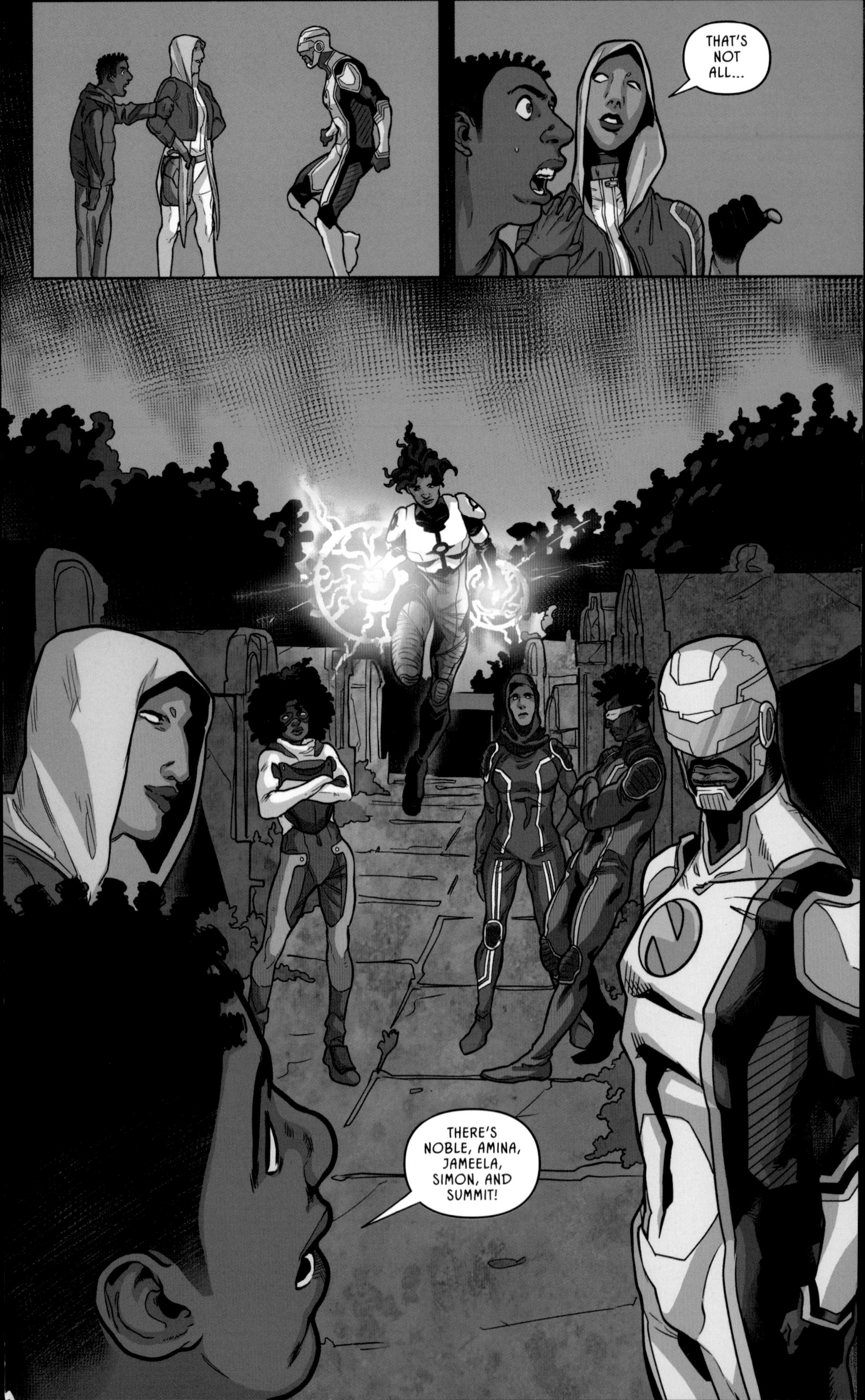
THAT'S NOT ALL...
THERE'S NOBLE, AMINA, JAMEELA, SIMON, AND SUMMIT!

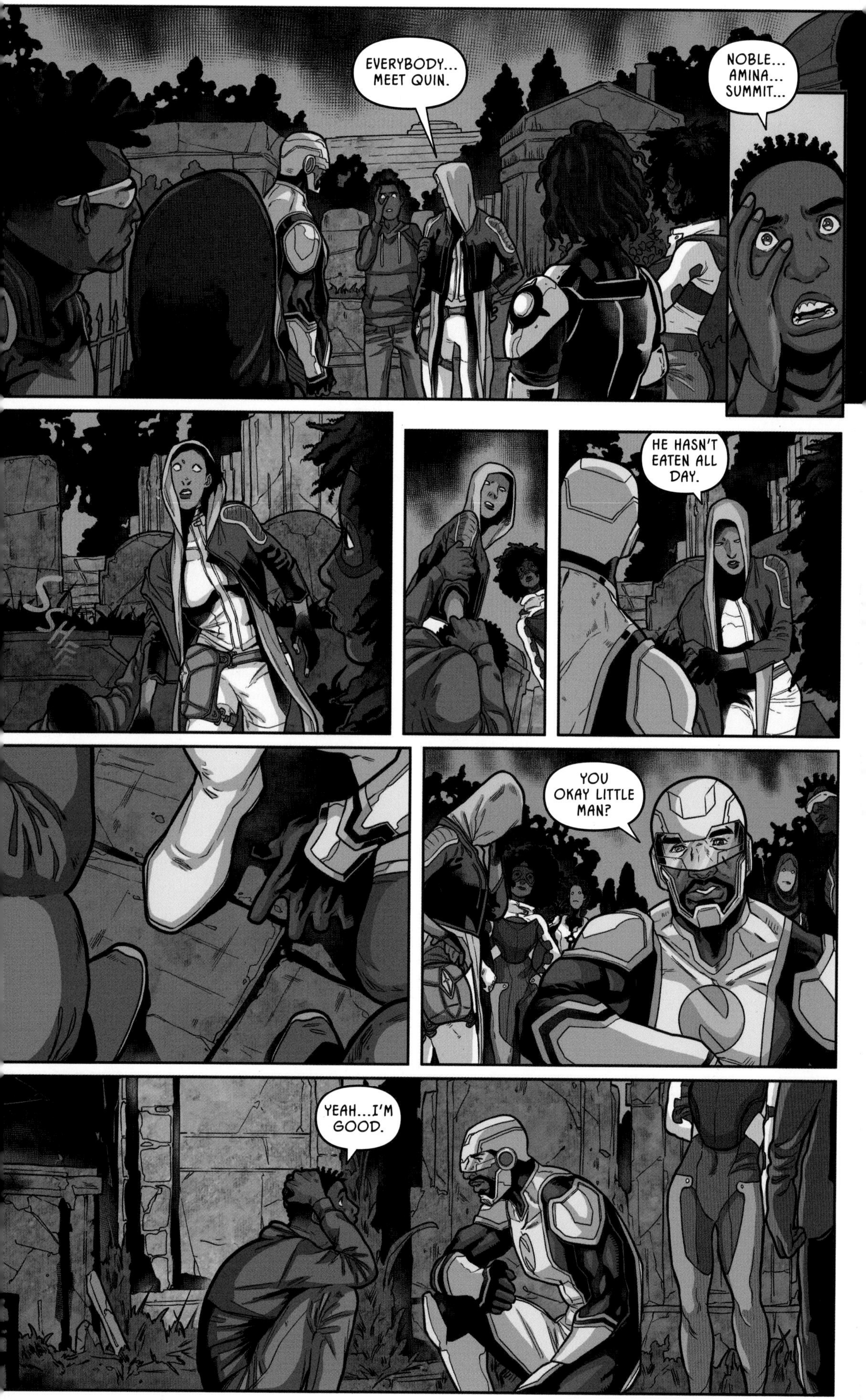
EVERYBODY... MEET QUIN.
NOBLE... AMINA... SUMMIT...
SSHHH
HE HASN'T EATEN ALL DAY.
YOU OKAY LITTLE MAN?
YEAH...I'M GOOD.

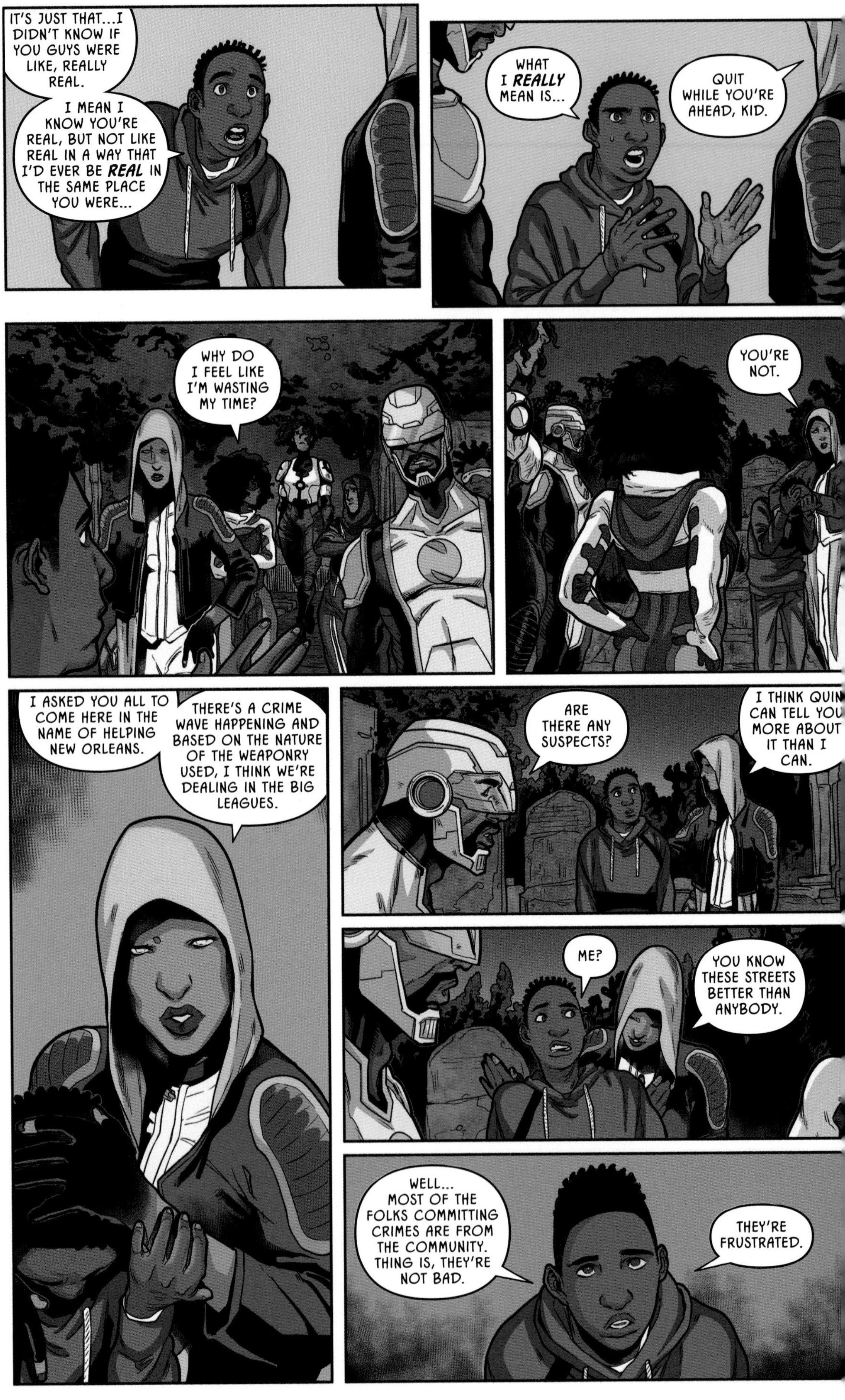
IT'S JUST THAT...I DIDN'T KNOW IF YOU GUYS WERE LIKE, REALLY REAL.
I MEAN I KNOW YOU'RE REAL, BUT NOT LIKE REAL IN A WAY THAT I'D EVER BE ***REAL*** IN THE SAME PLACE YOU WERE...
WHAT I ***REALLY*** MEAN IS...
QUIT WHILE YOU'RE AHEAD, KID.
WHY DO I FEEL LIKE I'M WASTING MY TIME?
YOU'RE NOT.
I ASKED YOU ALL TO COME HERE IN THE NAME OF HELPING NEW ORLEANS.
THERE'S A CRIME WAVE HAPPENING AND BASED ON THE NATURE OF THE WEAPONRY USED, I THINK WE'RE DEALING IN THE BIG LEAGUES.
ARE THERE ANY SUSPECTS?
I THINK QUIN CAN TELL YOU MORE ABOUT IT THAN I CAN.
ME?
YOU KNOW THESE STREETS BETTER THAN ANYBODY.
WELL... MOST OF THE FOLKS COMMITTING CRIMES ARE FROM THE COMMUNITY. THING IS, THEY'RE NOT BAD.
THEY'RE FRUSTRATED.

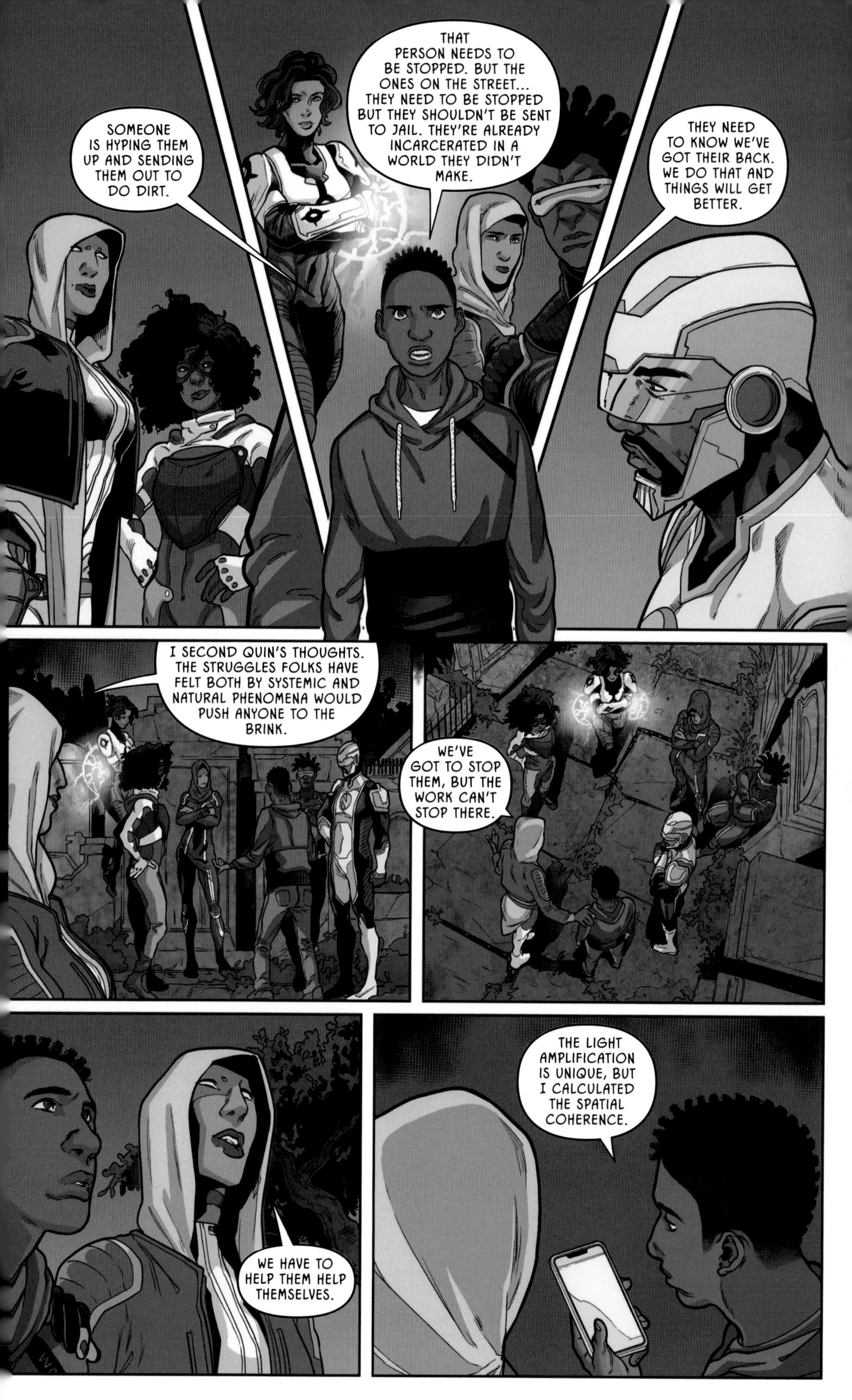
SOMEONE IS HYPING THEM UP AND SENDING THEM OUT TO DO DIRT.
THAT PERSON NEEDS TO BE STOPPED. BUT THE ONES ON THE STREET... THEY NEED TO BE STOPPED BUT THEY SHOULDN'T BE SENT TO JAIL. THEY'RE ALREADY INCARCERATED IN A WORLD THEY DIDN'T MAKE.
THEY NEED TO KNOW WE'VE GOT THEIR BACK. WE DO THAT AND THINGS WILL GET BETTER.
I SECOND QUIN'S THOUGHTS. THE STRUGGLES FOLKS HAVE FELT BOTH BY SYSTEMIC AND NATURAL PHENOMENA WOULD PUSH ANYONE TO THE BRINK.
WE'VE GOT TO STOP THEM, BUT THE WORK CAN'T STOP THERE.
WE HAVE TO HELP THEM HELP THEMSELVES.
THE LIGHT AMPLIFICATION IS UNIQUE, BUT I CALCULATED THE SPATIAL COHERENCE.

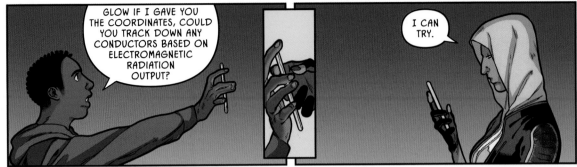

GLOW IF I GAVE YOU THE COORDINATES, COULD YOU TRACK DOWN ANY CONDUCTORS BASED ON ELECTROMAGNETIC RADIATION OUTPUT?

I CAN TRY.

IF YOU CAN CREATE A SIMILAR BEAM AND DISPERSE IT, IT MIGHT ACT AS A MAGNET TO A STRONGER BEAM SEEKING TO BOND WITH IT.

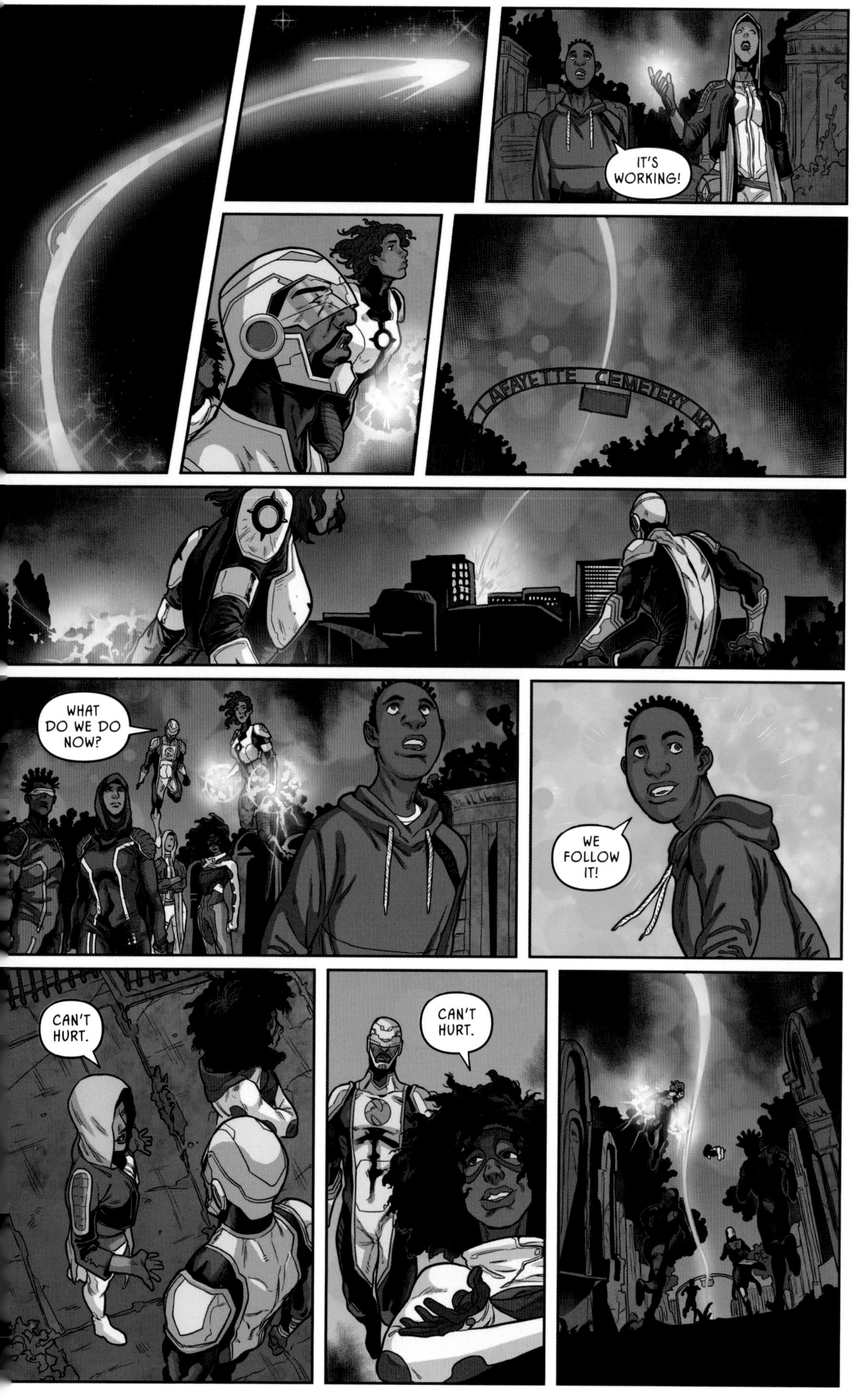
IT'S WORKING!
LAFAYETTE CEMETERY NO
WHAT DO WE DO NOW?
WE FOLLOW IT!
CAN'T HURT.
CAN'T HURT.

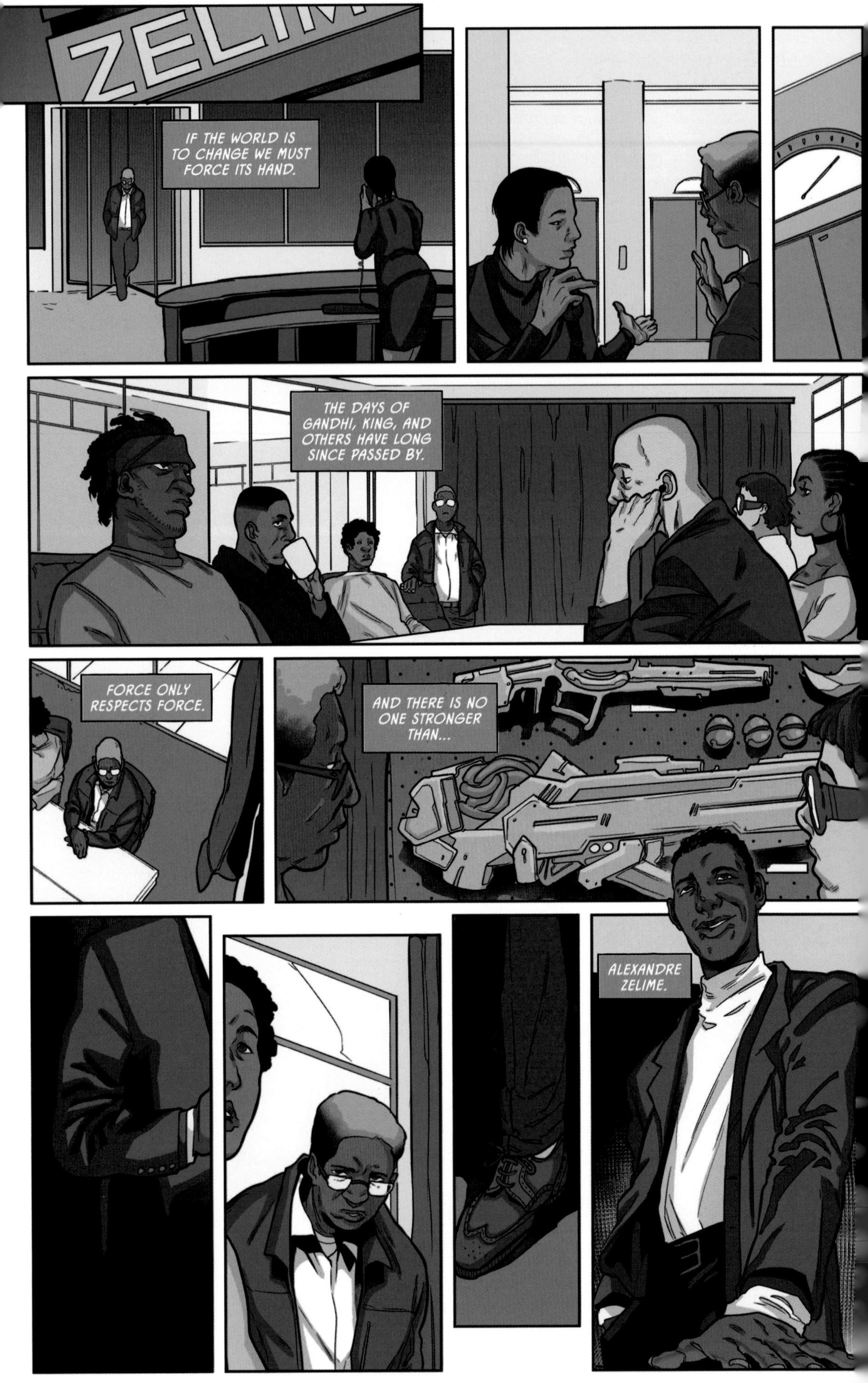

ZELIM
IF THE WORLD IS TO CHANGE WE MUST FORCE ITS HAND.
THE DAYS OF GANDHI, KING, AND OTHERS HAVE LONG SINCE PASSED BY.
FORCE ONLY RESPECTS FORCE.
AND THERE IS NO ONE STRONGER THAN...
ALEXANDRE ZELIME.

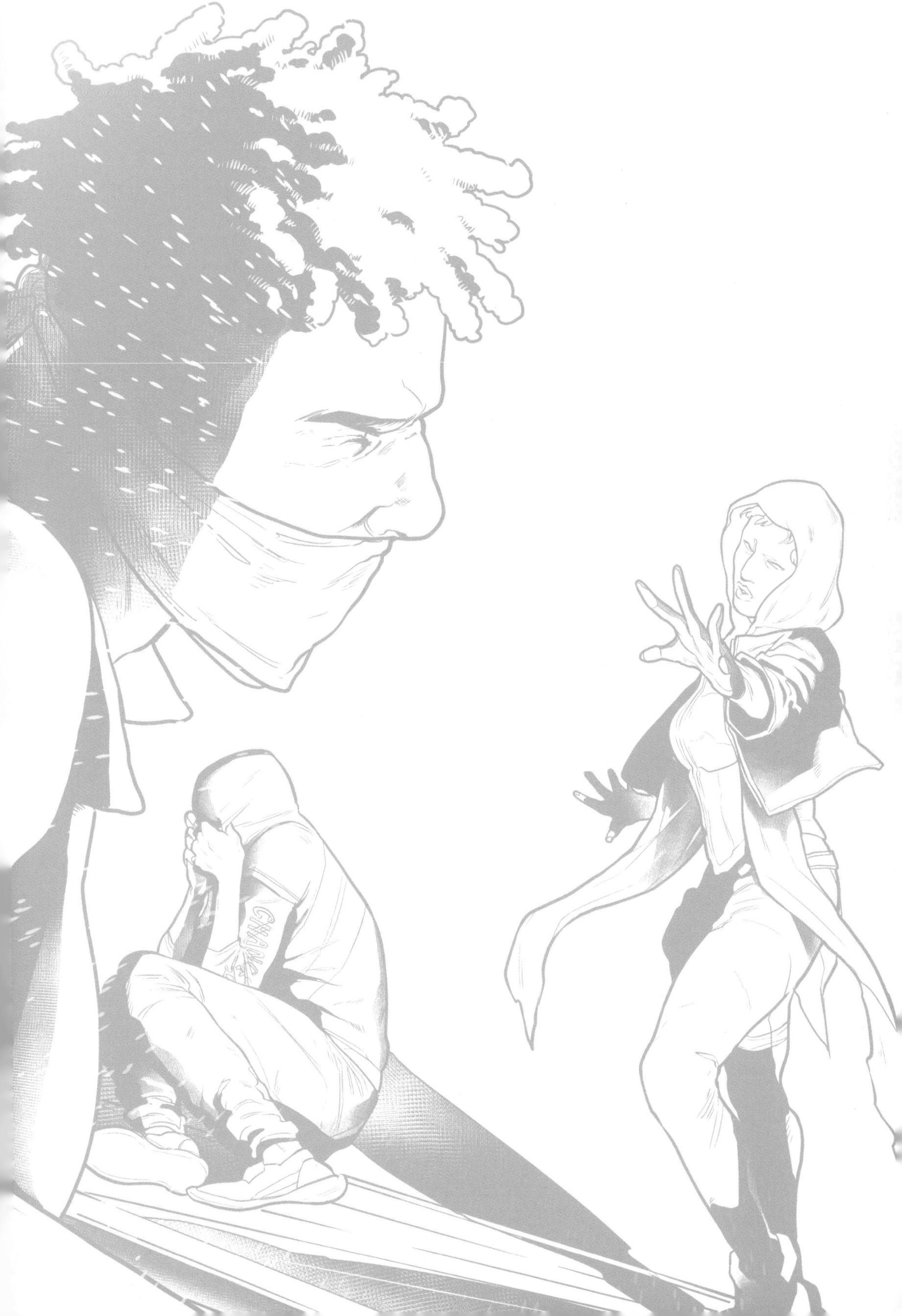

CHAPTER FIVE

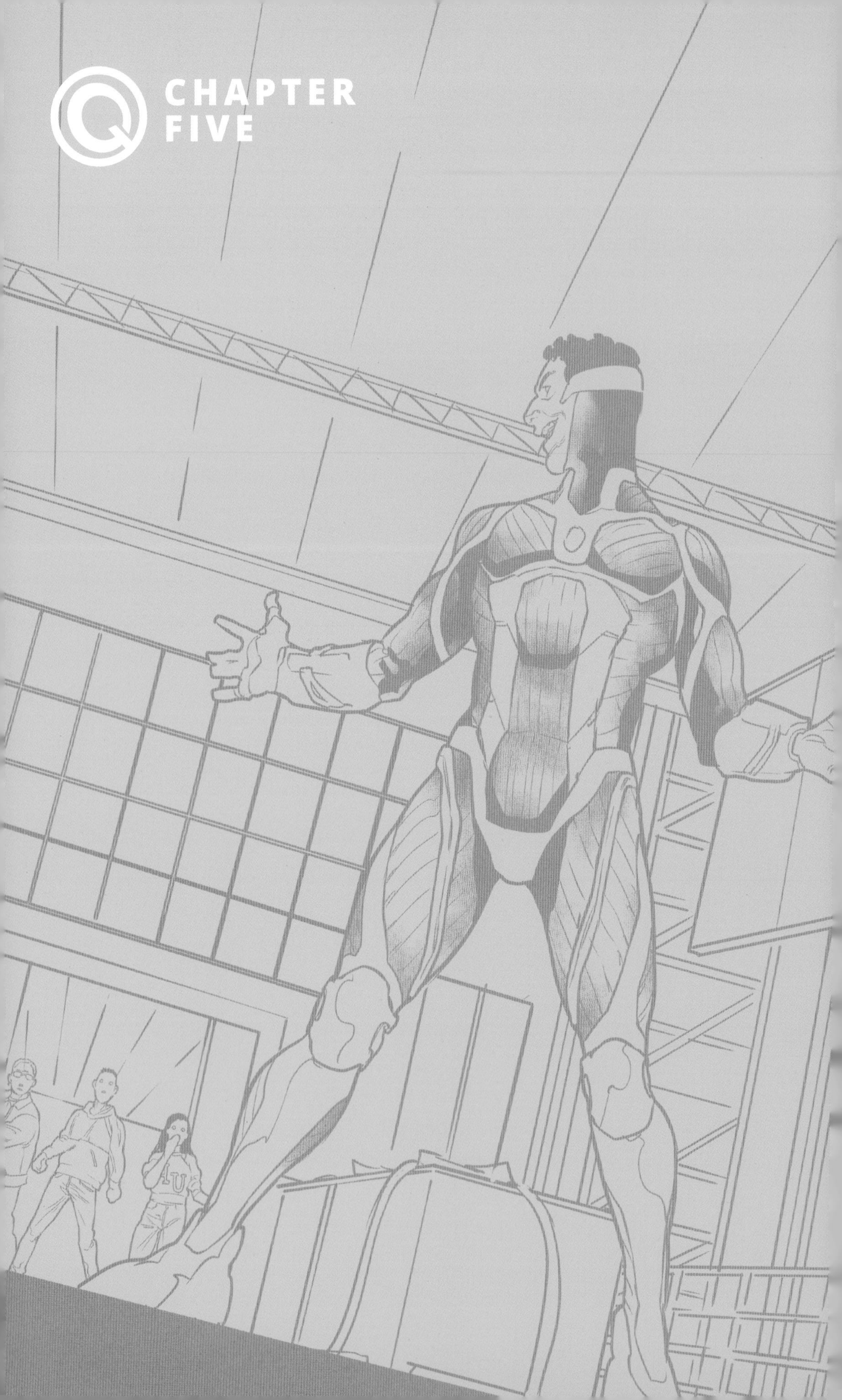

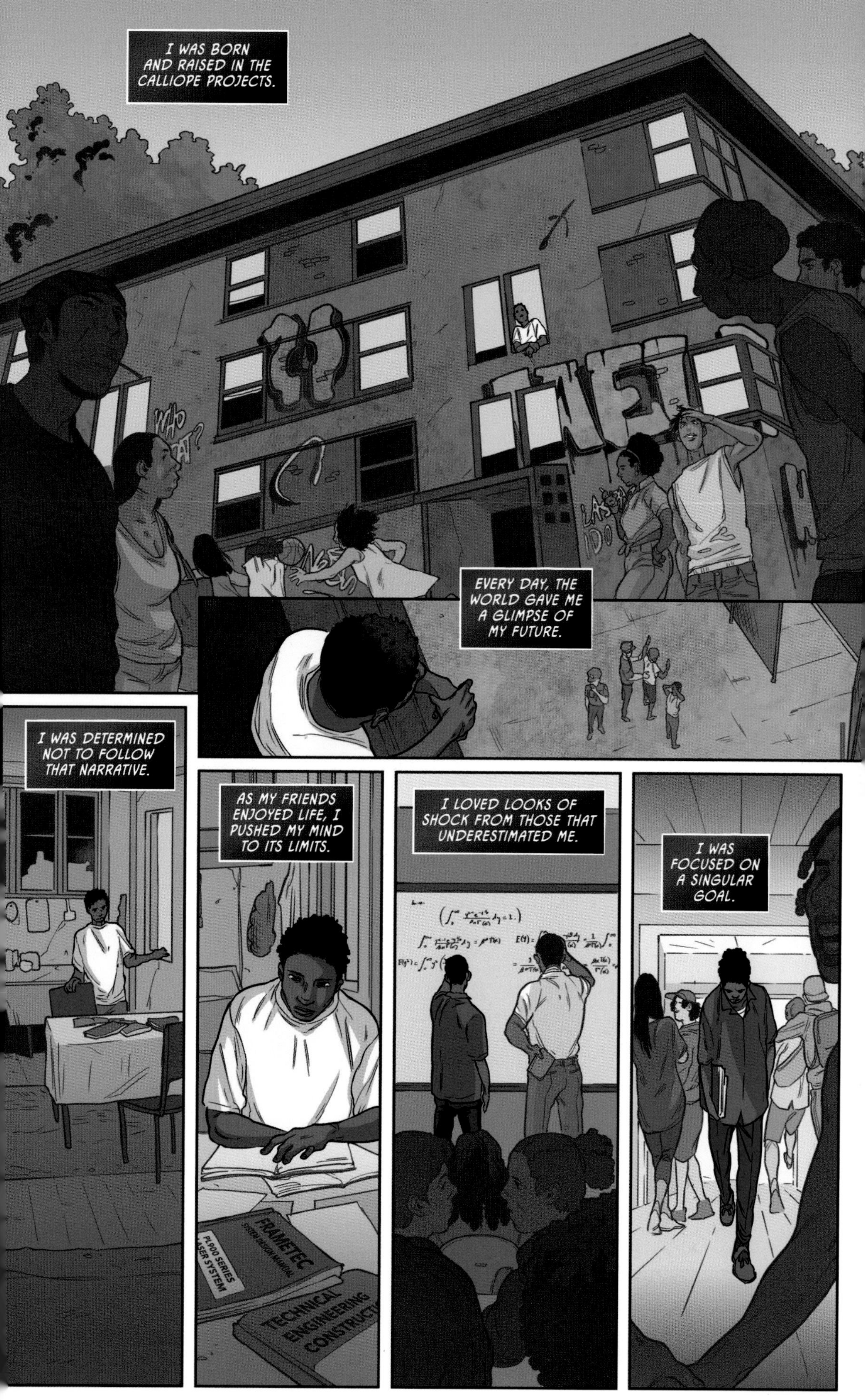
I WAS BORN AND RAISED IN THE CALLIOPE PROJECTS.
EVERY DAY, THE WORLD GAVE ME A GLIMPSE OF MY FUTURE.
I WAS DETERMINED NOT TO FOLLOW THAT NARRATIVE.
AS MY FRIENDS ENJOYED LIFE, I PUSHED MY MIND TO ITS LIMITS.
FRAMETEC
TECHNICAL ENGINEERING CONSTRUCT
I LOVED LOOKS OF SHOCK FROM THOSE THAT UNDERESTIMATED ME.
I WAS FOCUSED ON A SINGULAR GOAL.

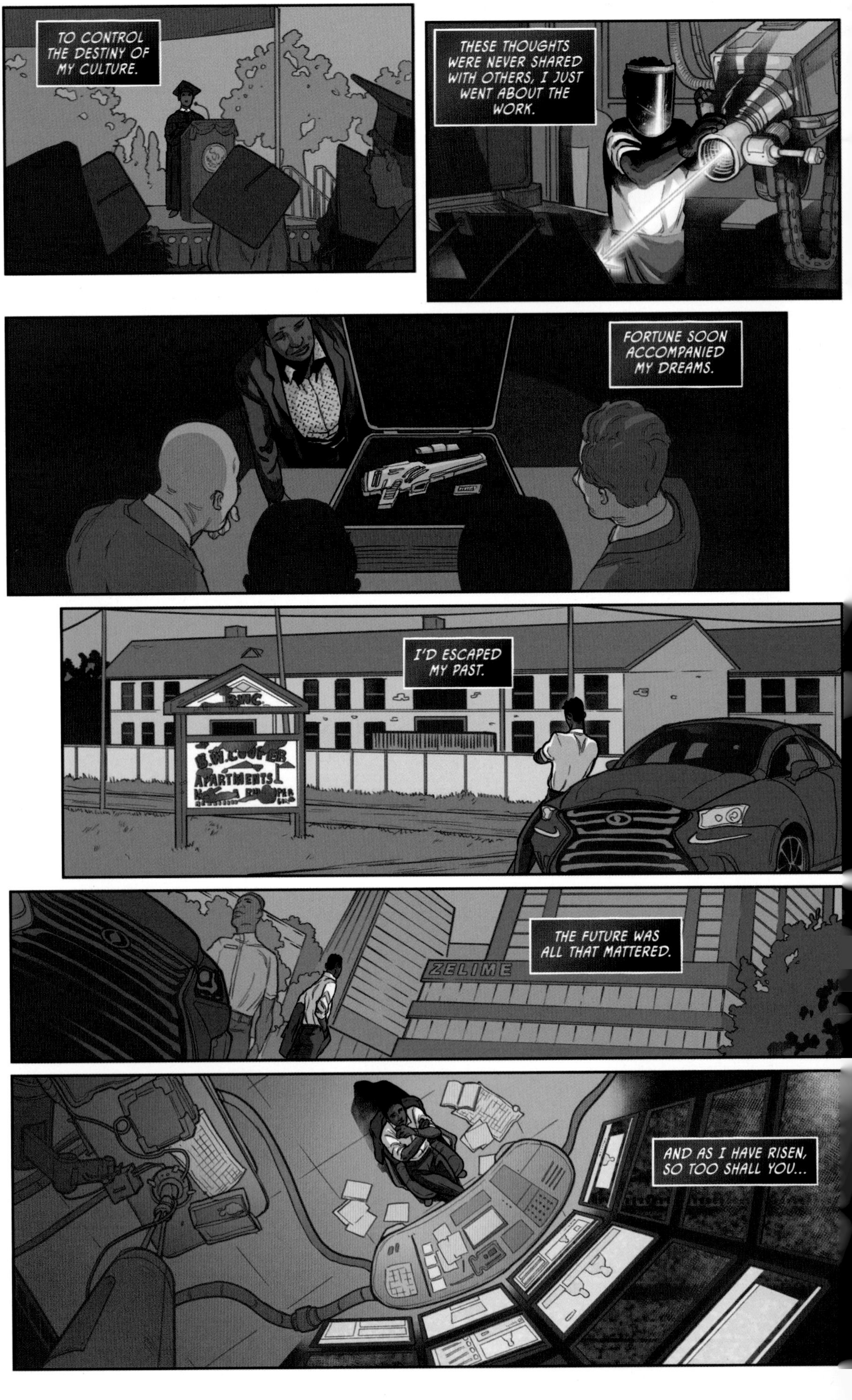
TO CONTROL THE DESTINY OF MY CULTURE.
THESE THOUGHTS WERE NEVER SHARED WITH OTHERS, I JUST WENT ABOUT THE WORK.
FORTUNE SOON ACCOMPANIED MY DREAMS.
I'D ESCAPED MY PAST.
B.W. COOPER
APARTMENTS
THE FUTURE WAS ALL THAT MATTERED.
ZELIME
AND AS I HAVE RISEN, SO TOO SHALL YOU...

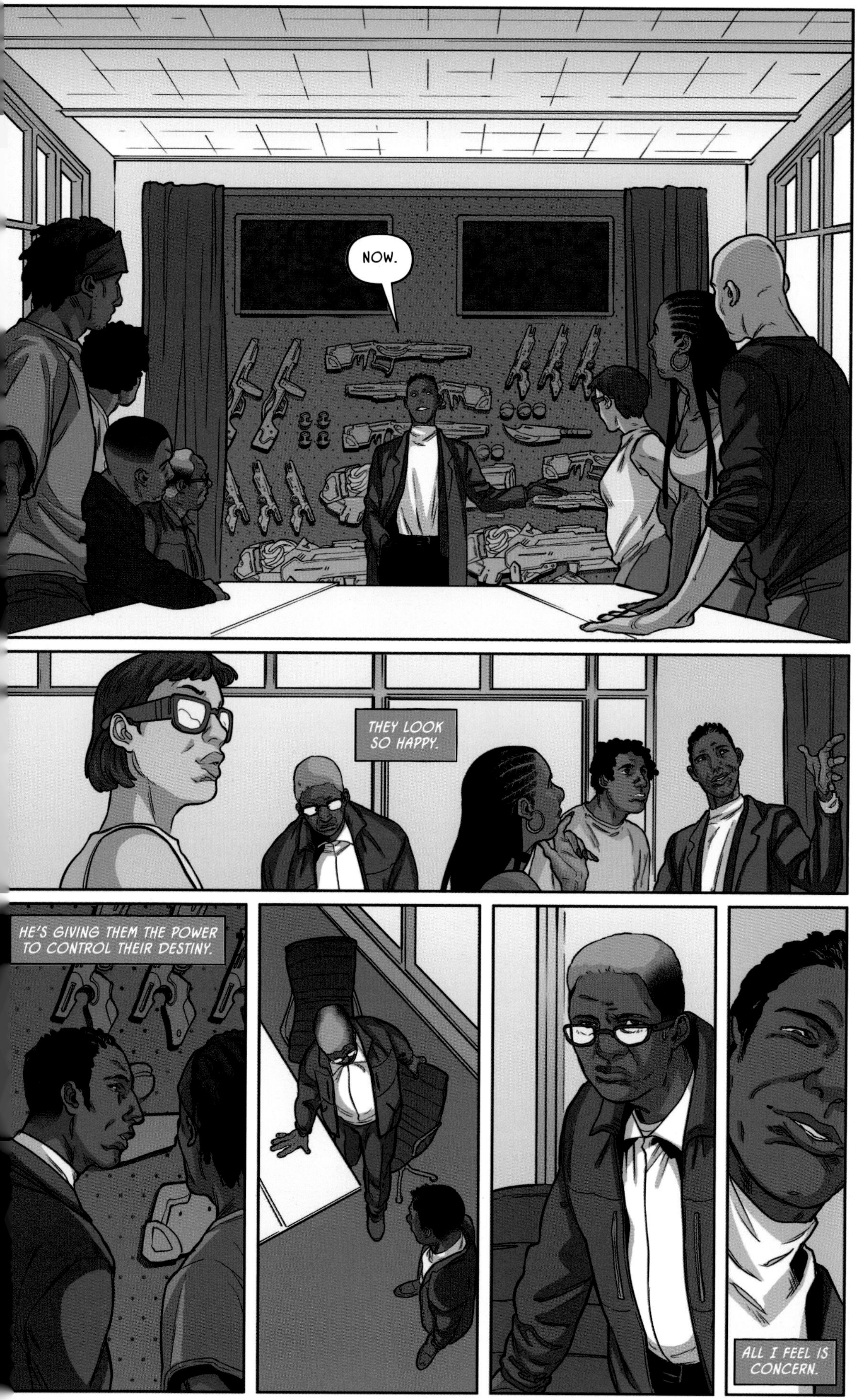
NOW.
THEY LOOK SO HAPPY.
HE'S GIVING THEM THE POWER TO CONTROL THEIR DESTINY.
ALL I FEEL IS CONCERN.

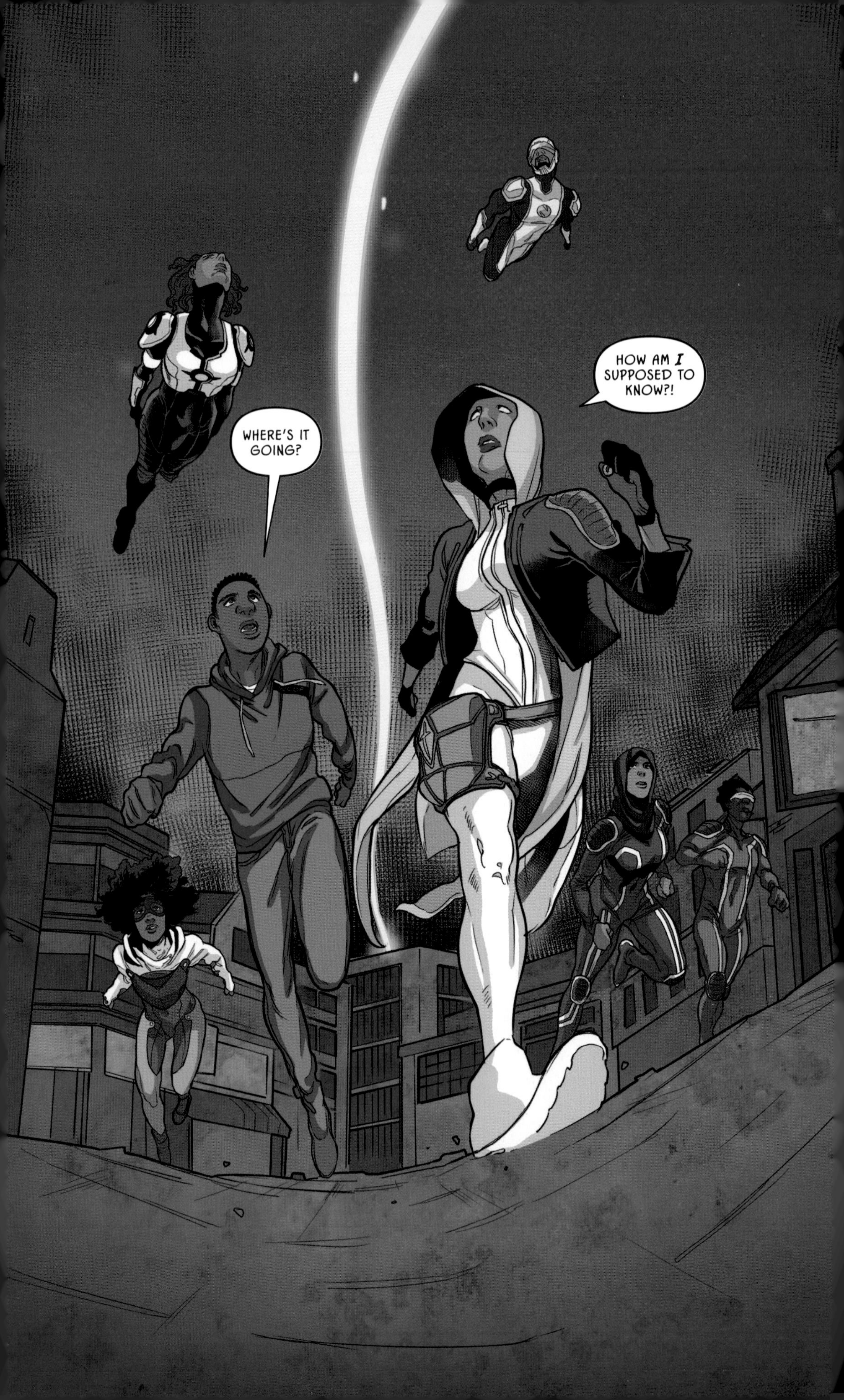
WHERE'S IT GOING?
HOW AM I SUPPOSED TO KNOW?!

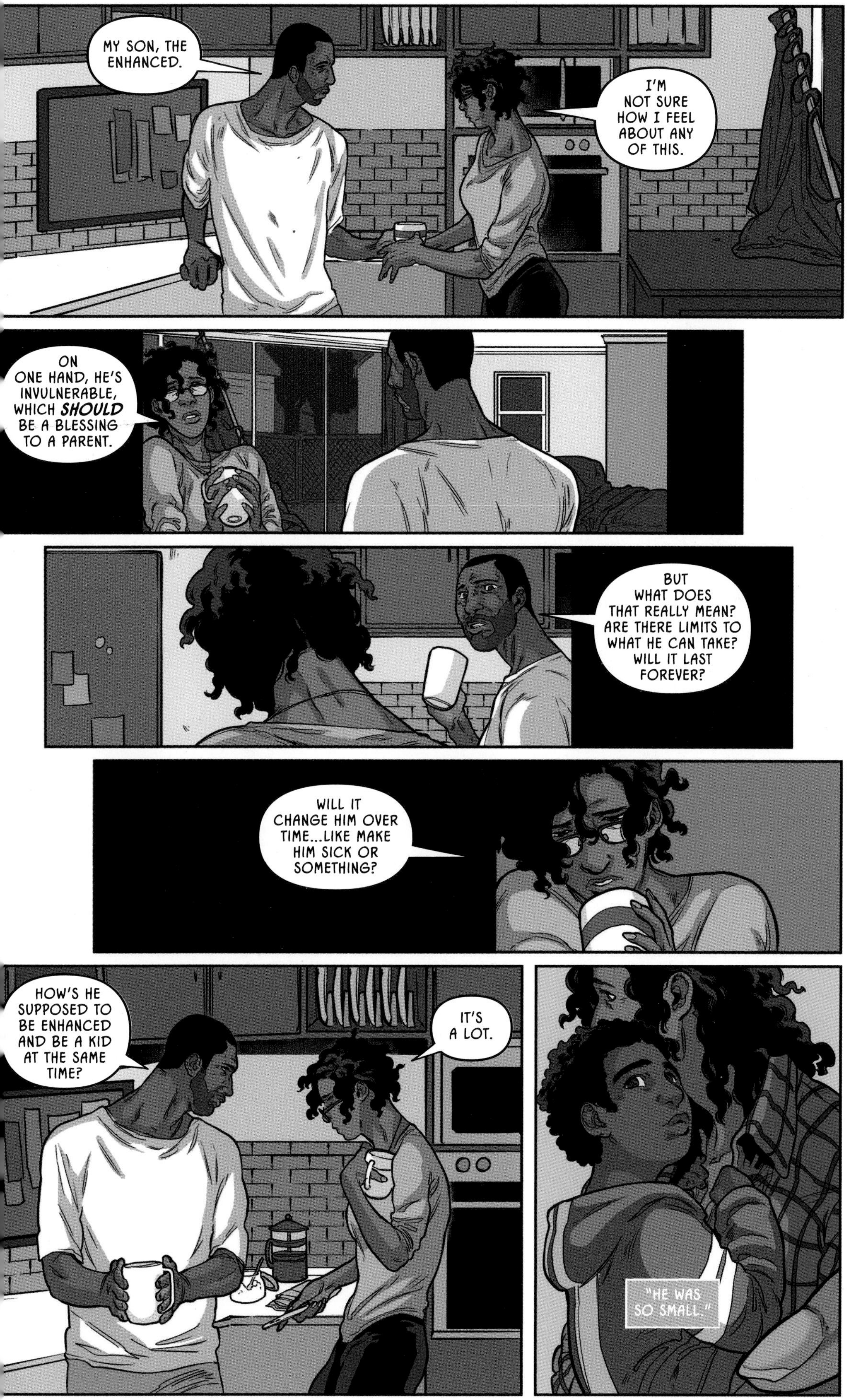
MY SON, THE ENHANCED.
I'M NOT SURE HOW I FEEL ABOUT ANY OF THIS.
ON ONE HAND, HE'S INVULNERABLE, WHICH **SHOULD** BE A BLESSING TO A PARENT.
BUT WHAT DOES THAT REALLY MEAN? ARE THERE LIMITS TO WHAT HE CAN TAKE? WILL IT LAST FOREVER?
WILL IT CHANGE HIM OVER TIME...LIKE MAKE HIM SICK OR SOMETHING?
HOW'S HE SUPPOSED TO BE ENHANCED AND BE A KID AT THE SAME TIME?
IT'S A LOT.
"HE WAS SO SMALL."

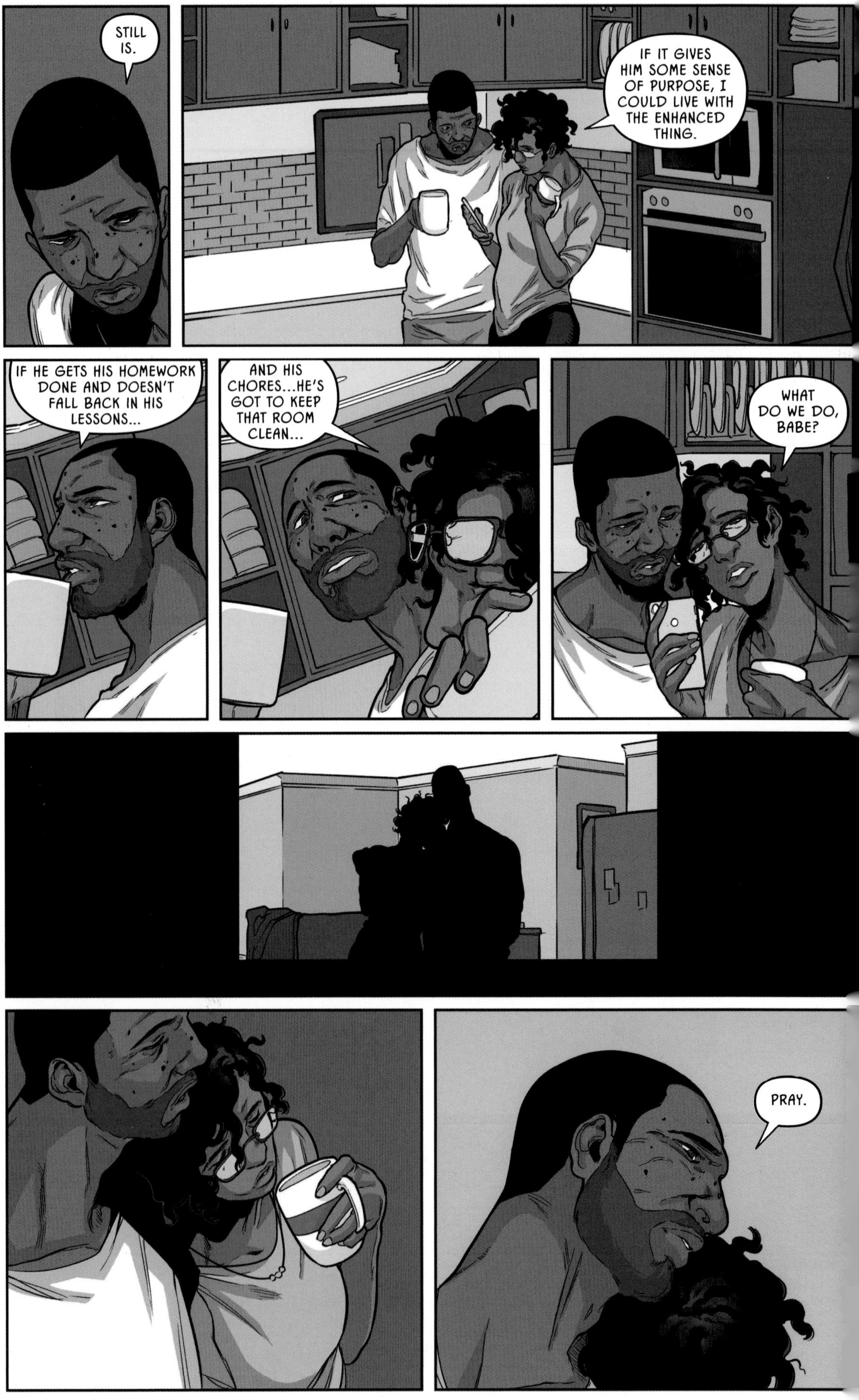
STILL IS.
IF IT GIVES HIM SOME SENSE OF PURPOSE, I COULD LIVE WITH THE ENHANCED THING.
IF HE GETS HIS HOMEWORK DONE AND DOESN'T FALL BACK IN HIS LESSONS...
AND HIS CHORES...HE'S GOT TO KEEP THAT ROOM CLEAN...
WHAT DO WE DO, BABE?
PRAY.

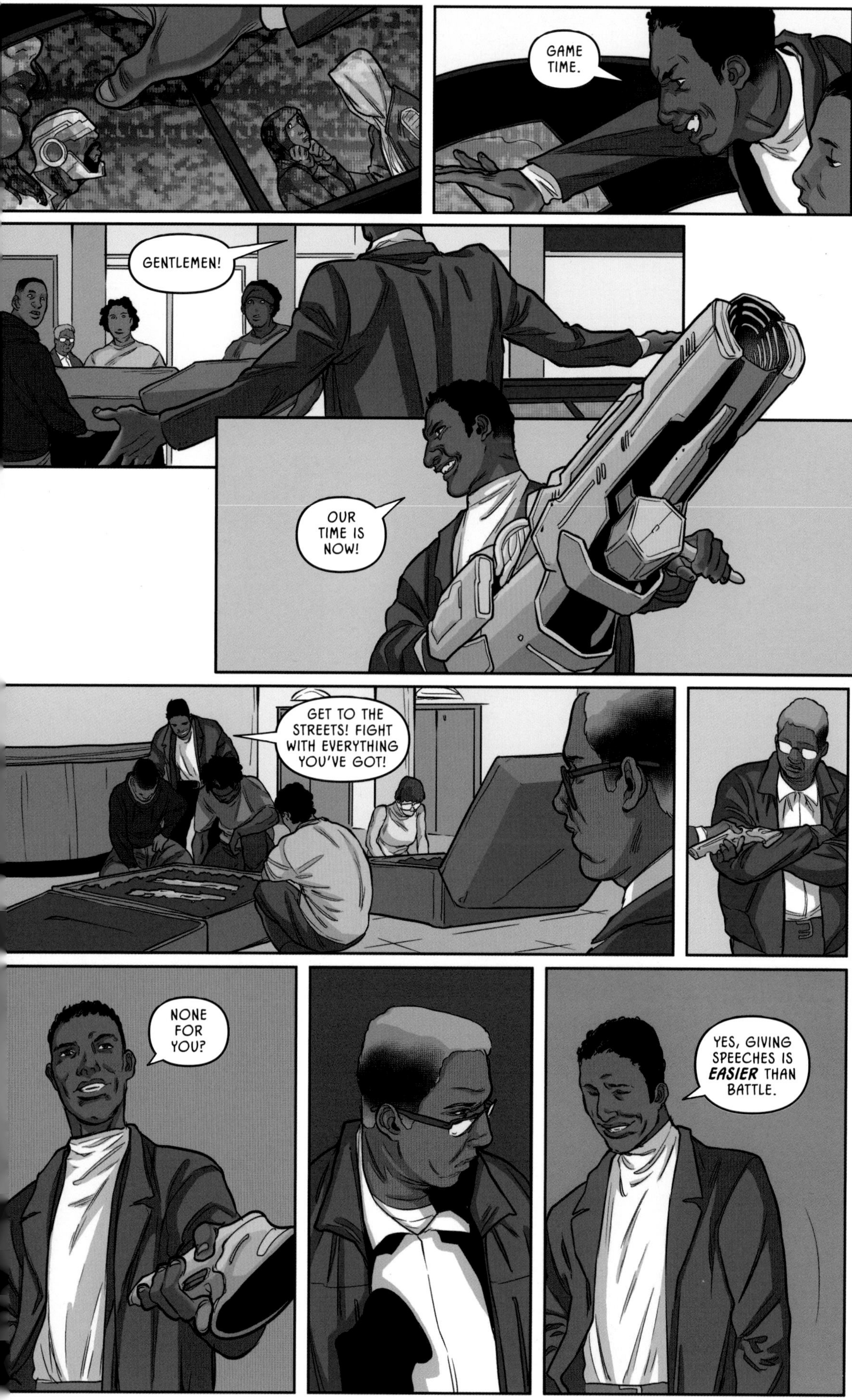
GAME TIME.
GENTLEMEN!
OUR TIME IS NOW!
GET TO THE STREETS! FIGHT WITH EVERYTHING YOU'VE GOT!
NONE FOR YOU?
YES, GIVING SPEECHES IS **EASIER** THAN BATTLE.

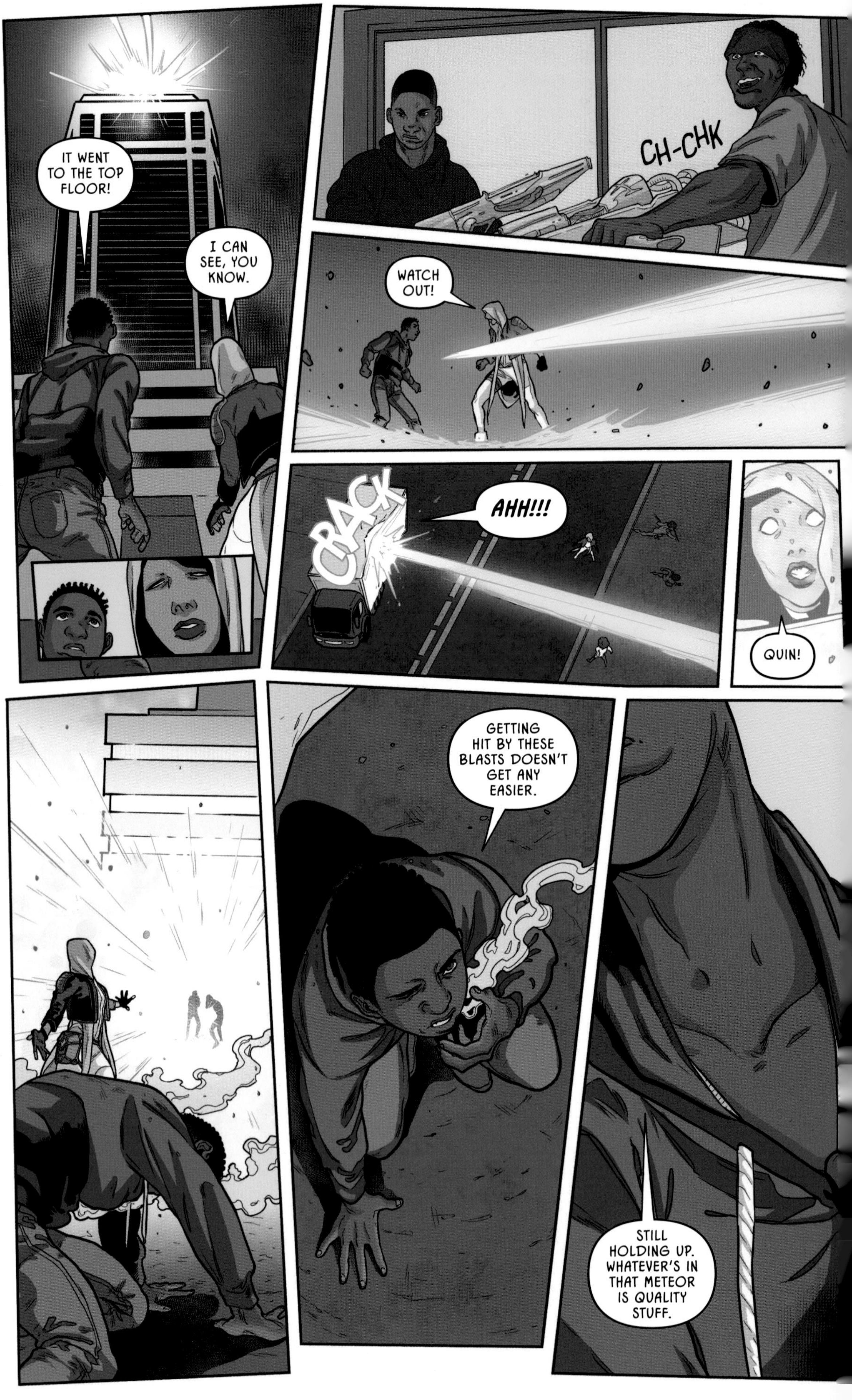
IT WENT TO THE TOP FLOOR!
I CAN SEE, YOU KNOW.
CH-CHK
WATCH OUT!
CRACK
AHH!!!
QUIN!
GETTING HIT BY THESE BLASTS DOESN'T GET ANY EASIER.
STILL HOLDING UP. WHATEVER'S IN THAT METEOR IS QUALITY STUFF.

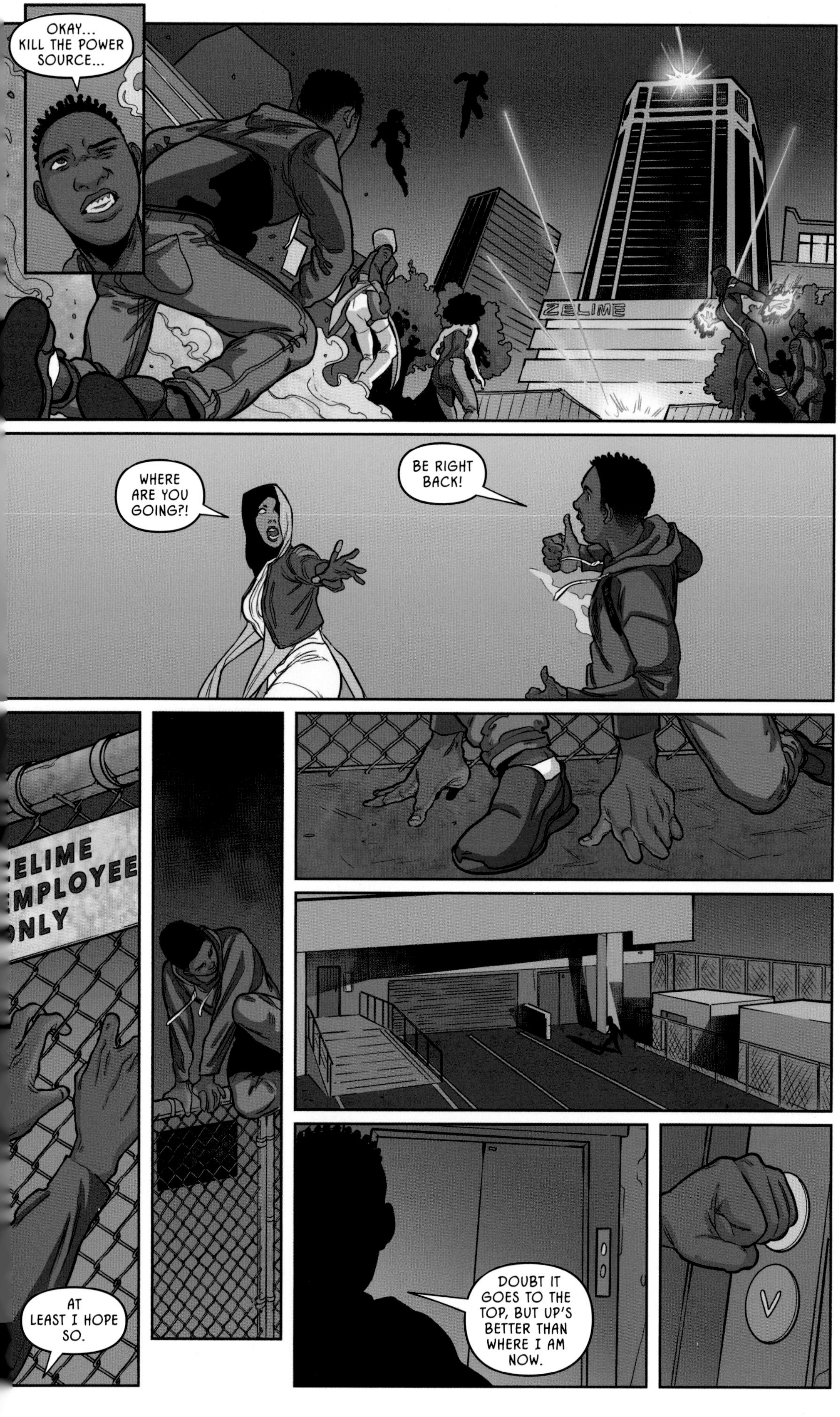

OKAY... KILL THE POWER SOURCE...
ZELIME
WHERE ARE YOU GOING?!
BE RIGHT BACK!
ZELIME EMPLOYEE ONLY
AT LEAST I HOPE SO.
DOUBT IT GOES TO THE TOP, BUT UP'S BETTER THAN WHERE I AM NOW.

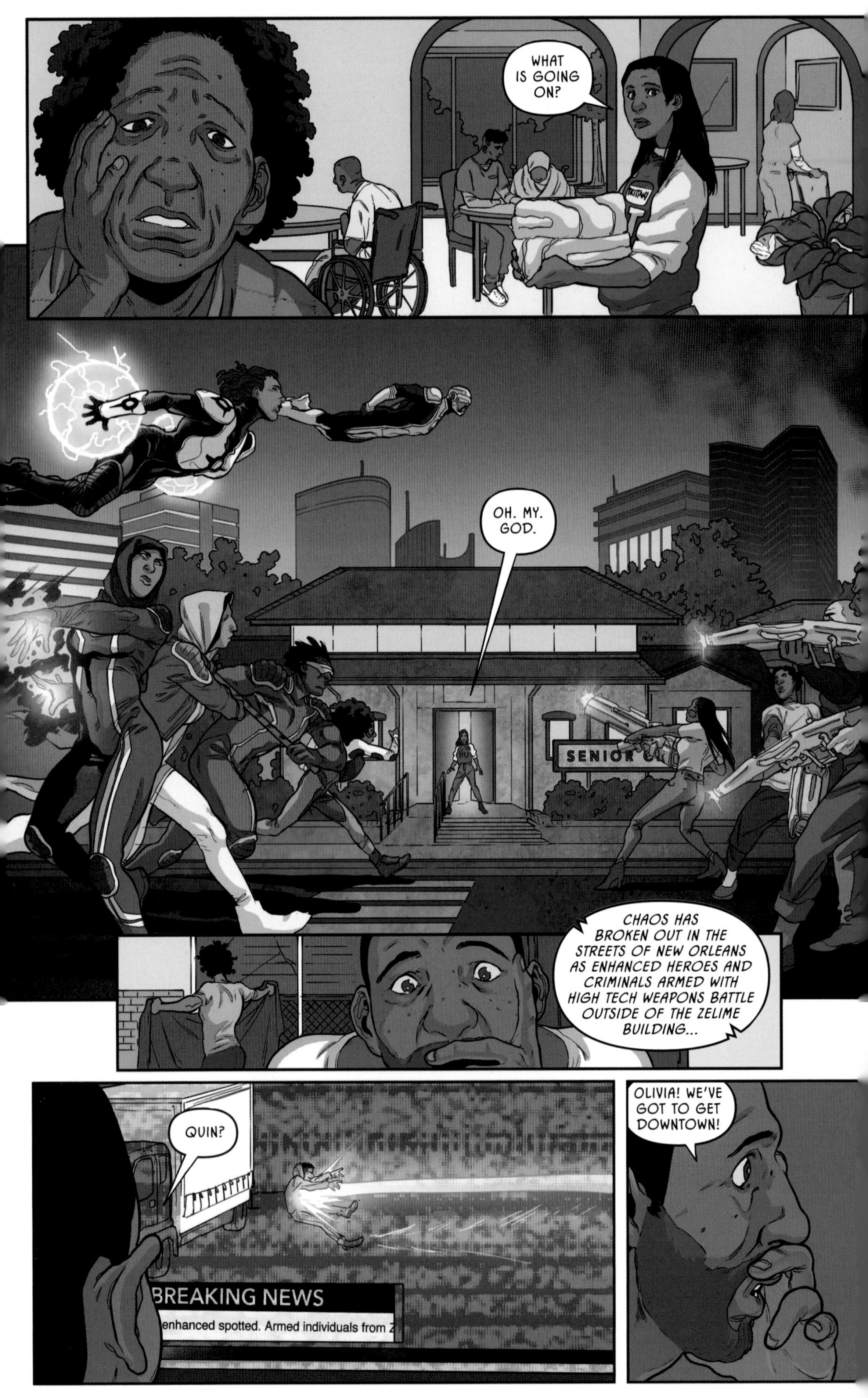

WHAT IS GOING ON?
OH. MY. GOD.
SENIOR C
CHAOS HAS BROKEN OUT IN THE STREETS OF NEW ORLEANS AS ENHANCED HEROES AND CRIMINALS ARMED WITH HIGH TECH WEAPONS BATTLE OUTSIDE OF THE ZELIME BUILDING...
QUIN?
BREAKING NEWS
enhanced spotted. Armed individuals from Z
OLIVIA! WE'VE GOT TO GET DOWNTOWN!

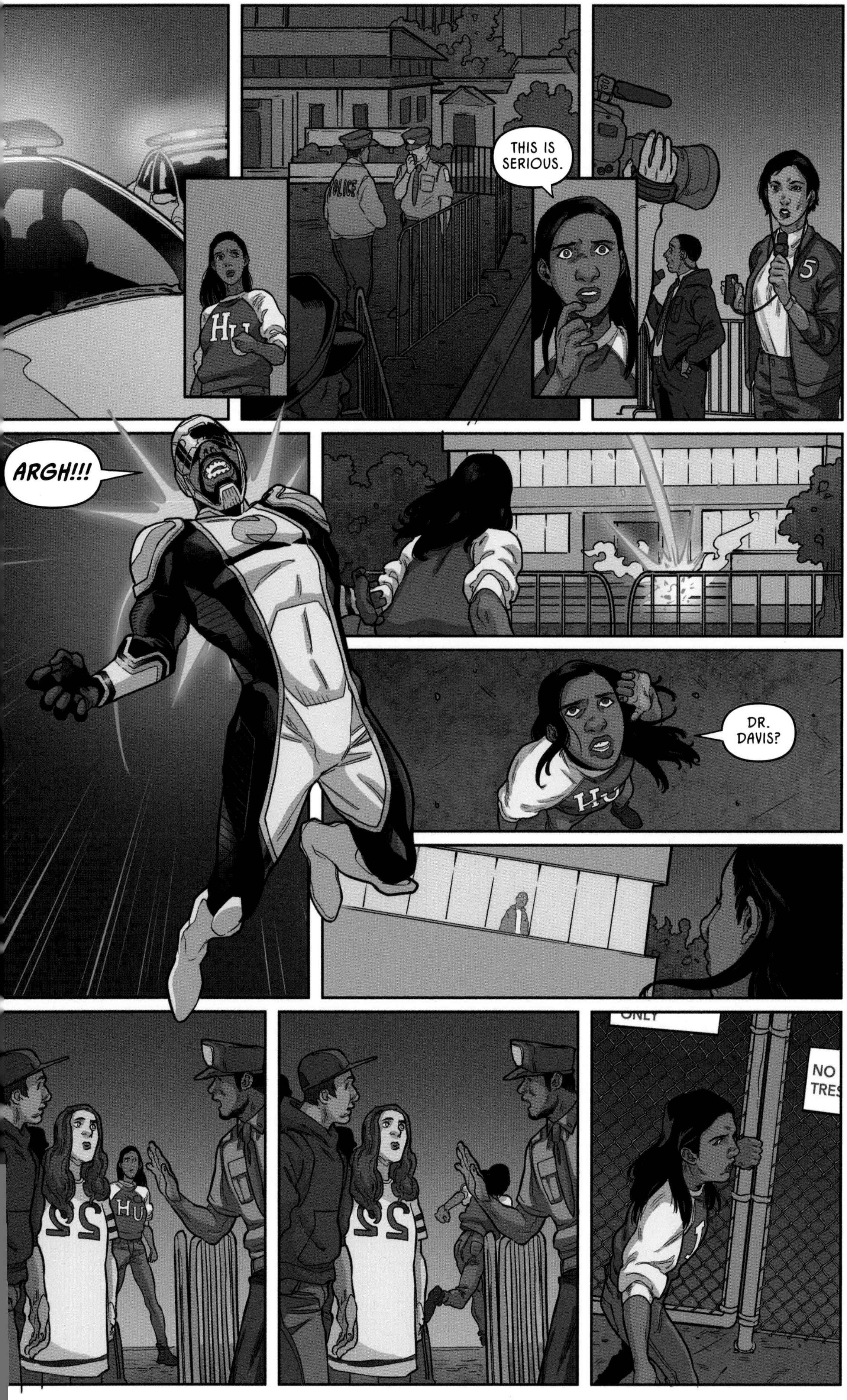

POLICE
THIS IS SERIOUS.
HU
5
ARGH!!!
DR. DAVIS?
HU
ONLY
NO TRES
22
HU
22

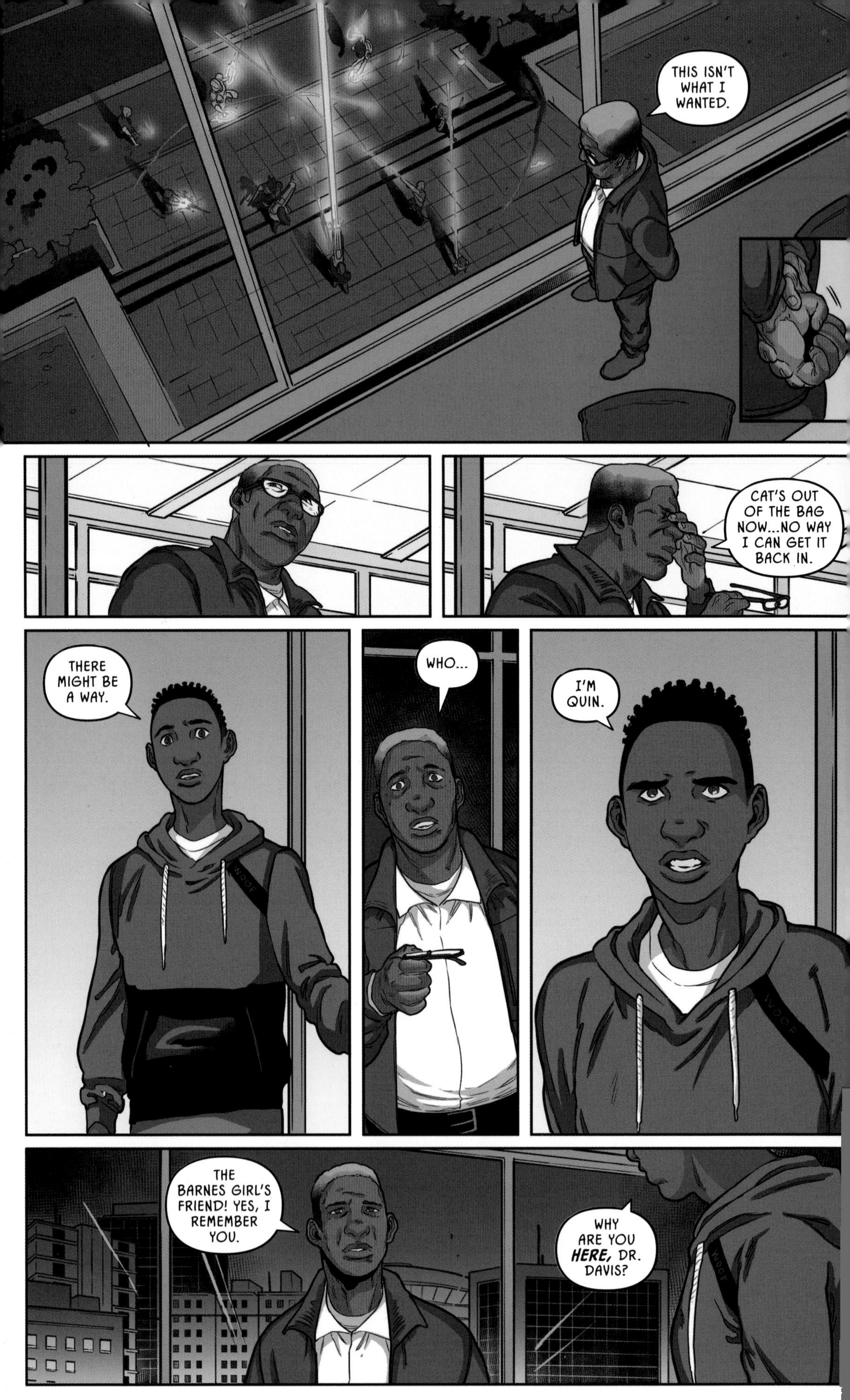
THIS ISN'T WHAT I WANTED.
CAT'S OUT OF THE BAG NOW...NO WAY I CAN GET IT BACK IN.
THERE MIGHT BE A WAY.
WHO...
I'M QUIN.
THE BARNES GIRL'S FRIEND! YES, I REMEMBER YOU.
WHY ARE YOU *HERE,* DR. DAVIS?

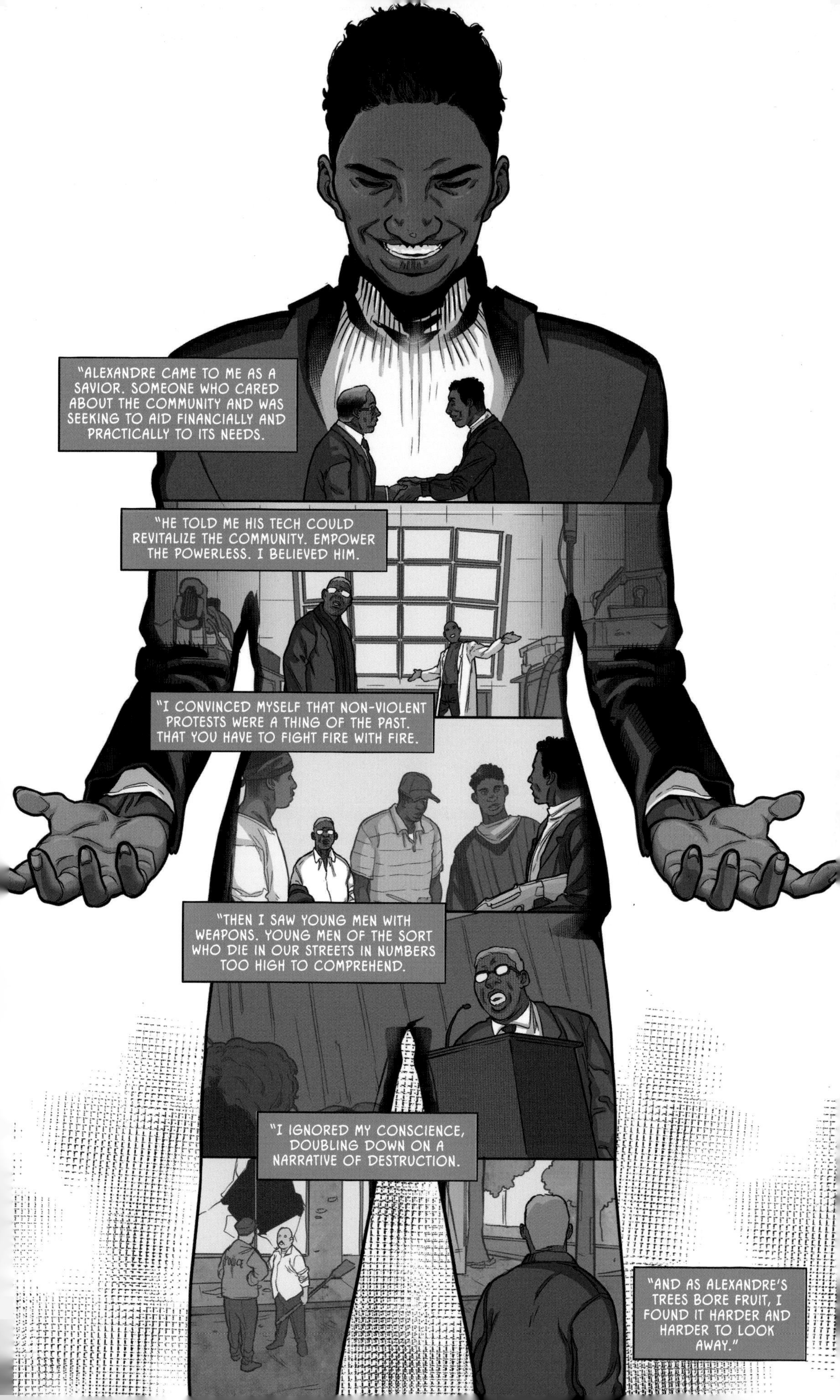
"ALEXANDRE CAME TO ME AS A SAVIOR. SOMEONE WHO CARED ABOUT THE COMMUNITY AND WAS SEEKING TO AID FINANCIALLY AND PRACTICALLY TO ITS NEEDS.
"HE TOLD ME HIS TECH COULD REVITALIZE THE COMMUNITY. EMPOWER THE POWERLESS. I BELIEVED HIM.
"I CONVINCED MYSELF THAT NON-VIOLENT PROTESTS WERE A THING OF THE PAST. THAT YOU HAVE TO FIGHT FIRE WITH FIRE.
"THEN I SAW YOUNG MEN WITH WEAPONS. YOUNG MEN OF THE SORT WHO DIE IN OUR STREETS IN NUMBERS TOO HIGH TO COMPREHEND.
"I IGNORED MY CONSCIENCE, DOUBLING DOWN ON A NARRATIVE OF DESTRUCTION.
"AND AS ALEXANDRE'S TREES BORE FRUIT, I FOUND IT HARDER AND HARDER TO LOOK AWAY."

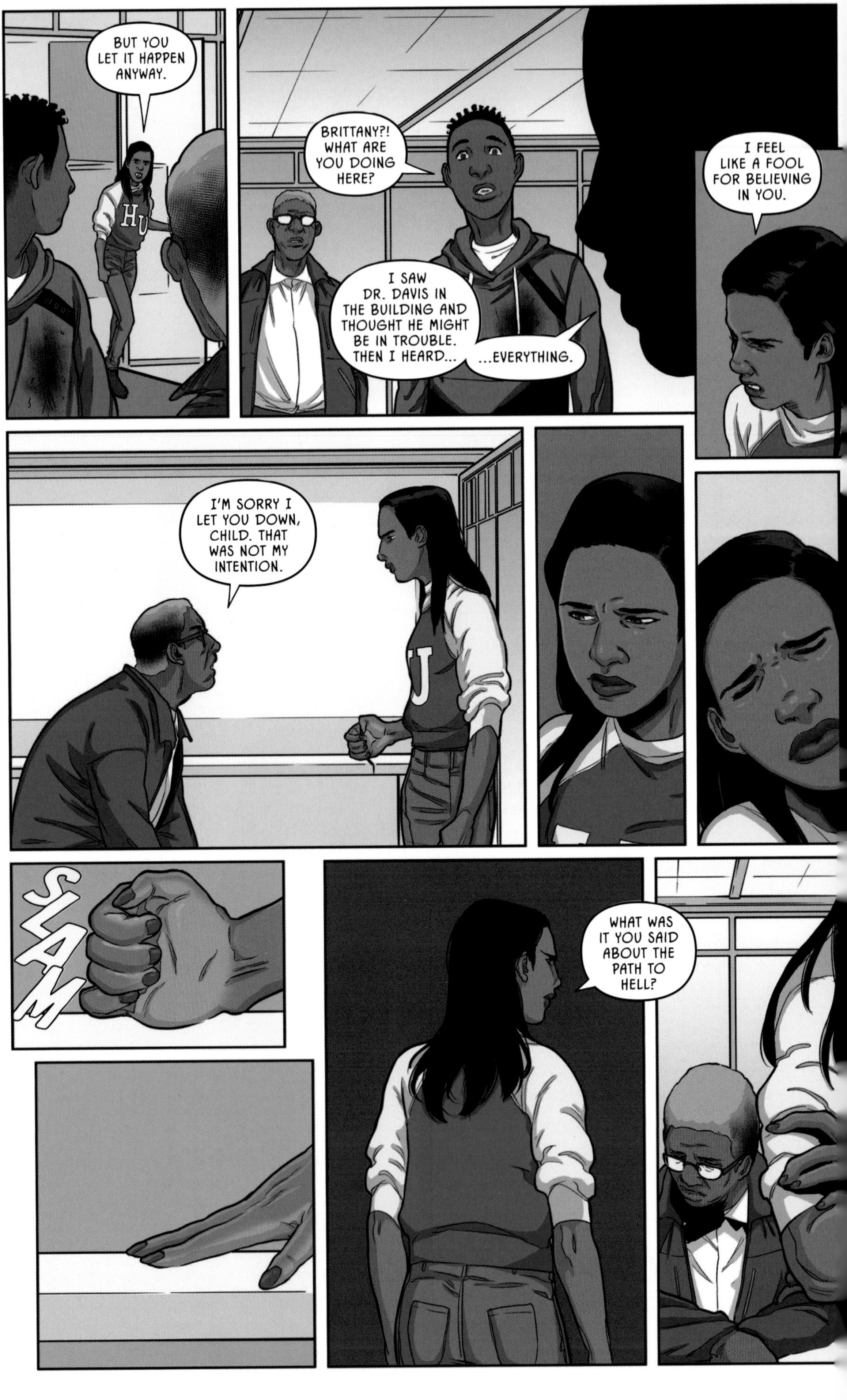
BUT YOU LET IT HAPPEN ANYWAY.
BRITTANY?! WHAT ARE YOU DOING HERE?
I SAW DR. DAVIS IN THE BUILDING AND THOUGHT HE MIGHT BE IN TROUBLE. THEN I HEARD...
...EVERYTHING.
I FEEL LIKE A FOOL FOR BELIEVING IN YOU.
I'M SORRY I LET YOU DOWN, CHILD. THAT WAS NOT MY INTENTION.
SLAM
WHAT WAS IT YOU SAID ABOUT THE PATH TO HELL?

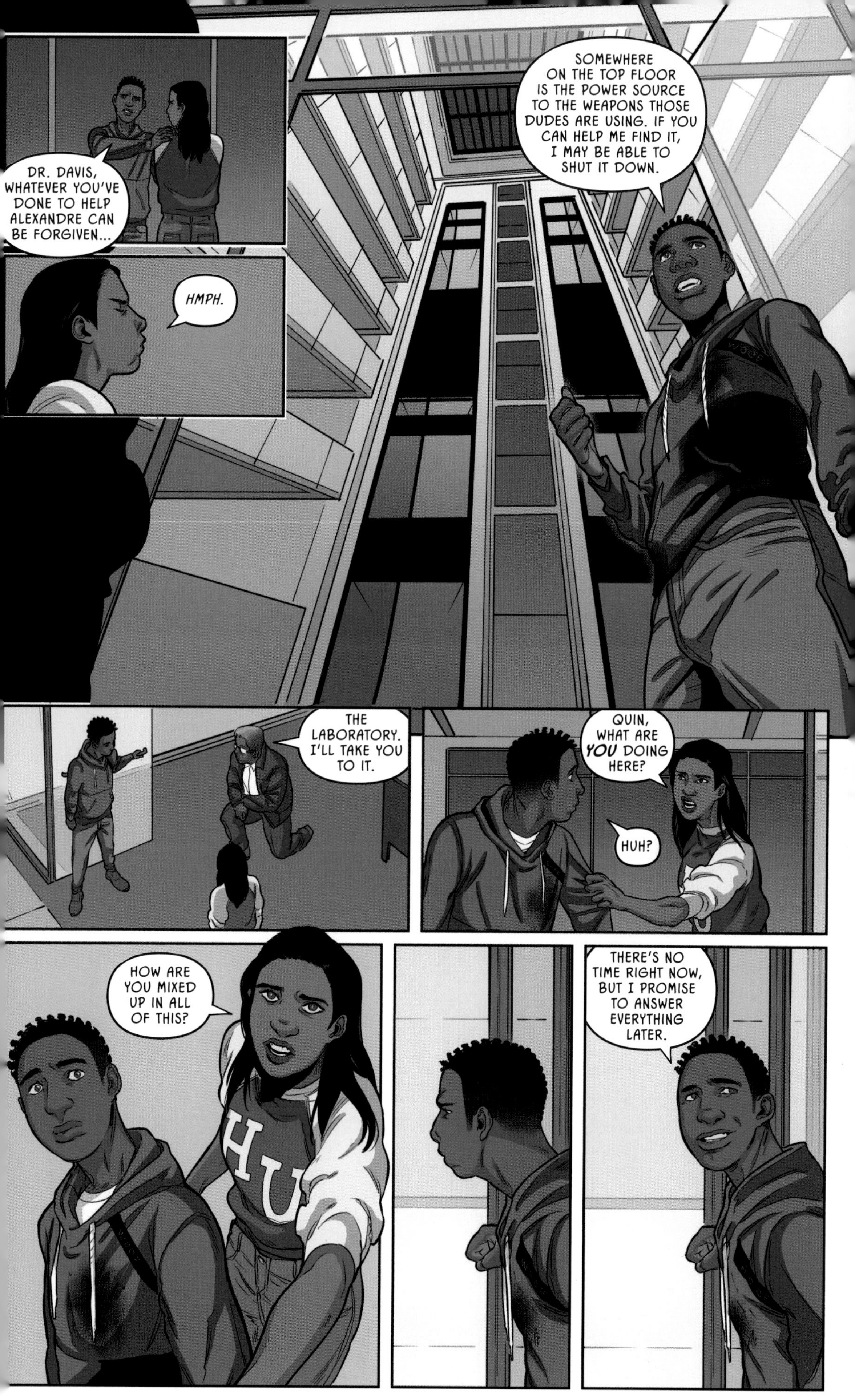
DR. DAVIS, WHATEVER YOU'VE DONE TO HELP ALEXANDRE CAN BE FORGIVEN...
HMPH.
SOMEWHERE ON THE TOP FLOOR IS THE POWER SOURCE TO THE WEAPONS THOSE DUDES ARE USING. IF YOU CAN HELP ME FIND IT, I MAY BE ABLE TO SHUT IT DOWN.
THE LABORATORY. I'LL TAKE YOU TO IT.
QUIN, WHAT ARE *YOU* DOING HERE?
HUH?
HOW ARE YOU MIXED UP IN ALL OF THIS?
THERE'S NO TIME RIGHT NOW, BUT I PROMISE TO ANSWER EVERYTHING LATER.

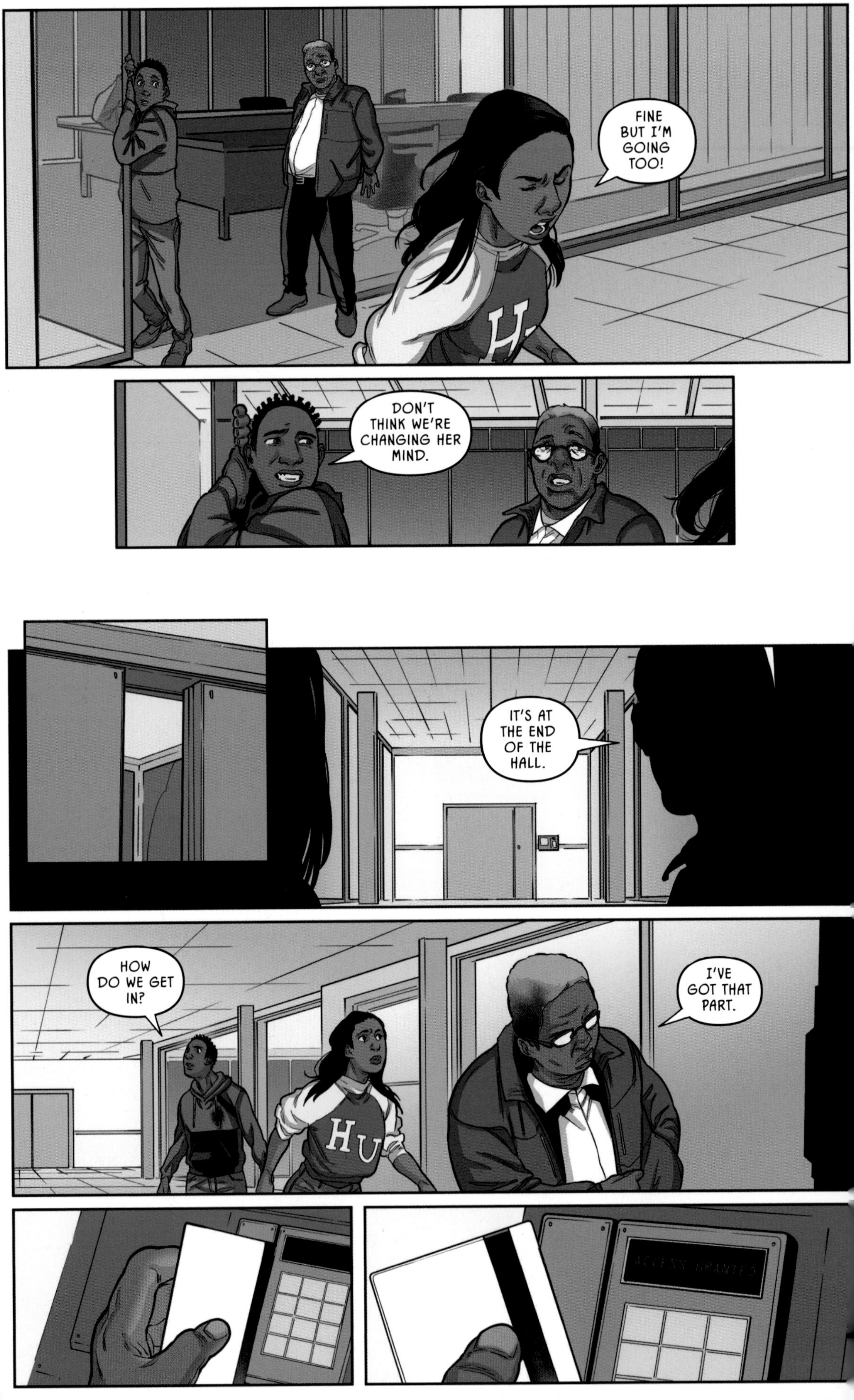
FINE BUT I'M GOING TOO!
DON'T THINK WE'RE CHANGING HER MIND.
IT'S AT THE END OF THE HALL.
HOW DO WE GET IN?
I'VE GOT THAT PART.
ACCESS GRANTED

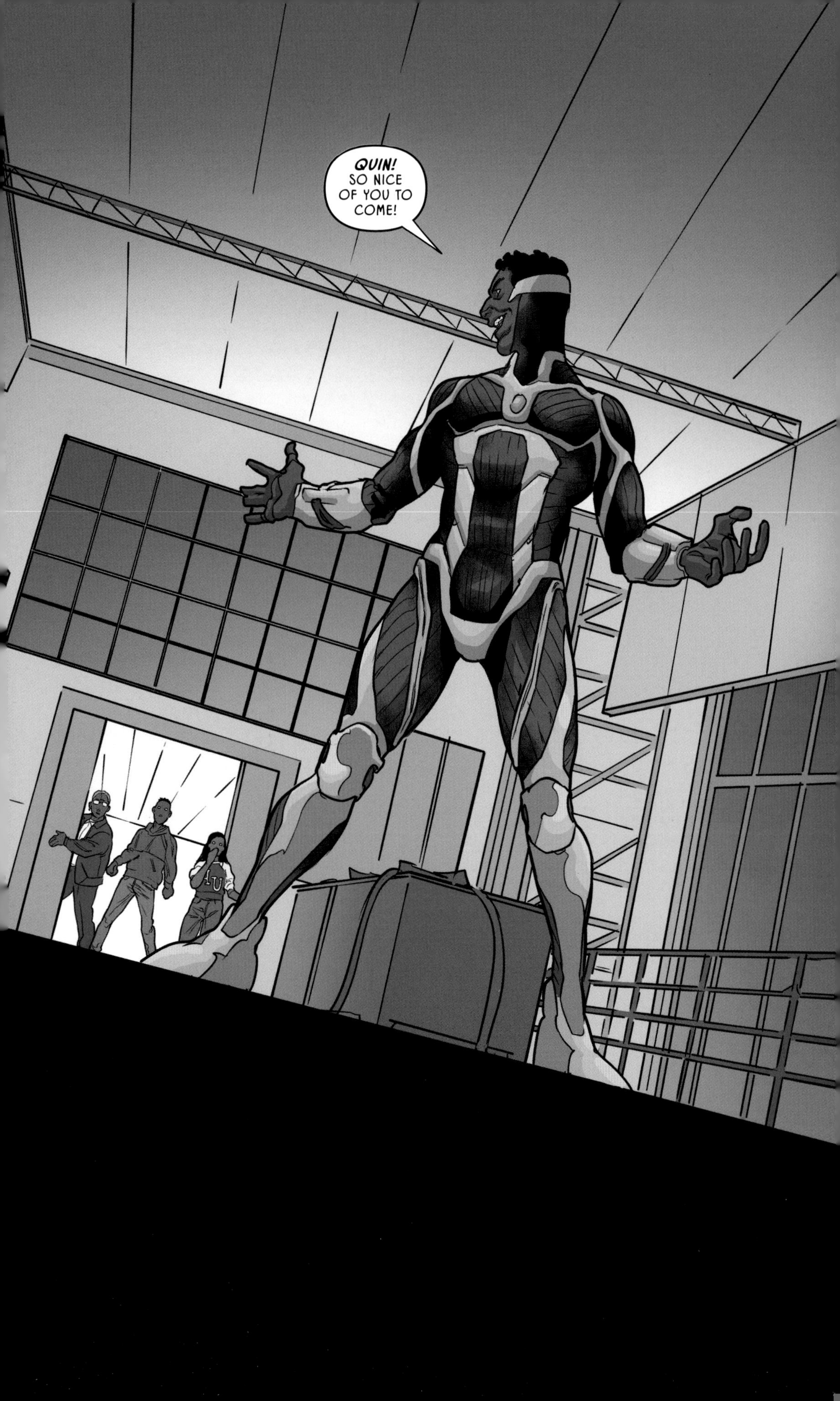
QUIN! SO NICE OF YOU TO COME!

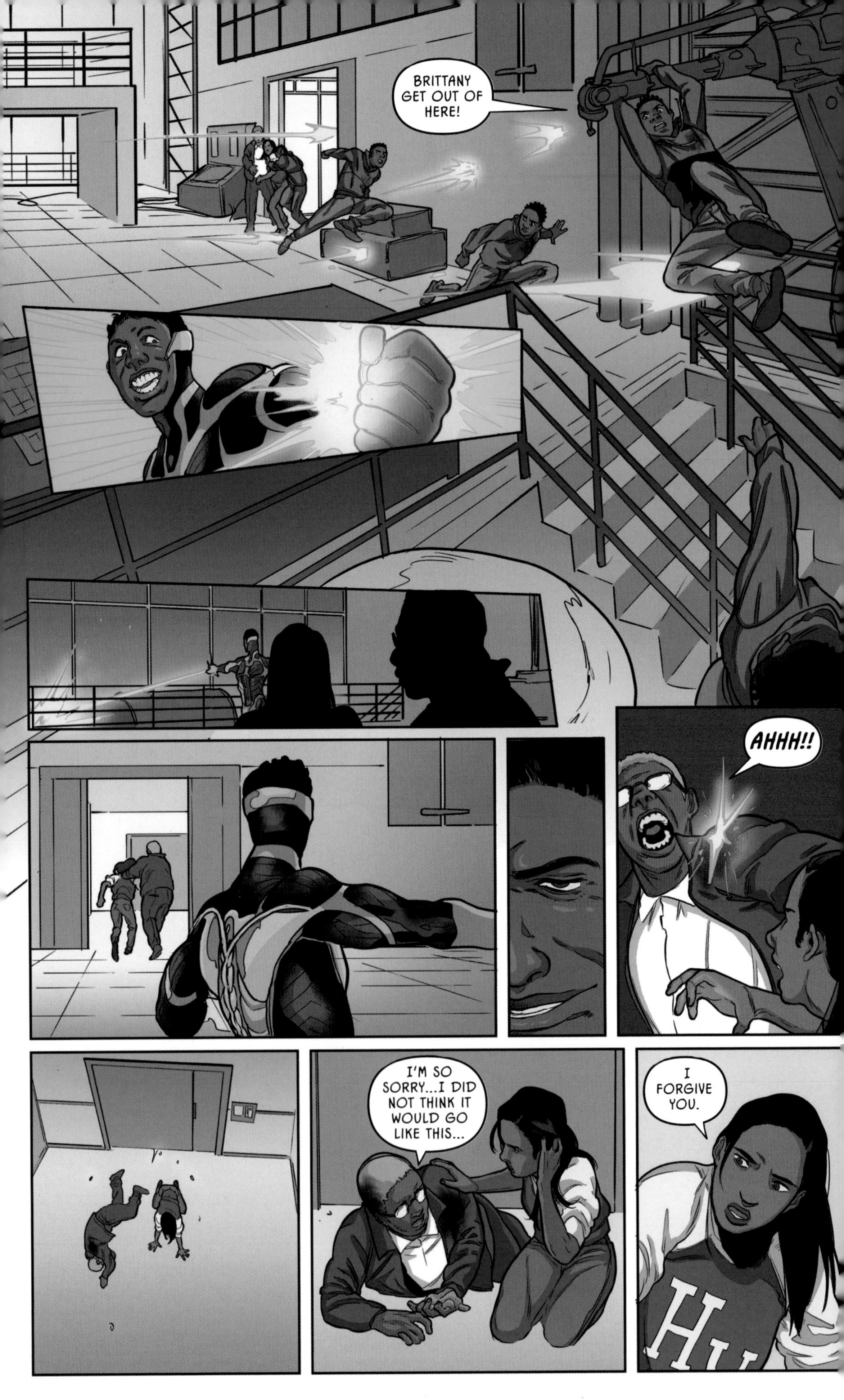
BRITTANY GET OUT OF HERE!
AHHH!!
I'M SO SORRY...I DID NOT THINK IT WOULD GO LIKE THIS...
I FORGIVE YOU.

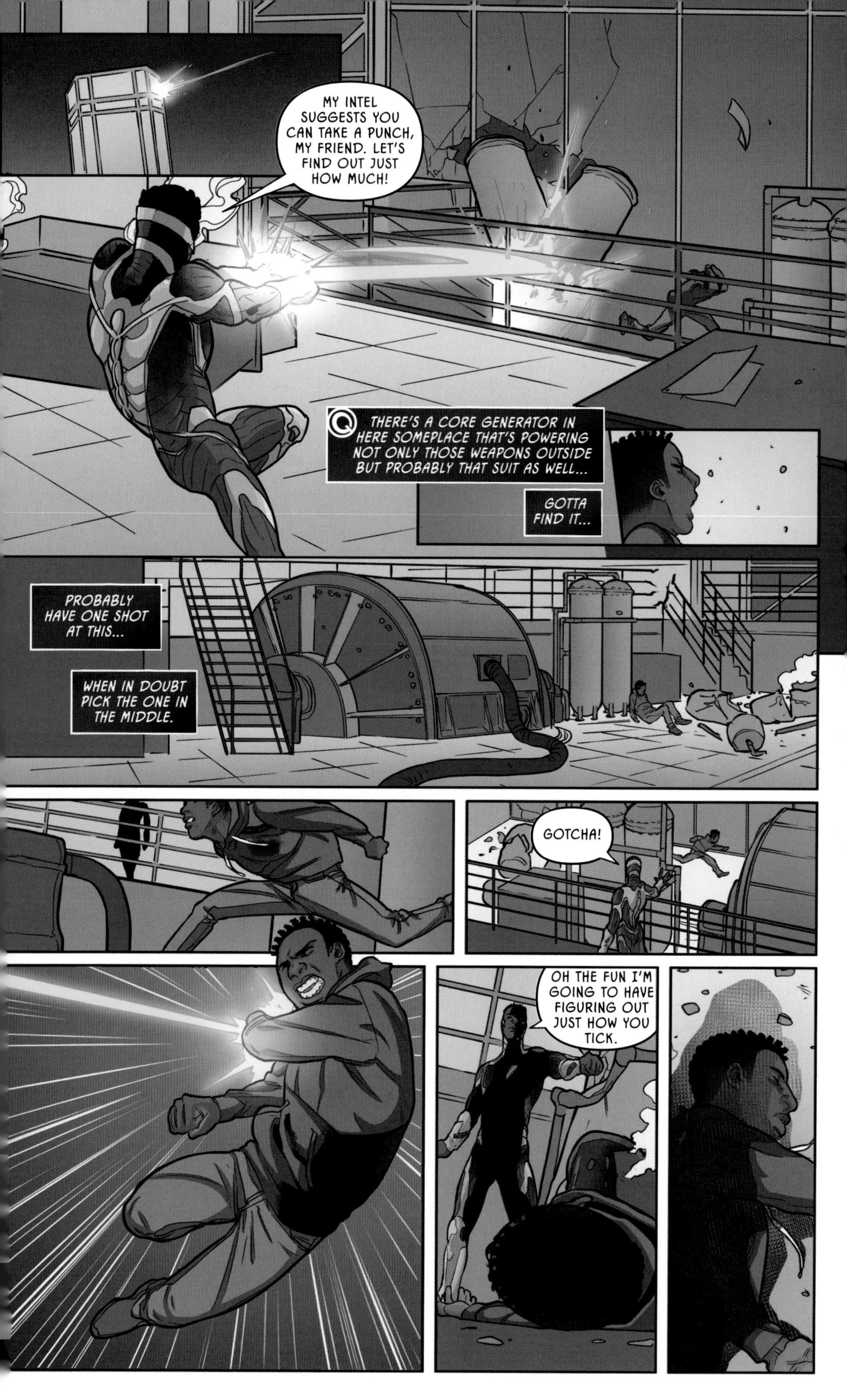
MY INTEL SUGGESTS YOU CAN TAKE A PUNCH, MY FRIEND. LET'S FIND OUT JUST HOW MUCH!
THERE'S A CORE GENERATOR IN HERE SOMEPLACE THAT'S POWERING NOT ONLY THOSE WEAPONS OUTSIDE BUT PROBABLY THAT SUIT AS WELL...
GOTTA FIND IT...
PROBABLY HAVE ONE SHOT AT THIS...
WHEN IN DOUBT PICK THE ONE IN THE MIDDLE.
GOTCHA!
OH THE FUN I'M GOING TO HAVE FIGURING OUT JUST HOW YOU TICK.

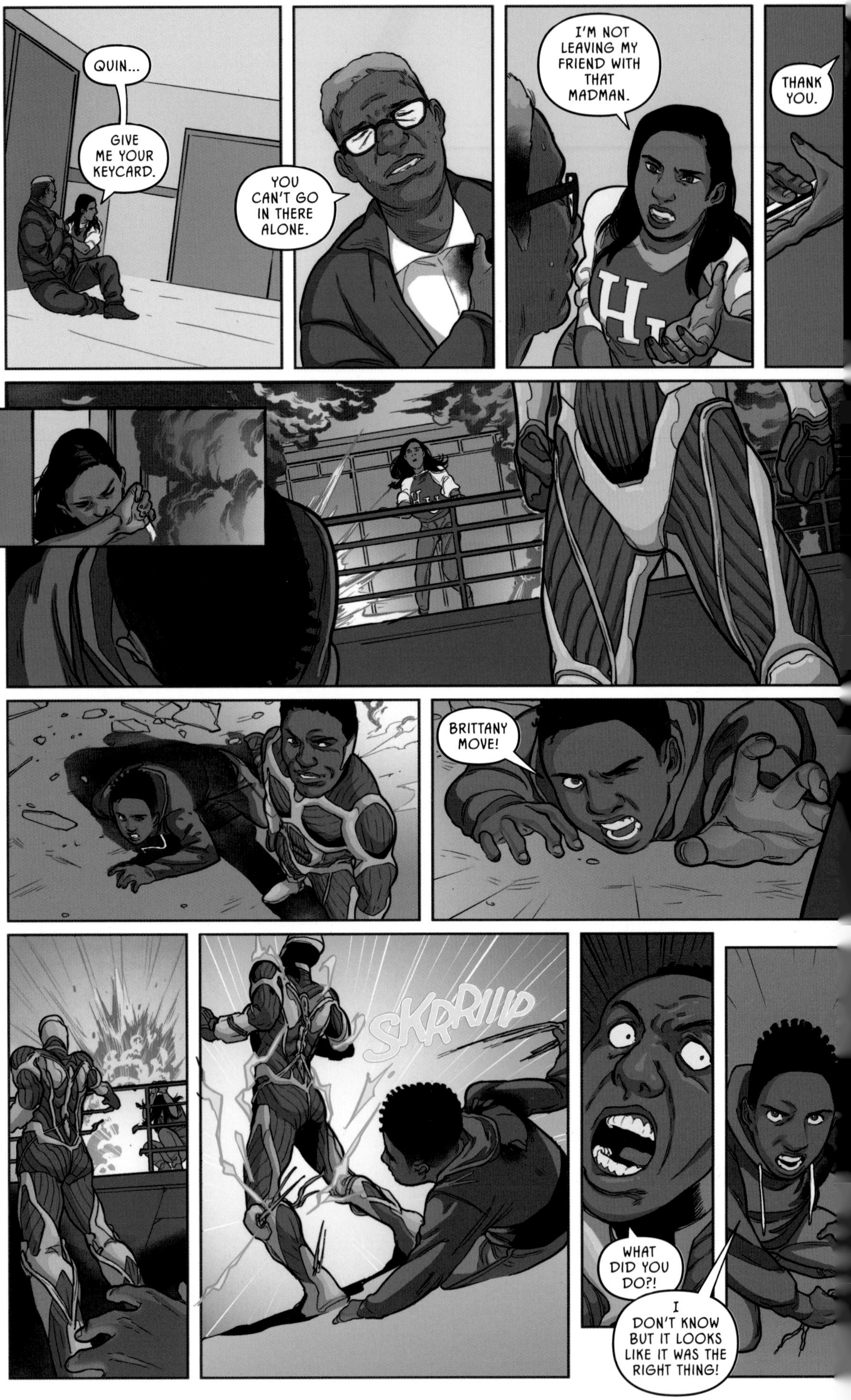
QUIN...
GIVE ME YOUR KEYCARD.
YOU CAN'T GO IN THERE ALONE.
I'M NOT LEAVING MY FRIEND WITH THAT MADMAN.
THANK YOU.
BRITTANY MOVE!
SKRRIIIP
WHAT DID YOU DO?!
I DON'T KNOW BUT IT LOOKS LIKE IT WAS THE RIGHT THING!

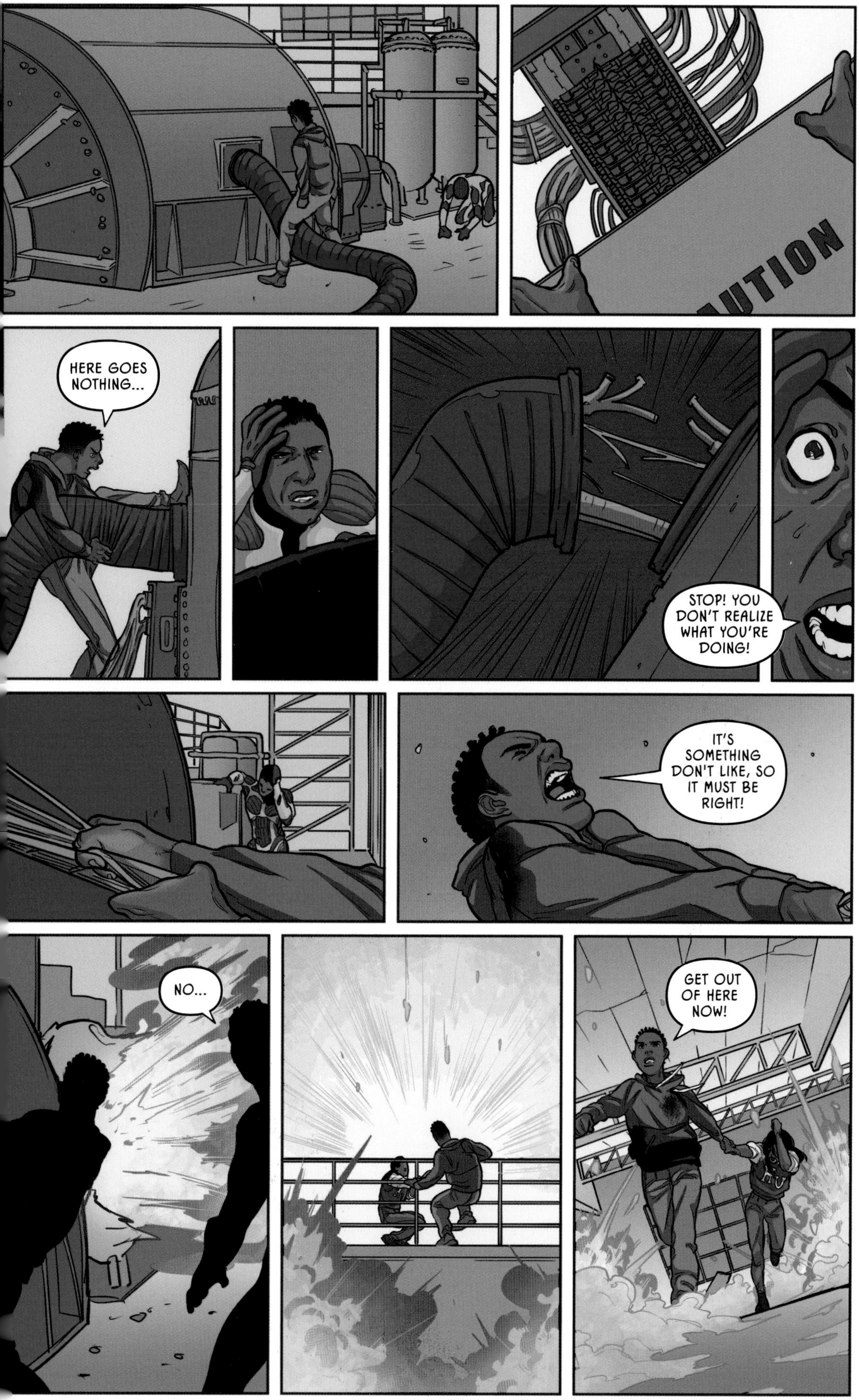
AUTION
HERE GOES NOTHING...
STOP! YOU DON'T REALIZE WHAT YOU'RE DOING!
IT'S SOMETHING DON'T LIKE, SO IT MUST BE RIGHT!
NO...
GET OUT OF HERE NOW!

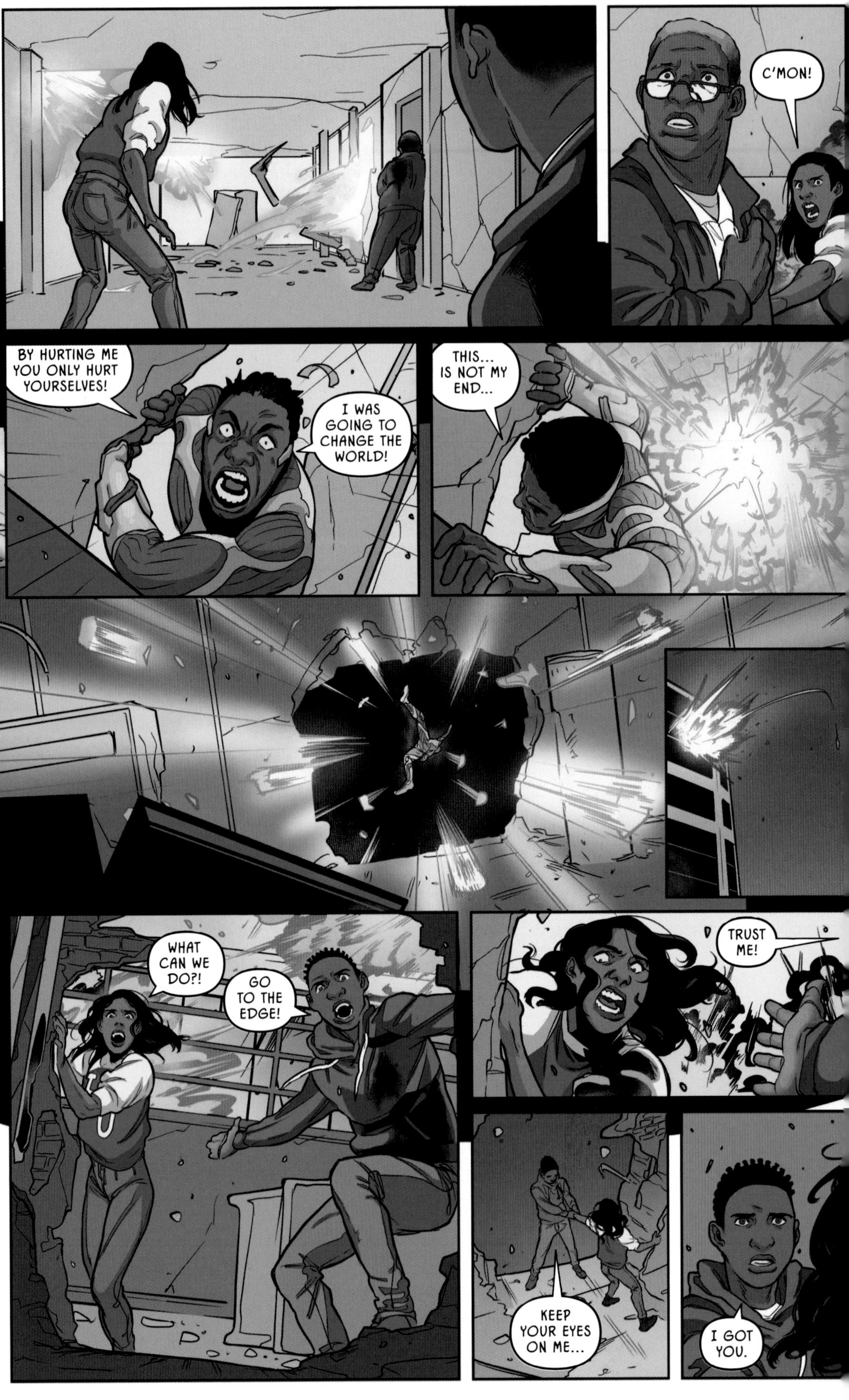
C'MON!
BY HURTING ME YOU ONLY HURT YOURSELVES!
I WAS GOING TO CHANGE THE WORLD!
THIS... IS NOT MY END...
WHAT CAN WE DO?!
GO TO THE EDGE!
TRUST ME!
KEEP YOUR EYES ON ME...
I GOT YOU.

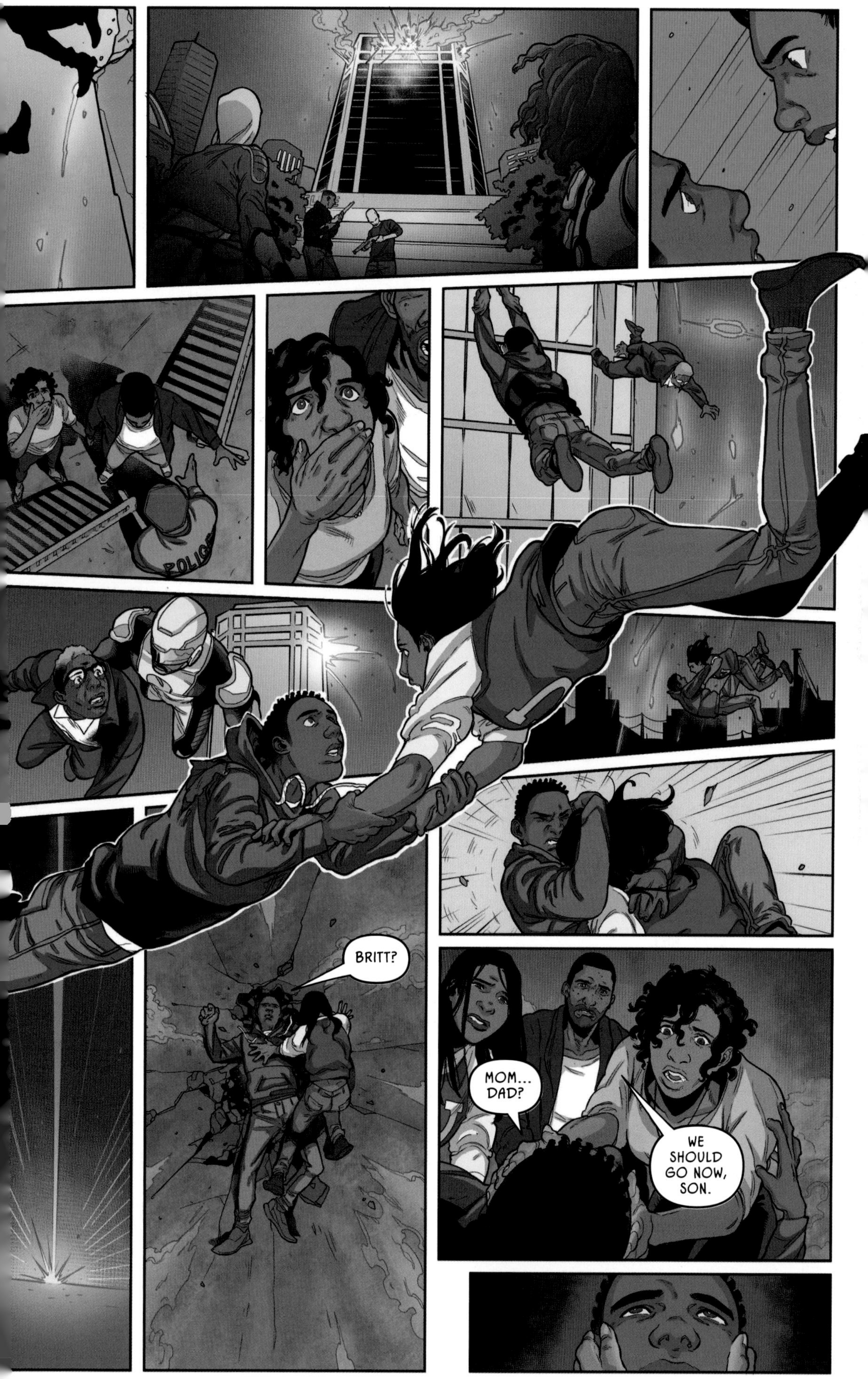
POLICE
BRITT?
MOM... DAD?
WE SHOULD GO NOW, SON.

BACK TO THE ROUTINE.

DR. DAVIS COOPERATED WITH THE D.A. SO HE DIDN'T GET ANY TIME FOR HIS INVOLVEMENT WITH ALEXANDRE'S PLAN.

THEY NEVER FOUND ALEXANDRE.

THE DUDES THAT SIDED UP WITH ALEXANDRE?

CITY STARTED A PROGRAM TO HELP THEM GAIN THE SKILLS NECESSARY TO COMPETE IN THE WORLD.

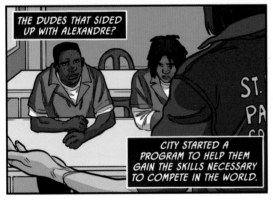

BRITT AND I HAVEN'T HAD OUR TALK YET. I CAN WAIT.

NOT SURE WHERE I GO FROM HERE...

BUT I'M EXCITED ABOUT THE JOURNEY.

THE END

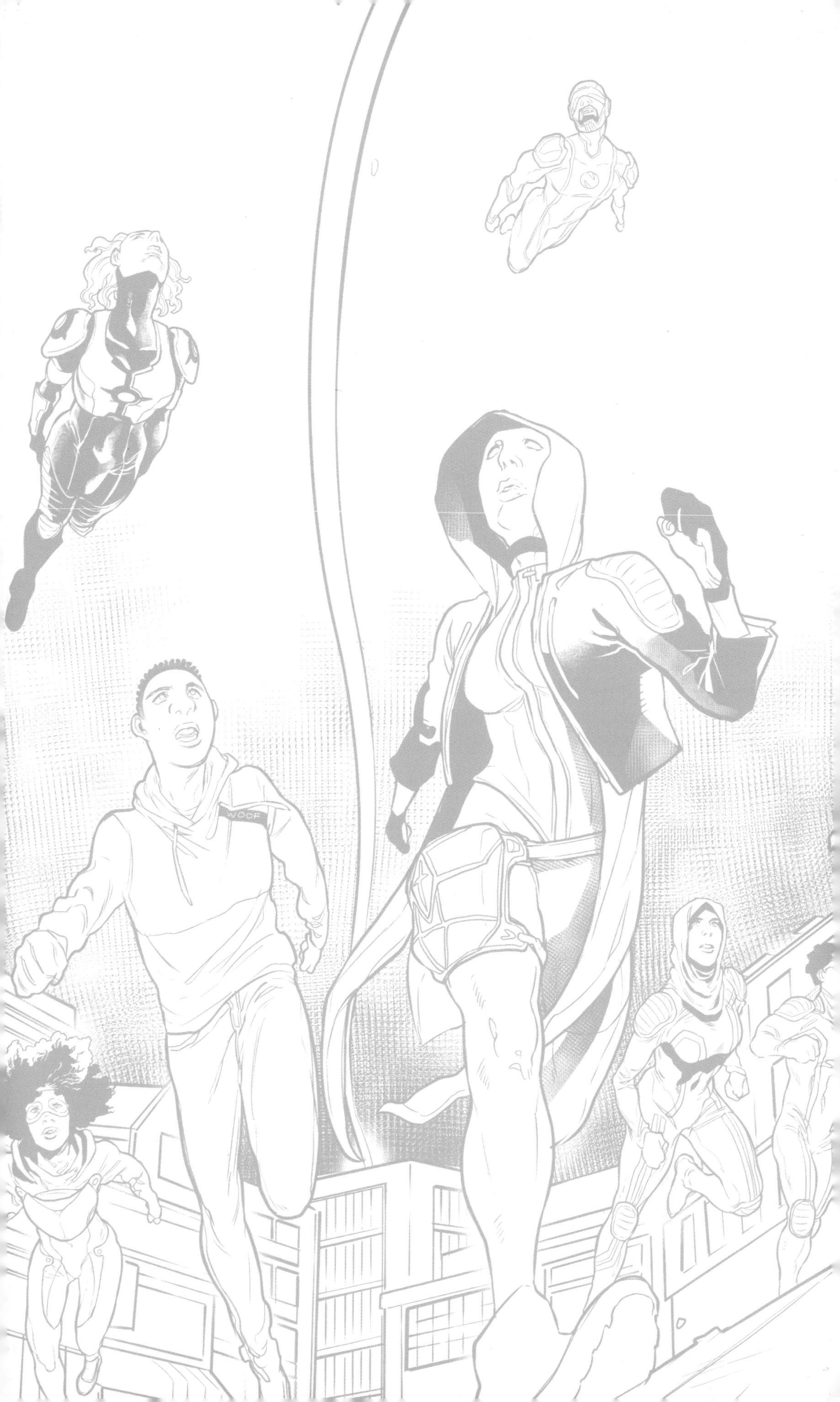
WOOF

COVER GALLERY

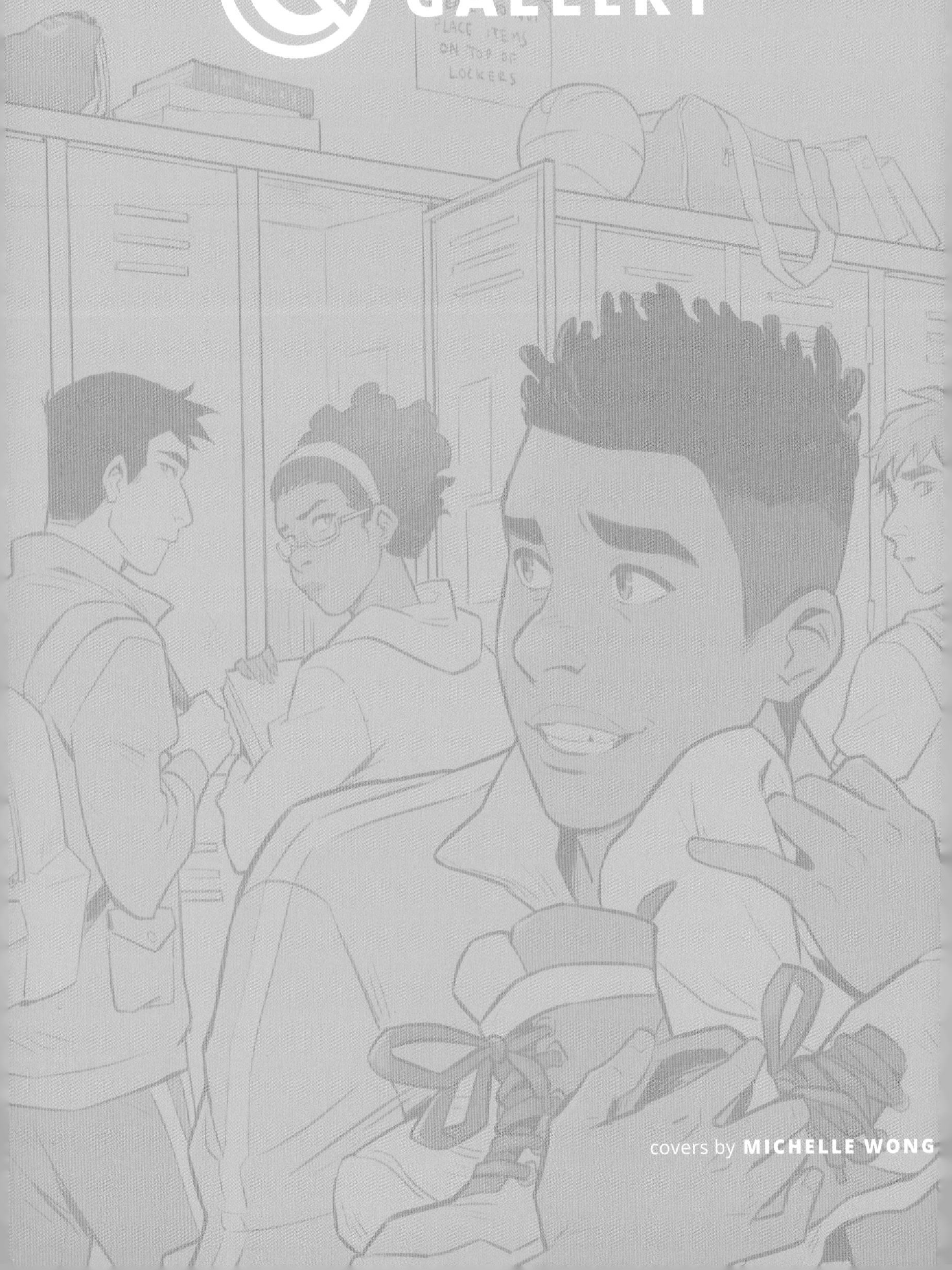
PLACE ITEMS
ON TOP OF
LOCKERS

covers by **MICHELLE WONG**

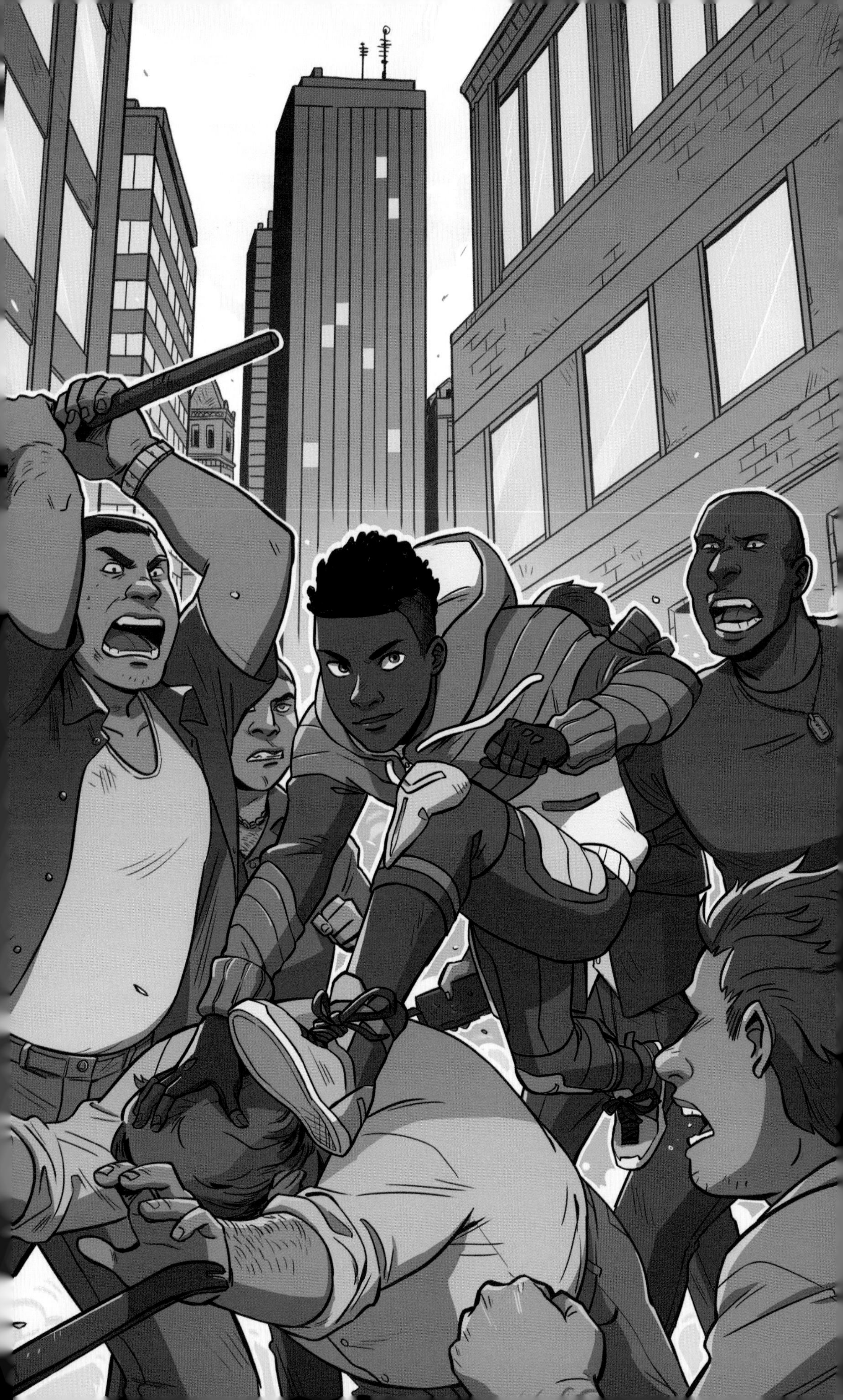

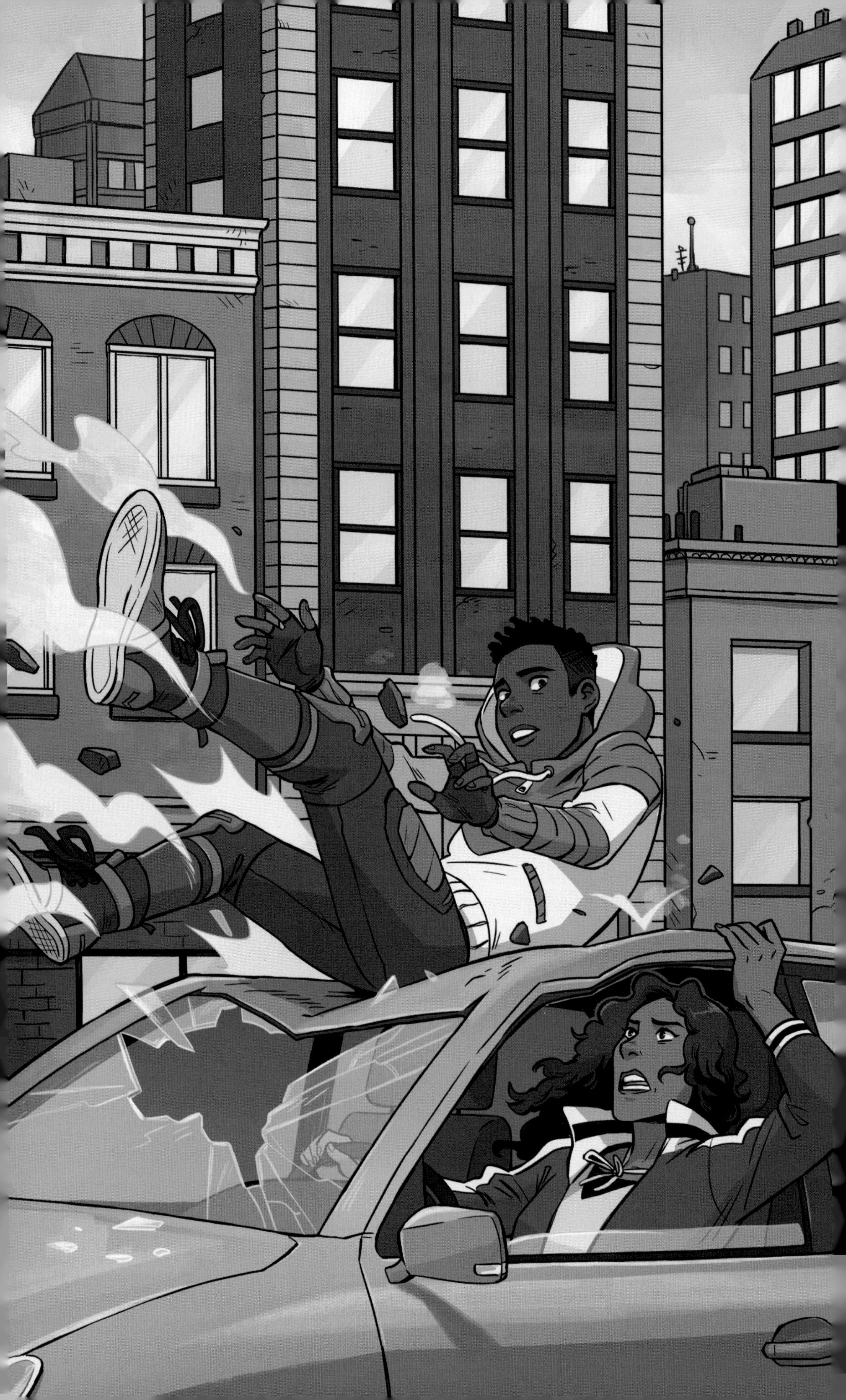

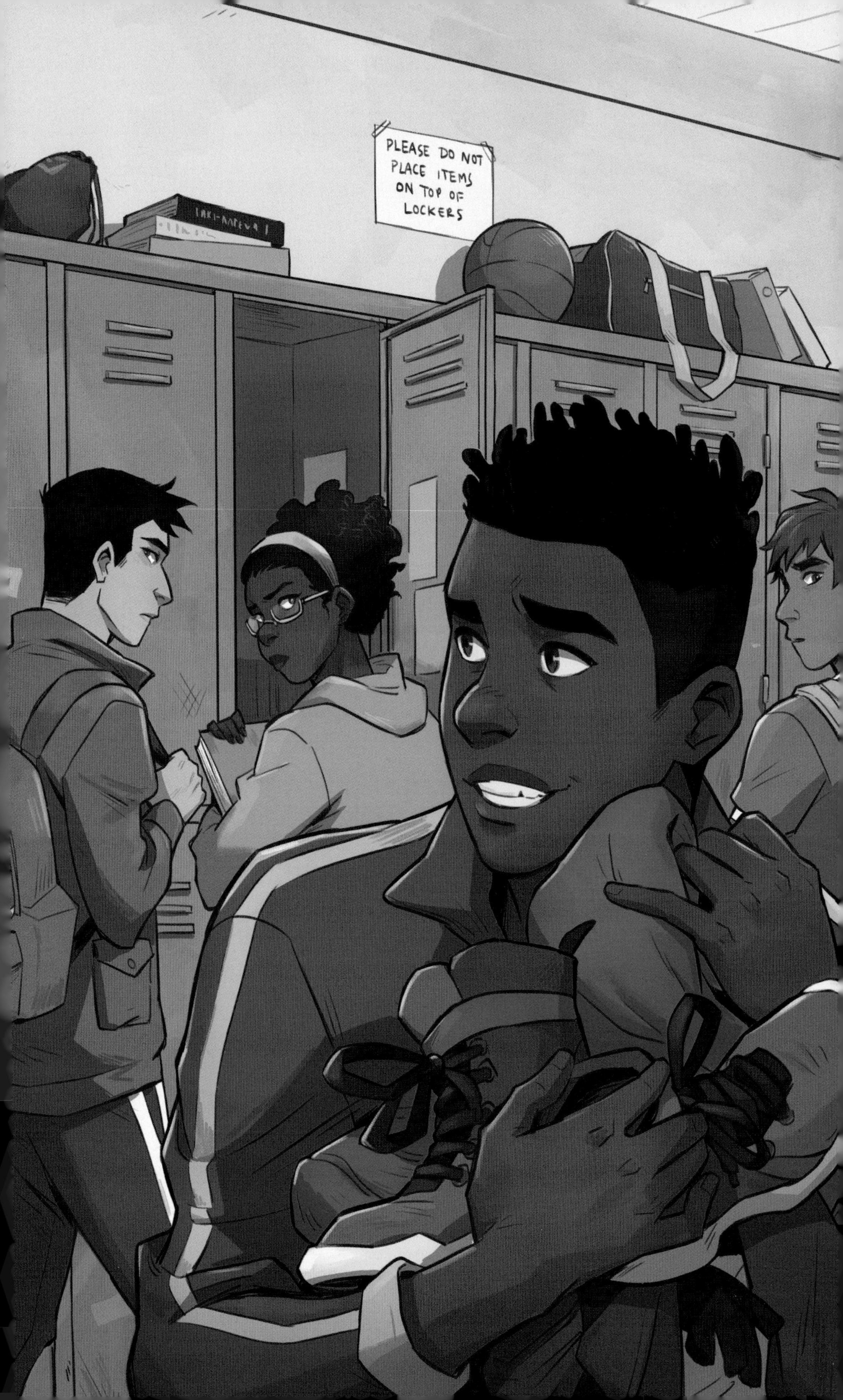
PLEASE DO NOT PLACE ITEMS ON TOP OF LOCKERS

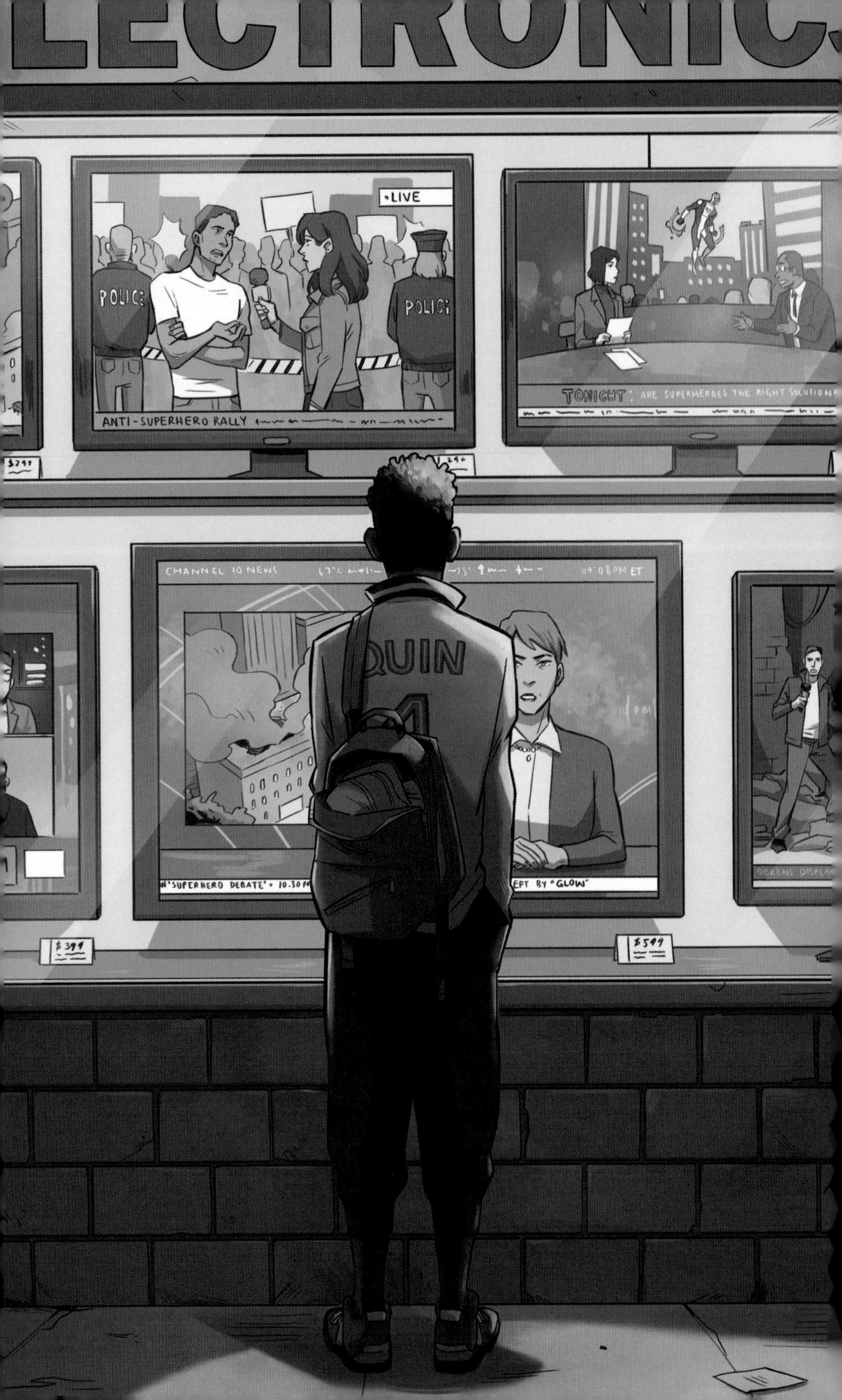
LECTRONIC
•LIVE
POLICE
POLIC
ANTI-SUPERHERO RALLY
TONIGHT: ARE SUPERHEROES THE RIGHT SOLUTION
CHANNEL 10 NEWS
09:08PM ET
QUIN
1
'SUPERHERO DEBATE' • 10:30
EPT BY "GLOW"
$399
$599
DOZENS DISPLA

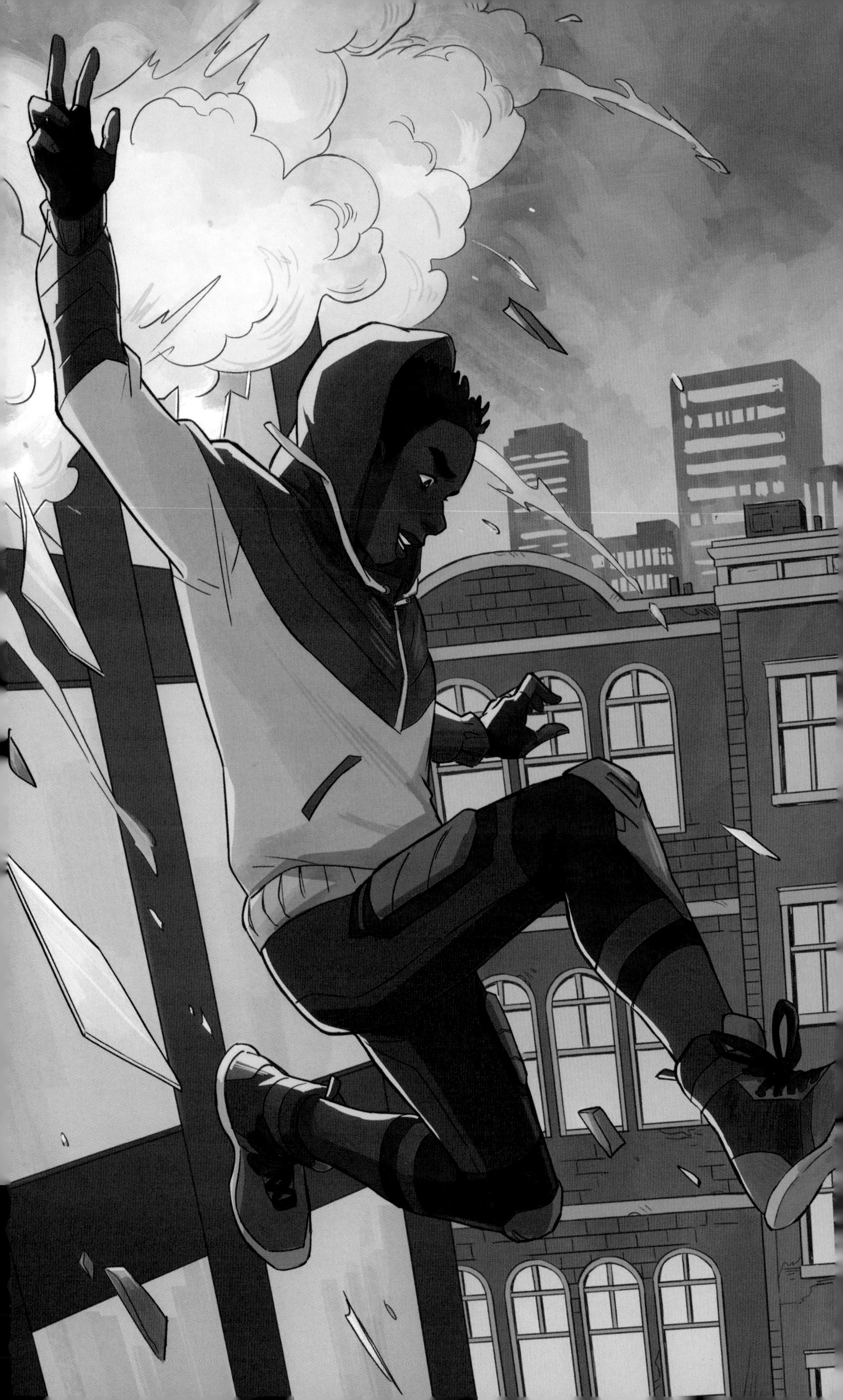

MAKING OF QUINCREDIBLE

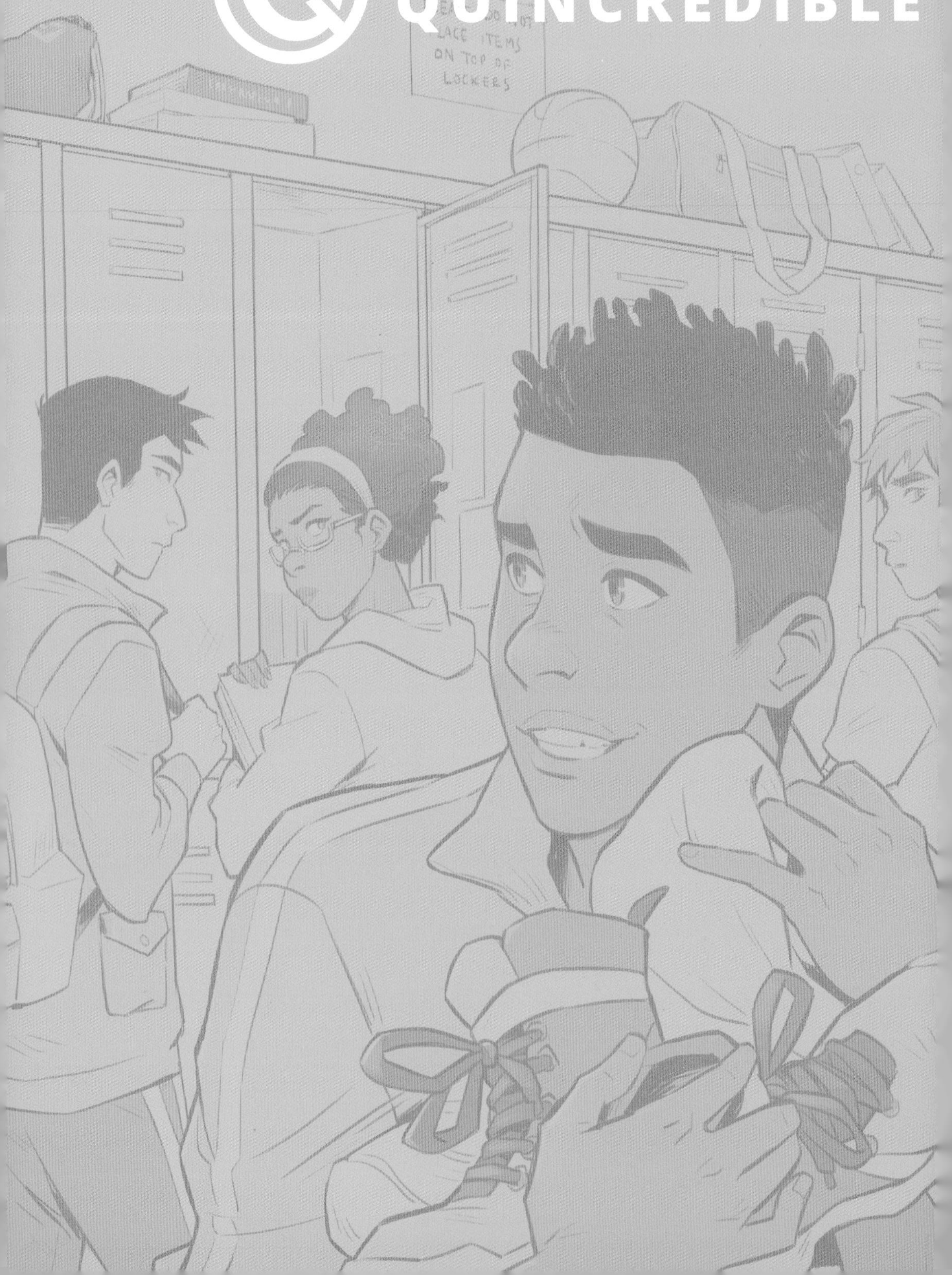
ON TOP OF
LOCKERS

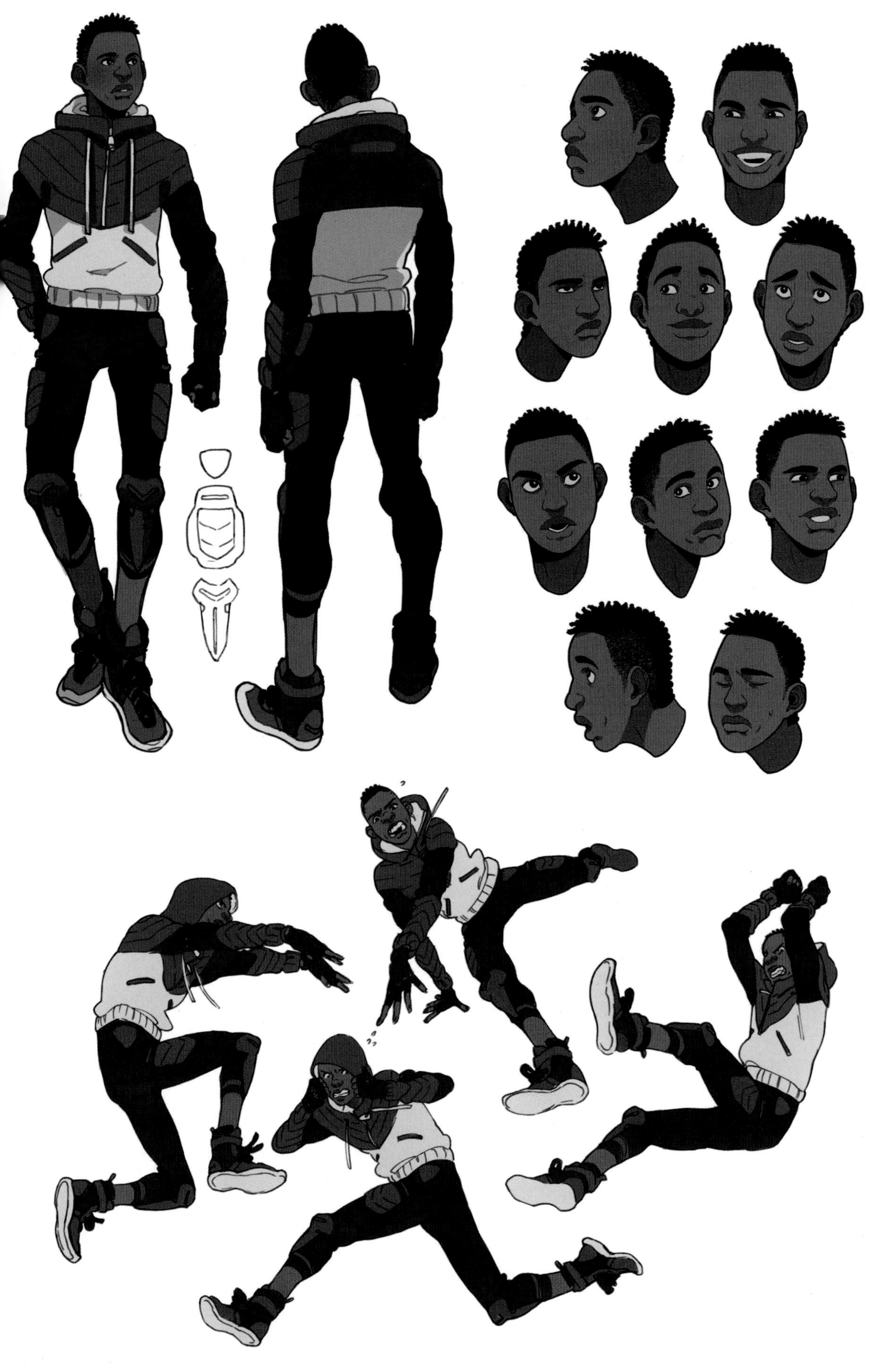

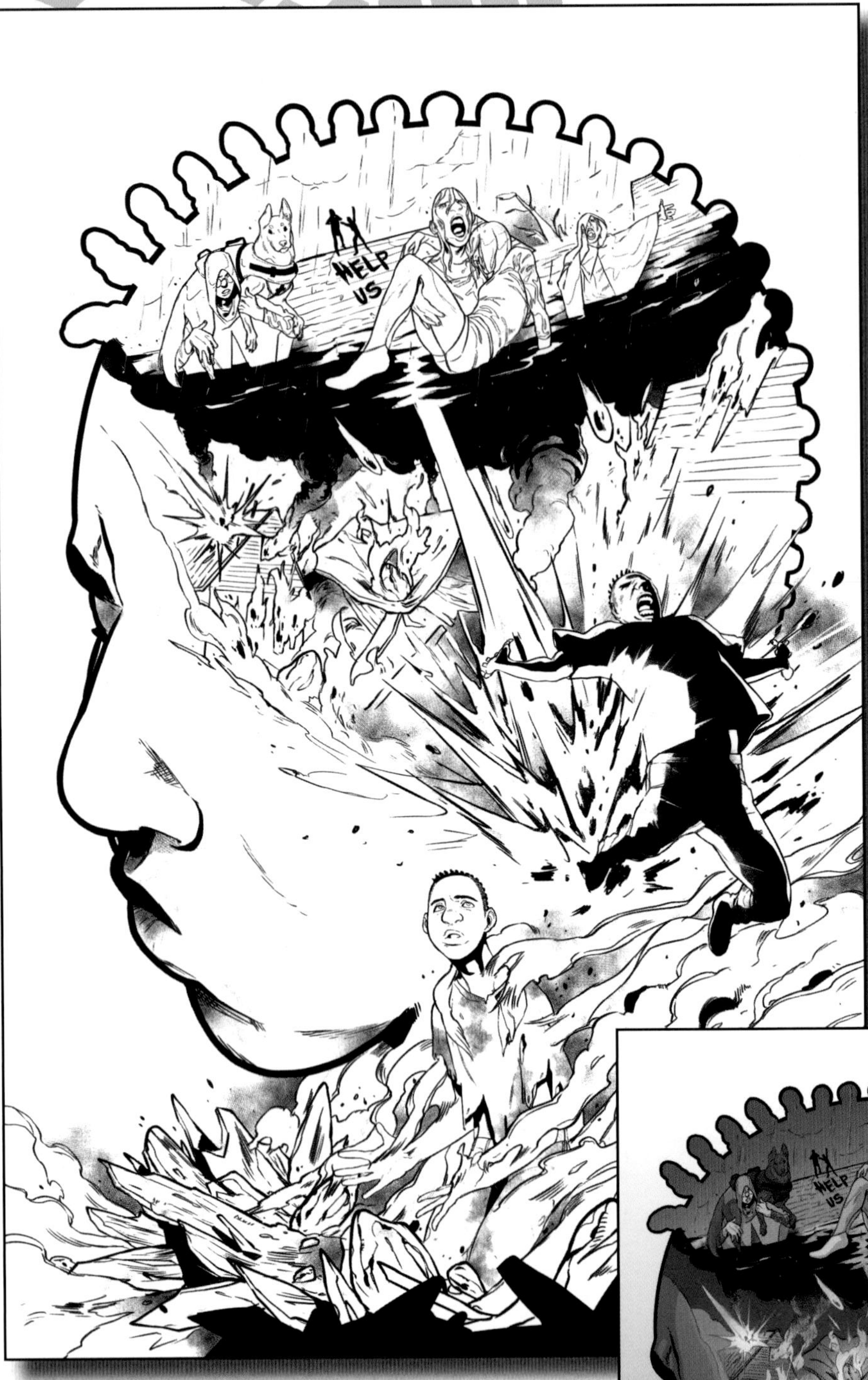
HELP
US

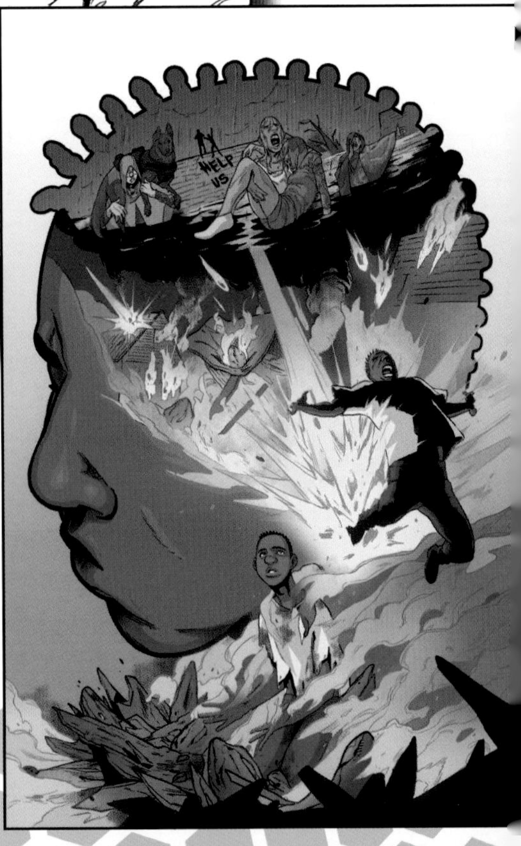
HELP
US

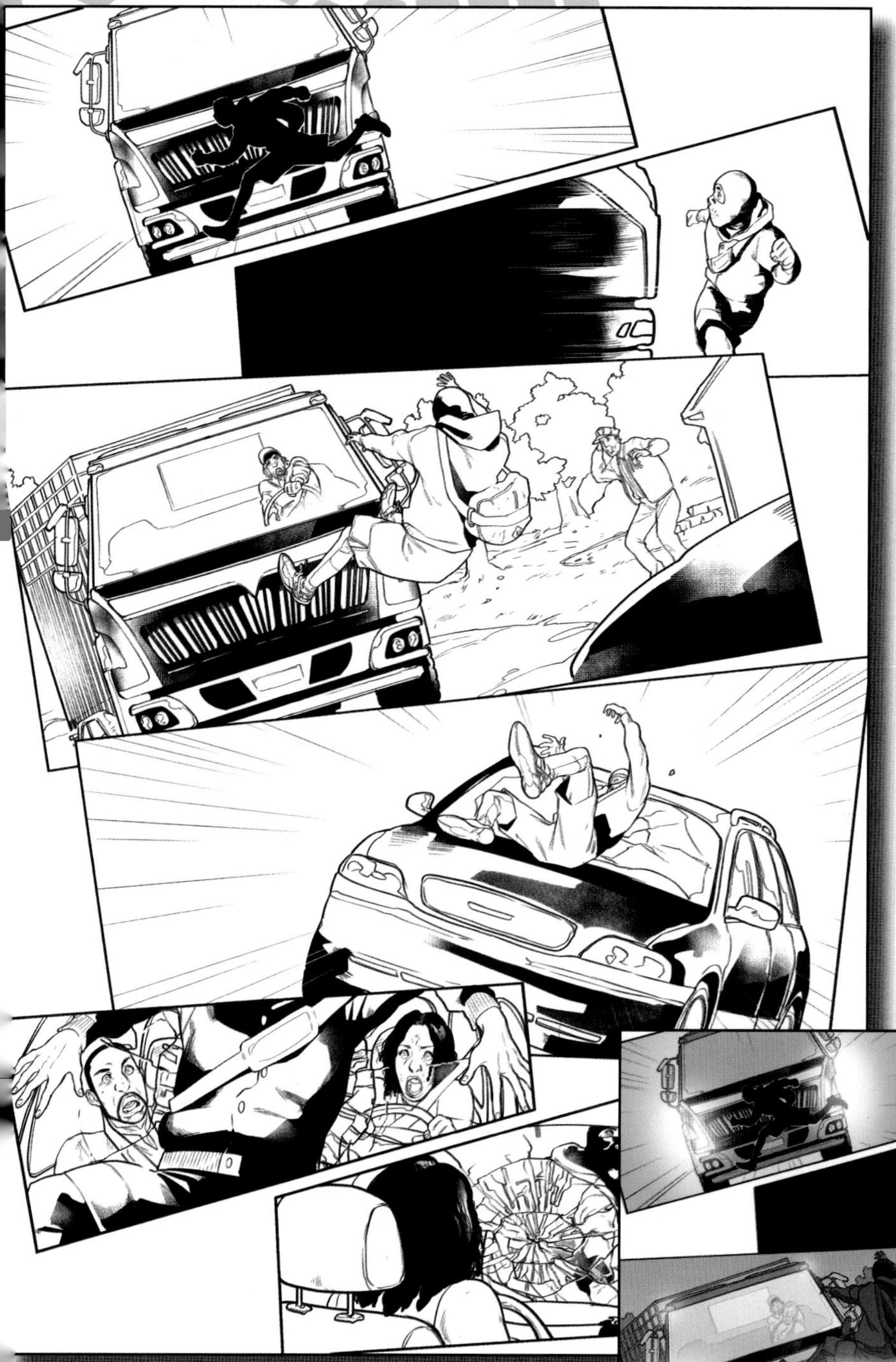

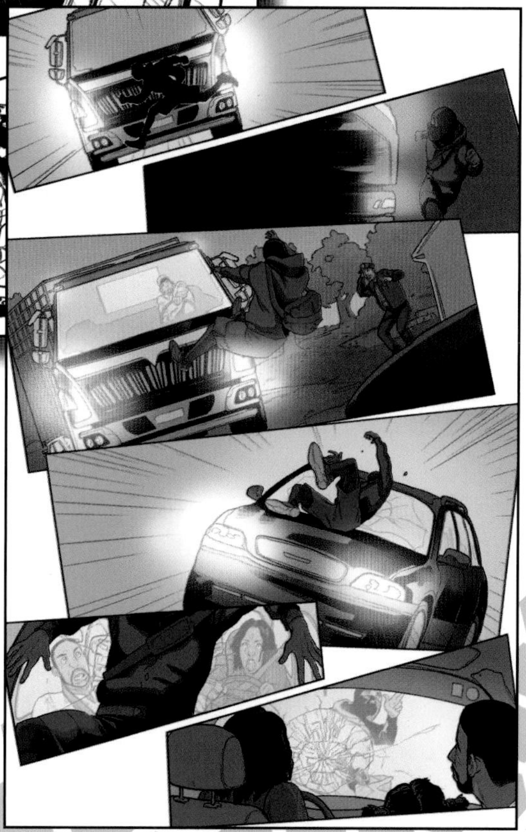

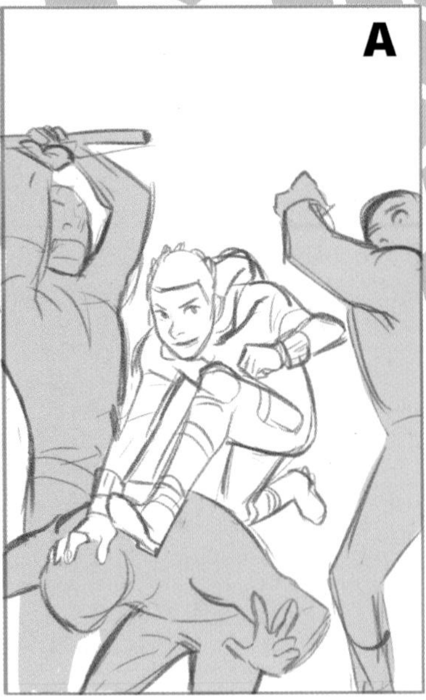
A

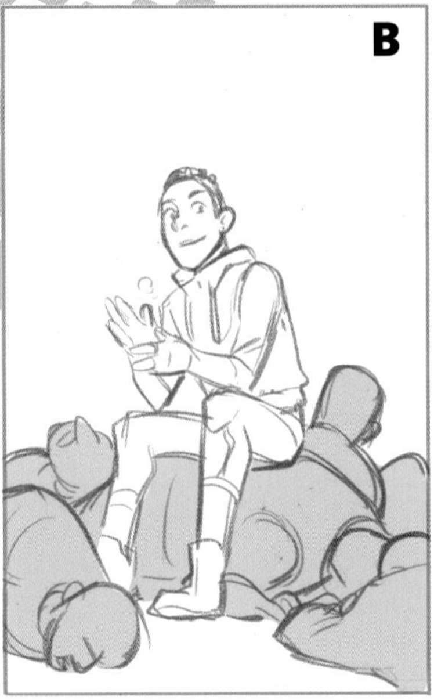
B

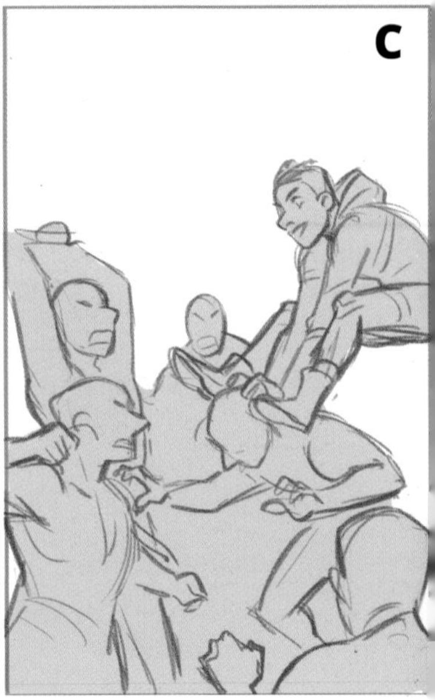
C

CONCEPT SKETCHES

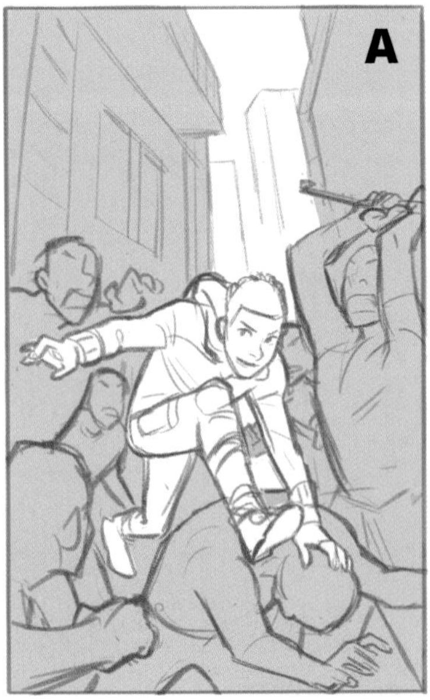
A

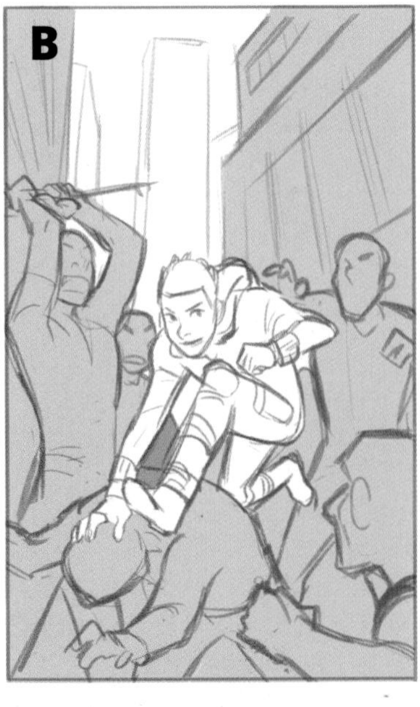
B

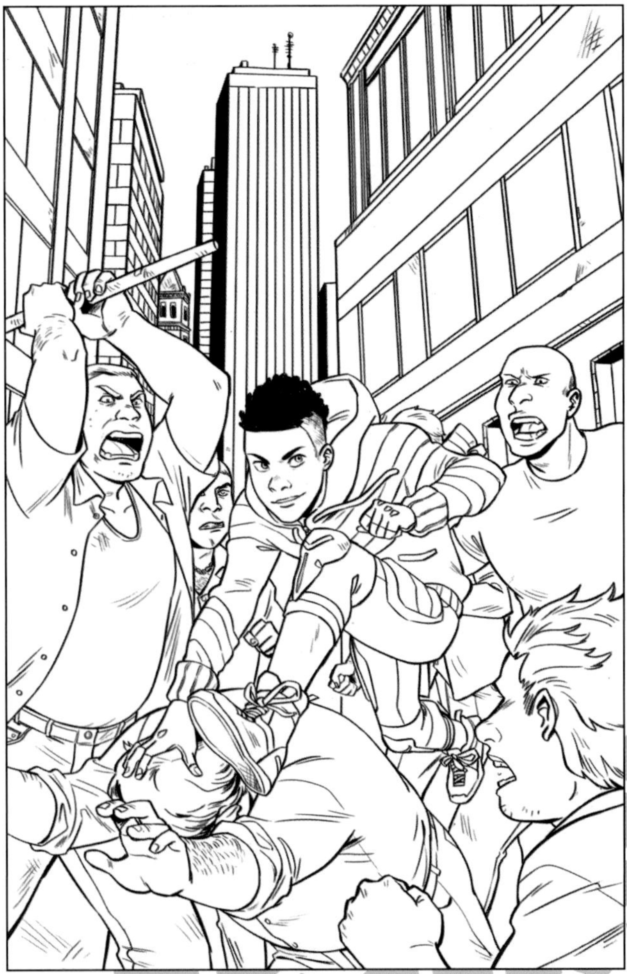